We Are #ALTGOV

We Are #ALTGOV

Social Media Resistance
from the Inside

AMANDA STURGILL

ROWMAN & LITTLEFIELD
Lanham • Boulder • New York • London

Published by Rowman & Littlefield
An imprint of The Rowman & Littlefield Publishing Group, Inc.
4501 Forbes Boulevard, Suite 200, Lanham, Maryland 20706
www.rowman.com

86-90 Paul Street, London EC2A 4NE

British Library Cataloguing in Publication Information Available

Library of Congress Cataloging-in-Publication Data

ISBN 978-1-5381-6209-5 (cloth : alk. Paper)
ISBN 978-1-5381-6210-1 (electronic)

CONTENTS

AUTHOR'S NOTE

AltGov is an anonymous movement that includes, among others, some who faced losing their jobs or other attacks if their names were known. Rather than refer to them by awkward Twitter handles, they agreed to the following temporary names for this book. Most are intentionally gender neutral and I refer to all accounts with the masculine pronouns he/him/his. This is not a statement of their gender identity, but an anonymizing device.

Alex is @AltCyberCommand. "Not the actual US Cyber Command"

Amadi is @AltNatSecAgency. "Former USMC SIGINT Analyst. He/him Deep State Operative™ Alleged Antifa Leader™ POG LEG REMF™. Astronaut Diaper™. Vampire™. May be spying on you right now."

Asher is @AltWASONPS. "NPS Unofficial Washington D.C. Office Resistance Team. Protect & Preserve the U.S. from Fascism."

Booker is @AltUSPressSec. "Hello, I am the Alternative United States Press Secretary. All of my statements have a basis in reality. Blocked by Trump."

Cameron is @AltSpaceForce1. "Boldly Going Where No Jedi Has Beamed Before Proud member #AltGov #AltFam #AltGovCares Earth is our spaceship."

Carter is @Alt_Mars. "Mars planetary science and perspective on human activities from 225 million km. Turns out, Mars has no govt so I must be the legit Mars account. Who knew."

Charlie is @ActualEPAFacts. "When the 'elected' government lets you down, turn to us. We've got your back, America."

Chris is @AnotherRogueAcct. "Just another cog in the immigration machine."

Colby is @NastyWomenNPS. "The Unofficial Resistance team of nasty lady rangers your elected officials warned you about. We may even be in a park near you! #OroftheBison#altgov."

Dallas is @alt_fda. "Not the FDA, but close enough we can micro swab them."

Dana is @lynnstahl7. "Award-winning Baltimore based web developer, mother of dragons, baking enthusiast. #civtech #resist #altfam."

Drew is @SaveEPAA2. "We are former USEPA employees at the National Vehicle and Fuel Emissions Laboratory in Ann Arbor MI . . . Supporting federal protections for people & our planet."

Gary is @altGS_rocks. "Minerals dept. of The Resistance. Posts on mining, maps & more. AltGov. Super-duper parody account."

Gefen is @OldTenahu -OT. 2021: Happiness and renewed purpose. Social contracts matter. Don't break them.

Gerry is @WickedSmartFace. keeping up with the keepings on. musician. 32-bit owl, hoping for an upgrade before 2038 @CEDRdigital #NEISvoid.

Greer is @realShawnEib. "Disinformation researcher. #OSINT #SMINT Politics/military history junkie. Personal account. All opinions are my own and do not reflect those of my employer."

Hansa is @Prickles. 2nd generation geologist, volcanology, water quality, general geology | incremental theorist | runner reader skier tweeter eater.

Hunter is @alt_jabroni. "Alt Jabroni has returned to AltGov to fight for the resistance! We are all on the same side. It's time to UNITE! We troll those who troll our Alts. ESTP-A."

Jelani is @AltHomelandSec. "Not with DHS. Opinions are my own. "Reasonable af"— @Senatorshoshana // Ephesians 5:11 #countryoverparty // FNU LNU // #PipeLayer."

Kim is @bartenderResist. "#Welcome2TheResistanceBar Always #AltGov WE WON!! Get vaccinated!! Continue to wear a mask, wash your hands and social distance."

Lee is @Rogue_VHA. "Snopes verified VHA who can handle severe bleeding OR severe sarcasm. Does NOT reflect the views of the DVA but the DVA would be better if it did. DO BLOCK."

Liron is @EmbryoResist. "Proud to say I'm AltFam. Just like Jaylah, "I like the beats and shouting." OSINT fan. ★Personal is not the same as important.★

Mickey is @AltMtRanier. "Focused on fact based reporting and analysis. The Mountain is out & tweeting! Producer at @altsafterdark and @birdwatch contributor."

Morgan is @AltScalesOfJust. "Commentary on American politics. Opinions are my own. No internal sensitive/leaked info, just my personal views on the current state of affairs. RESIST. AltGov."

Ning is @RogueEPAstaff. "Fed career staff gone rogue. Science is not fake news. In this house we do science. We do snark. We reduce #foodwaste. In this house, we Resist."

Noor is @thenationalgood. "We're not here to help ourselves. We're here to devote ourselves to the national good."

Parker is @RogueVBA. "Not official acct. VA is 3 pts VHA (med) VBA (ben) NCA (cem). We'll cover benefits, so don't ask me about your dr appts. F_ck Snopes, but we are Brooke verified."

Rahel is @RogueResistanceKnitter. "I've been told sarcasm is part of my charm. Wrangler of yarn. Animal lover. #TheResistance #Altfamily #MeToo #WhereAreTheChildren #WhyIDidntReport."

Reid is @Alt_4nTrade. "Only the devil, @AngrierWHStaff, & I know the whereabouts of my treasure, & the one of us who lives the longest should take it all."

Sabah is @AngryStaffer. "Trump White House. This is terrible. Sad! The Resistance/Views are my own and should not be taken as official government position or opinion."

Sam is @RogueNASA. "The unofficial 'Resistance' team of NASA. Not of official NASA account. Not managed by gov't employees. Come for the facts, stay for the snark."

Stacy is @twimprine. "Father, EMT, Diver Generally pragmatic—currently in Paramedic school."

Suuad is @AltNoods. "Haudenosaunee. White coded, bong loaded. I grow your food and sh_t. #NOODS4PREZ."

Tai is @MirthDAL "#215children. IRS Crisis Hotline—1-866-925-4419 Be safe. #WearAMask #Vaccinate #Resist #BLM."

Tanner is @Alt_Labor. "freak in the streets, tweets in the sheets."

Tate is @AltDIA. "An AltGov voice here to discuss Defense and Intelligence. Upholding the Constitution. Protecting the people."

Taylor is @WatchPresTrump. "altGov member from the US Mint. Blocked by usmint for going rogue. Possibly a Nasty Girl. Infantry. VetsAgainstTrump RESIST."

Terry is @alt_localgov. "Livin la vida local. Wherever you go, there you are. This is where the magic happens. Views are my own, but I'll share if you ask nicely. AltGov."

Valentin is @AltUSDA_ARS. "Data is power! Illegally blocked by Trump for calling him racist. The Constitution is at the top of my org chart."

Van is @AltGovDoc. "alt gov assistance for medical info #COVID19. Ask questions!—does not constitute a doc/patient relationship. Data should be soundly sourced, attributed, vetted."

Wilder is @alt_USCIS. "Misfit | Not on gov time/tax $. Not DHS USCIS views/opinions. The good work goes to reporters now. #Vote pronoun: That/This Mofo."

PREFACE

Like many Americans who use social media, I first became aware of the resistance within the government shortly after the inauguration of the 45th president, when Twitter accounts related to the US National Park Service began tweeting information relating to the crowd size at the inauguration, to climate science, and to other science issues. It seemed like an arms race. There would be a new story about the public losing access to a data source, matched by new accounts coming online with what they said was insider information about how the government was actually working. Resistance movements and leaks are nothing new, but the technology had changed. If these really were government employees, they had a chance to communicate directly with citizens in a digital public square.

As a professor of journalism who also studies digital marketing and analytics, my own Twitter account is mostly professional. I tweet about issues related to news, analytics, and social media. I was curious about this emerging movement, but I didn't want to appear biased by openly following those accounts. I made a Twitter list, locked and unhelpfully named "Politics" that I jokingly referred to as my "conspiracy Twitter" to my family and friends. It did feel like conspiracy and rumors. Sometimes, there were verifiable insights about existing policies and hints of things coming that turned out to be true. Other times, there were wild sounding stories about how many Krispy Kreme donuts the president required on an overseas trip or a detailed description of a chain of events that would lead to impeachment and so many government figures going to jail that Orrin Hatch would become president. I watched, mostly amused, looking for bits of truth. When the government issued a subpoena to Twitter to compel the social media site to release the identity for one of the accounts, I knew that some of what was being shared must be hitting close to home.

As I watched, the things those accounts changed over time. First, the scope broadened quite a bit. The first accounts in my list were affiliated with identifiable units in the government—usually an agency like the Environmental Protection Agency or sometimes a smaller subunit in an agency like national parks, a smaller portion of the Department of the Interior. Later additions, which I found because they engaged with those early accounts, shared facts about how the government works but didn't state that they were current or former employees. Their interactions changed as well. There was quite a bit of infighting that developed, with some accounts warning that other accounts were not what they seemed to be. All the while, the number of followers shot up, growing in both number and variety. There are tools to see who follows different accounts, and I could see that some of the accounts were being followed by well-known journalists, elected officials, celebrities. These alt and rogue accounts were starting to have impacts that went beyond Twitter.

Along with my research student, Andrew Scott, we decided to get systematic about what that impact might be. For an early paper, we focused on Andrew's passion: the environment, comparing a sample of Alt accounts with the official Twitter accounts of the agencies they paralleled. We found that there were real and significant differences. While official accounts mostly discussed policies, Alt accounts mostly discussed people. Official accounts were overwhelmingly positive in tone, while Alt accounts were more varied, with both positive and negative postings. Influence was an important difference. Influence cuts two ways: to whom you listen and who listens to you. AltGov accounts listened to government accounts, their followers, and to each other. Official accounts listened primarily to other government accounts. The official government accounts were older and had more than ten times more followers overall, but AltGov accounts had many more journalists, even out of that much smaller total number. Since media are an important way that people learn information, the AltGov accounts had serious potential to impact the national conversation. In the years since we collected this initial data in October of 2017, the influence and extent of the AltGov have grown.

That first paper led me to make contact with some of the AltGov accounts in the spring of 2018. They allowed me to do several interviews as well as to observe their interactions and work behind the scenes. Collecting this information helps to put what happens in public on Twitter in context. I found several things of interest. Overall, I found a unique community of overcomers. The AltGov is composed of people who face the limits of technology, their own diversity of background, purpose and skills, and the challenges of maintaining anonymity, even from each other. They overcome this to take action, in hope that they will better a nation that they have found extremely frustrating. Their story is fascinating and sheds light on the ways communities can form and be effective, even as technology appears to make us less engaged with each other.

And so, this book. Using my background both as a journalist and a social scientist, I look at the AltGov from multiple perspectives to see how the need for anonymity and flexibility affects postings in public and affects interactions in shared, private spaces. I also look at the effects of the movement, both for the army of followers who interact on social media and for the others who have been touched by their efforts, in tangible ways ranging from politicians who are hearing from their constituents to candidates running for office to animals in protected lands. The story of the AltGov is a fascinating one with important implications for civil society in a technology-driven age, and I am pleased to share it with you.

ACKNOWLEDGMENTS

M y most sincere thanks go first and foremost to the members of Alt-Gov and to their followers, who worked with me for years to accomplish this project. The story is theirs and they were unfailingly accommodating with information, interviews, and encouragement throughout the process. Particular thanks to Ning, who first reached out about allowing me to have access to their conversation spaces and a chance to observe some of their projects in action.

Second, to my family, David, Claire, and Lucy, who put up with my late-night Twitter chats, my shutting them out of the room before an interview, and my endless conversations about what I was finding out and what it meant. Your patience made this possible and I love you forever. Thank you also to my parents, Bob and Dale Colson, for their endless love and encouragement over the years. Big jobs are always easier with cheerleaders, and they were always mine. I appreciate it more than you can know.

Finally, thank you to my agent, Amanda Jain, of Bookends Literary Agency, for taking a chance on an academic writer hoping to write a popular book and for her thoughtful editing of the proposal, and to my editor, Natalie Mandziuk, who has worked with me through the disruptions of a pandemic to help bring this story to life.

"It began with a defiant, and now infamous, tweet from Badlands, because of Trump's intentional disregard for science. Soon after, the #AltNPS and #AltGov was formed, most standing in unity with Badlands.

That's why we are here, since the beginning, and we aren't going anywhere.
First and foremost, that is our mission. To ensure that facts and scientific information remains.
We will fight for it for a variety of ways.

Data preservation

And calling out blatant ethical violations.

We point out propaganda.

Sometimes we also just flat-out troll Trump or bring attention to those who have.

Other times we call out what we believe is questionable activity that impacts our followers.

We also help others to sift through the trolls, the bots, and misinformation

And assist with humanitarian efforts.

We are not here for the fame or the glory, and we won't accept payment.

We are here to fight for what's right, to bring awareness, and to ensure that facts and science remain.

This is what it's about. This is our mission. And we are not alone.

#WeAreAltGov"

@AltWASONPS. (Asher)

1

1

TRANSITIONS

It was a nice day for the late fall near the nation's capital—partly sunny, a little warm for November, and Asher enjoyed leaving work a little early. He had to go vote and then run by the store to get some supplies for his Election Night party. It's been a tradition to get together with the neighbors and some long-time friends for a few games, some laughs and libations, and to watch the succession of power in the United States. "We welcome anyone over for a drink and some food so long as they vote," he said. So in between the drinks and sushi and little sandwiches, there was some banter over which states would do what and even a few friendly bets among a diverse group that included Democrats, some Republicans and Libertarians. This election cycle had been a dictionary's worth of adjectives. Crazy. Exciting. Fascinating. Unbelievable.

At home in another DC suburb, Morgan's house was quieter and more somber. As he was fixing cheese tortellini for family dinner, his phone buzzed occasionally with a text from his fiancée, who lived several states away, asking if he was doing OK. She knew he had strong feelings about the election. Morgan and the kids were living back in Northern Virginia after some time away and Morgan was working as a manager for a major section of the Department of Justice. He waited a while to respond to some texts and tried to put on a nonchalant face in front of the children, but he was not OK. At all. He was very worried about the presidential election, both as a civil servant and as a person. He had a painful experience with a malignant, dramatic personality before and thought he was seeing it again. He couldn't imagine what it might mean to put that personality in the White House.

Early on, the news on the East Coast wasn't far from what was expected. By 8:00 p.m. the media had called the race for Donald Trump in

Indiana, Kentucky, and Oklahoma. They said Hillary Clinton had won a host of more northeastern states—Delaware, Maryland, Massachusetts, New Jersey, and DC. Electoral vote count: Trump 26, Clinton 38. At Asher's house, most of the neighbors had paid their respects and left, and only close friends remained. TVs were on in the background; the beer was cold and the conversation warm and jovial both in the room and with far-off friends over video calls. Electoral votes added up slowly. South Carolina, Tennessee, Alabama for Trump, Rhode Island for Clinton, Mississippi for Trump, Illinois for Clinton.

On Morgan's TV, John King's touchscreen map on CNN turned more and more red with each call, but again, nothing unexpected. The kids stayed engaged—they had talked about the election before. "When they talked on the news about things Trump did that I didn't like, such as the *Access Hollywood* tape, I would talk to the kids (at a high level) explaining why I didn't approve of his behavior and didn't think he was a very nice or honest man." They were watching the returns with interest, but it was getting late, so he put his six-year-old daughter to bed. His eleven-year-old son wanted to stay up with Dad. They watched together as the news called New York for Clinton. Kansas, the Dakotas, Texas, and Wyoming went for Trump. "I tried to appear calm to the kids," he said, "but I feel sure they could tell I was more subdued than normal and was nervous."

Over the next hour, the tone at Asher's party turned sober. "By eleven the mood was changing. It wasn't looking so good. There was still a chance, but it wasn't looking so good. And while our friends are diverse, we all have one thing in common. None of us wanted Trump to win." They discussed the impact of the email controversy on Clinton's chances. On the probabilities for the remaining states. "By this time, most of the conversation had shifted to what it would take for him not to win, the chances that those places would flip, etc." Trump won four electoral votes in Nebraska and two more southern states: Arkansas and Louisiana. Clinton took tiny Connecticut, with its seven electoral votes. Trump took Montana. Clinton, New Mexico. Trump, Missouri. Then a big blow: Trump took Ohio, with its eighteen electoral votes.

Morgan's iPhone still buzzed with the occasional texted welfare check. Morgan said his fiancée "knew how upset the thought of him becoming president made me. I responded to her as best I could, but it was honestly pretty halfhearted, and I went long periods without looking at my phone, so I wasn't very prompt about answering." Right before eleven o'clock, the AP called Florida for Trump. Morgan turned off the TV and sent his son to bed. He went to bed himself. "I laid there in the dark with my mind roiling over what a Trump win would mean for the country, and for my ability to work in the government. I saw all the signs of serious personality disorder and was angry and baffled that so many couldn't see it." It was a long, disrupted night, punctuated with rising periodically to check the returns on his MacBook. He finally fell asleep around 2:30 a.m. when the outcome was certain.

"By about 12:30 a.m., most of us had given up hope," Asher said. Some locals left. Others, staying over, headed to bed. A few persisted until about 3:00 a.m., when they resigned themselves to the results. Asher had scheduled a vacation day for the ninth, a day he recalls as "kinda surreal. Like not bad, but we certainly knew things would change."

Morgan's children had a school holiday, and he got up late. "When I did eventually wake the kids, the first thing they both asked was who won. I told them Trump did. My daughter was sad but handled it just fine. My son was angry and asked what was wrong with people. He wanted to know how so many people could vote for such an immoral man. I just told him I truly didn't know." Morgan had to go to work, and, in a small, barely perceptible gesture, he dressed for a funeral. Black suit. Dark charcoal grey shirt. Black and white patterned tie. He stepped onto the DC Metro, headed back to his job and the preparations for the transition at the top of the government. He, and others, would have to find a way to keep things together.

Wednesday was rough. Chris was working for the Department of Justice, and he had been part of the immigration court system for a while—since the Obama administration. Even before the election, the court was already not a great place to work. It was ranked in the 300s out of all government agencies, and in frustration even its own judges referred to it as "second-rate" at times. Policy conflicts and changing attorney general rulings and judicial quotas make it difficult to run a justice system that is both fair to potential immigrants and as efficient as demanded. Throughout the campaign, as employees watched the run-up to the election, Trump's campaign promises included a great deal about immigration issues. The employees feared that if he won, his new administration would make things even worse. The day after the election, "It f_cking sucked," Chris said. "I apologize for the vulgarity, but that is the most succinct way of putting it." He had a lot of company in fellow employees who shared his concerns. He said some people in his office ended up taking part of Wednesday off. "We were terrified of what was to come and a lot of our fears have been realized."

Although federal employees can have strong opinions, they have to set them aside. The day after an election that changes the controlling party is also a day to get down to work. For all civil servants, the transition between presidents is usually an intensely busy time as they prepare for new appointees who will be coming in to lead their agencies. "At work, we begin an extreme effort to finish/close out projects," Asher said. "Not just because of Trump, but because anytime the admin changes, things change. And it's never a good idea to have unfinished work during a transition because it has a tendency to get scrapped unless absolutely critical," he added. He was hopeful at first. "I was a little bummed that my choice didn't win but wasn't sure exactly where everything would go. Still though, I had hoped that it was mostly just a personality quirk and that the government more/ less would function as normal." He slowly realized it would not.

In many ways, the men and women who do the work of the federal government across presidential administrations are responsible for keeping the ship of government stable across changing political seas. For Asher and other senior civil servants, there is always an element of being prepared. "We are often attempting to strategize and predict what the likely positions of Congress and the White House will be," as an election approaches. This is balanced by long-term planning that stretches four or even five years into the future. It's a game of strategy that's played in both formal and informal ways. Asher said he is watching as the electoral field winnows down. "We keep tickers," he said on candidate communications—website mentions of the agency in speeches and interviews. It's across the levels too. Local, state, and federal mentions matter, as well as those about a specific department. An individual park has a plan that feeds into a larger plan for the National Park Service as a whole and then into a plan for the entire Department of the Interior. "We run the scenarios," he said, "and we get prepared for 'worst case' activities."

It's not just presidential-level concerns. "And while we are also doing all this planning on the administration side, we have to do the same thing with Congress and [the] Senate. Since budget drives everything, they hold the purse." As a new Congress is seated, civil servants are paying attention to more than which side has the majority and thus controls the schedule. They carefully watch who gets assigned to which committees. No department is an island, so loose networks of civil servants also share information. Asher said he has occasional meetings with people who do jobs similar to his that he meets either through work or because they belong to the same professional organization. "We'll meet up for drinks," he said, and "talk shop, going out well past the official four- to five-year plans and strategizing out of over the next ten to twenty years." They are discussions he calls "boring stuff," but it leads to big ideas and cross-department alliances that help to modernize the government.

It's not always such big-picture concerns. Lee had served in the army, enlisting at seventeen. Before he joined the civil service at the Veterans Health Administration (VHA), he had seen wars on two continents and across multiple presidencies. He said that in the military, changes in the administration were "super important or seemed that way." He said the interest was because of the nature of the work. "What makes it feel like a big deal is that, when you're in the military, you are generally the pointy end of America's foreign policy, so you know you're going to be used for political or military purposes." Enlisted service members don't have much say in the workings of government, but some still find it fascinating, he remembers. "We all still chattered at the barber, at the gym, at chow." Now that he works for the VHA, one of three divisions of the Department of Veteran's Affairs (VA), the interest is a little different. In his civil service job, there was "the sense that it's a political hot potato anyway and we all knew he wanted to privatize." Especially at the VA, he said, "there is such a massive disconnect between what is actually happening and the political talking points or what pundits say that it's a joke to us all so it kind of feels like 'OK. Good luck with that.'"

Parker also had a military background before he joined the Veterans Benefits Association (VBA), another VA division. There, political transitions have effects, but they usually aren't felt much because "we're too big to fail." Political appointees come into the agency with their ideas and the civil servants try to balance that with the agency still being able to meet its mission—in Parker's case providing veteran benefits like home loans, vocational counseling, and the GI Bill support for education. "They give the idea," he said, "it gets down to the business line responsible and then we try to incorporate their ideas into programs still in development and current operations." Those ideas from the newly elected aren't always feasible, though, he said. For example, appointees came in with an idea to prioritize claims for veterans with service-related injuries that would require VBA to "stop ALL work and manually search through 200K claims to find those with a Purple Heart because of poor data sharing and archaic IT" or a desire to develop a self-service option for veterans that would have meant employees would have had to violate existing laws.

Like any presidential transition, this one was a time of uncertainty. Some tried to keep an open mind. Asher said he hoped the quirky personality at the top would not keep the government from meeting its obligations.

After all, personality aside, just the inertia behind government systems and structures can impact newly elected leaders' ability to make big changes. Sabah said, "I was obviously a Republican who didn't vote for Trump, so I expected it to be something of a dumpster fire. . . . I've also witnessed how the gravity of the office has a way of dragging people to the center and changing their most radical campaign rhetoric." Others were more focused on contingency. Booker said that he and others from his job with a government contractor spent the night after the election at a local bar "laying groundwork on what to do if events unfolded worst-case."

The staff who do the work of the federal government aren't all federal employees. There are slightly more than two million federal employees, and that sounds like a lot. Their ranks are bolstered by four million workers, others who are essentially paid with government money but work for private companies on federal contracts, doing everything from food service to cybersecurity. Civil servants have jobs to do on behalf of the will of the public, and that will is expressed through elections. But the "politicals" who are elected sometimes have little comprehension of how an agency is set up. It can be a delicate balance. "Say the new admin wants to do something like reorg an entire agency," Asher said. "We are obligated to put together a plan for it, regardless of whether we like the idea or not. But if we don't think it's a good idea, or if it will create issues, we also have a responsibility to put that out there, but not in an underhanded way. The truth of the matter is they don't really know what the impact will be unless you tell them." This can mean figuring out what the new bosses value. Cutting a popular program, for example, could mean unfavorable news coverage that could hurt future political aspirations. "Things like this tend to be calculated," he said.

As the transition went along, "Over the many following days, I just kept seeing more and more of what is bad about Trump coming to light and/or being affirmed through evidence," Asher said. An immediate concern was science information, particularly about climate change and the environment. In fact, the transition itself was the first sign that things would go badly. Ning worked for the Environmental Protection Agency (EPA) and had been proud of his ability to get along and do good work no matter who was in power at the White House. He was a veteran of political transitions and said he had a good idea of what to expect. But this time, he said, was odd from the outset. Usually, the incoming administration has people come in to learn about how the agency works from the career staff. There's not much time between the election and the inauguration, so the career staff expected to see political appointees right away. This is what usually happens. They had spent months preparing a lot of transition materials—binders, presentations. Through all the chaos of the election, Ning and others like him focused on doing their jobs so they would be ready, but no one came. "We had no political staff at [the] EPA because they were so unprepared to win," he said. "That was the first indicator that this was a president that was not equipped to lead in a good way."

The president had campaigned on, among other things, backing out of the Paris Climate Agreement, and he had tweeted in 2012 that climate change was a Chinese plot to suppress US manufacturing, so there was already some doubt and uncertainty about how the administration would treat the agency. They had to wait to find out. "We had no political oversight, so we were just on standby for days. And then we waited for weeks," Ning said. At the same time, the incoming administration was raising alarms about how it would treat environmental issues by the way it enacted policy and asked questions in other agencies. For example, the transition team asked the Department of Energy to provide a list of civil servants who had even attended working group meetings on the social cost of carbon, an Obama administration initiative. When political appointees did start showing up at the EPA, "The people that were appearing were coming in with a history of. . . . It was clear that they were coming in with a viewpoint that they wanted to stop the work of the agency to protect the environment and human health," Ning said. This was a huge issue for employees at the agency, people he describes as being very mission-driven.

Much of what we know about climate, the environment, and human health is either from research data directly collected by government scientists or funded at universities and private laboratories through government grants awarded by agencies like the National Science Foundation and the National Institutes of Health. Civil servants throughout the government joined other scientists and activists from the private sector in fear that the data collected with public money would either become publicly inaccessible or more difficult to find. It had happened before in another country. In Canada in 2013, the government closed or consolidated federal libraries with resources from the parks, environmental, and natural resources branches of the government among others. Years of monitoring data was discarded or moved into forms that would be harder for future researchers to gain access to. So, in the United States, when Myron Ebell was named the head of the transition team at the EPA, US scientists were worried. Ebell was a leader of environmental policy at a Libertarian think tank partially funded by fossil fuel companies. He also chaired the "Cooler Heads Coalition," a group with a goal of dispelling myths about global warming.

He had told PBS's *Frontline* that the strategy for mitigating concern about climate change was to "keep banging away on the science." The fear of losing valuable data escalated as anonymous sources close to the government were telling journalists that the EPA did indeed plan to remove data like the Obama Climate Action Plan. Groups of university researchers, independent coders, librarians, scientists, and archivists worked in weekend hackathons to download and back up government data, in some cases hosting repositories in other countries. Those news reports were combining with the delays in getting the transition going to make for a tense work situation.

The transition was filled with challenges that were both hard to work with and hard to swallow. Throughout the government, uncertainty spread. Sam kept up with a growing database of news reports about the new administration's actions against science. Wilder also saw the transition as unsettling from the first. He saw the same concerning lack of professionalism as Ning had, but also saw more. "The new administration had a rough startup," he said, noting that a month and a half went by before representatives of the new government even began showing up where he worked as well. Like Asher, Wilder's days at work became full, and what started as worry over the process became fear about the goal. When it came to immigration, his area of expertise, he believed that "They're coming to literally tear it apart."

As the transition went along, the lack of respect for experience became more concerning. Morgan had recently returned to a government role at the Department of Justice, taking a substantial pay cut to go back into public service because he believed his skills made a difference there: working for the people, and not just for a bottom line. As the days marched forward from his angst-filled election night to the inauguration, he grew increasingly upset. "I felt that Trump was intentionally ignoring anyone he felt had political experience or better insight than he had," he said. As the incoming president vetted candidates for his cabinet, that feeling worsened. For example, the secretary of energy typically has a deep understanding of science. The Obama secretary of energy, Ernest Moniz, was an MIT physics professor who was well-versed in the technical issues in negotiating nuclear program restrictions. Trump's nominee was Rick Perry, a former governor of Texas with a bachelor's in animal science who had called for the department to be abolished in a presidential debate. Trump's pick for secretary of housing and urban development was Ben Carson, a distinguished neurosurgeon whose spokesman told National Public Radio that a major qualification was having lived in public housing. Carson had no professional experience with housing policy. Carson and Perry had both run for the Republican nomination but ended up dropping out and en-dorsing Trump. The news about the transition kept getting worse, and the day before the inauguration, Morgan had already turned to an anonymous voice, writing more than 1,500 words in an anonymous Reddit posting in the form of an open letter to the incoming president. "I see you for what you are. And what you are is pathetic," he wrote, calling the president-elect incompetent, abusive, criminal, and bigoted. It didn't work. Reddit users show support for ideas with a like and dislike system that determines which ideas get boosted higher on people's screens. His words didn't get a lot of traction, he said, and "most comments just pointed out that it was overly emotional and hysterical." It wasn't clear that an anonymous voice in the wilds of social media could make much of a difference. It wasn't clear what would.

But Ning knew something had to be done. He shared a tweet from the president-elect:

@RealDonaldTrump

Look how things have turned around on the Criminal Deep State. They go after Phony Collusion with Russia, a made-up Scam, and end up getting caught in a major SPY scandal the likes of which this country may never have seen before! What goes around, comes around!

Ning added, "This Trump tweet is why I decided to stand up for civil servants through my AltGov account," he said. "Trump's characterization of career staff is not just offensive and absurd. It also demonstrates a funda-mental misunderstanding of how America's work gets done."

I really hope that people understand that federal employees, by and large, are just humans having careers. We're not part of the political class, we're not part of the political warfare, we don't have agendas that we're after. We're a highly skilled workforce that cares deeply about supporting Americans.

So when we get riled up about something, it should be a cautionary flag. I really hope that through interacting with the accounts, people continue to get a better understanding of who we are and have a little bit more respect for the federal workforce. The politicians will malign us, and the general public lumps us in with politicians. We get it from both directions. Really, we're just trying to do our jobs, and not make as much money as we would in the public sector, because we care about what we do.

@RogueEPAStaff (Ning)

2

FIRST DAY PROMISES

A sher had spent his entire career working for the government. He started by joining the Marines, a segment with the largest workforce: defense. His story wasn't one of connections and privilege. He grew up in a small town in the South, the kind of place he described as not having "much of anything—to do, or for a future." His family included his mother and his siblings, mostly, as his father died when he was a young child. "I never really knew my dad," he said, "but often heard stories about him. . . . Mostly the idealized stories about him being a great guy, super smart." School was easy, he said. He was the kind of kid who would read the books before class and be able to correct the teacher. He found some challenge on the math team, and even won a small scholarship. Outside of school, going hunting and fishing, playing video games, and joining primitive internet chat sessions weren't enough to keep him engaged, and he also "got into a whole lot of trouble—usually just silly things like egging a house."

As he got older, his mother realized he needed more challenge and sent him to a private school. The classes were better, he said, but the school was "not exactly accredited." And when he got further along in high school, he realized that college was going to be a problem, because he'd have to repeat some of his high school classes somewhere that was accredited. His mom had to work two jobs already to take care of herself and his sibling, so he'd also be on his own to pay for it. He opted to drop out and get a GED while he thought about next steps. He decided to go into the military. His dad had been a marine and a sibling served in the navy. He could trace military service in his family back to World War I. The decision "changed my life for the better," he said. "It ultimately got me to where I am today. My wife, my education, and my job at NPS are a result of me joining." The specialized training Asher got from the Marines directly translated to the job he got with headquarters at the National Park Service.

For federal employees who work in the Washington, DC, metro area, Inauguration Day is a day off, designed to have fewer people on the roads as citizens travel to the capital to watch the transfer of power. Freshly inaugurated, President Donald Trump took the podium in front of a crowd filling the space in front of the Capitol and some of the National Mall. His words painted an alarming picture of a country in decline, in which schoolchildren were "deprived of all knowledge." In a speech carried live on broadcast, streamed and recorded on YouTube, Trump promised "America First" and that he would unite the country. With regard to science, he said, "We stand at the birth of a new millennium, ready to unlock the mysteries of space, to free the Earth from the miseries of disease and to harness the industries and technologies of tomorrow." Yet, that same Inauguration Day, references to climate change disappeared from Whitehouse.gov, the official White House website. A page from the Obama administration concerning lesbian, gay, bisexual, and transexual issues also disappeared as the White House website came under the control of the new administration.

The Trump administration wasted no time blocking information from the public. According to articles in the Huffington Post, *Scientific American*, and BuzzfeedNews, employees at the United States Department of Agriculture and the Environmental Protection Agency (EPA) were told the Monday following the inauguration, that they were not to talk about their agency's research to the press. At both agencies, the president's choices of leadership had records of being hostile to research that supported climate change. Incoming agriculture secretary Sonny Perdue wrote in the *National Review* that one cause of climate change is farm animals: their way of digesting food produces methane. Purdue's article called the notion "a running joke." The EPA was working under temporary leadership while Congress was reviewing Trump's pick Scott Pruitt. Pruitt was a former coal lobbyist who, as Oklahoma attorney general, had a LinkedIn page describing himself as an "advocate against the EPA's activist agenda." Background efforts to save copies of climate and other scientific data were matched by public outcry, as a group called 500 Women Scientists participated in the first Women's March, the day after the inauguration, Like others in the crowd, they wore pink pussyhats, and they wore white lab coats, emblematic of their concerns. A Facebook group formed within a week, planning a March for Science.

At nearly the same time that information was disappearing, the official Twitter account from the National Park Service threw shade with two retweets: one from the Twitter account of landscape designer @annetrumble about data deletion and one from the Twitter account of *New York Times* journalist Binyamin Appelbaum about inauguration crowd size, featuring a side-by-side comparison of a photo of a National Mall thickly filled with observers at Obama's event to a similar photo from Trump's, with large white patches suggesting a much smaller crowd. Appelbaum noticed immediately and retweeted it at 1:03 p.m. with the comment, "Looks like the Trump administration hasn't taken control of the @NatlParkService Twitter feed just yet." The Park Service had more than three hundred thousand followers at the time and the tweets quickly went viral, with thousands of reshares from both journalists and ordinary users. They also set off a flurry of activity within the Department of the Interior (DOI), the part of the federal government that houses the park service.

Government records show that DOI communication managers were alarmed, sharing their personal telephone numbers and emails in the early afternoon so they could stay in touch. They knew they had a crisis on their hands. According to the records, Larry Gillick, the deputy director of digital strategy for the DOI wrote, "I've been mulling over what to do if the tweet storm doesn't subside." It wasn't clear where the tweets had come from. Around 5:00 p.m., Gillick wrote to the department's Web Council saying he had met with the new communications director and that things had gone well. "And then, someone inadvertently tweeted an unwise and unflattering RT about the new administration to the public." A portion is redacted, and then continues, "The new administration says that the Department and all Bureaus will not tweet this weekend and will wait for guidance before returning to Twitter. Such guidance is not expected until Monday at the earliest." He summarized the new policy, "I'm not tweeting, we're not tweeting and none of our people are tweeting." Department accounts were asked to stop any tweets that were scheduled for automatic posting, but it was a weekend, and it wasn't clear that the right staff at the many sites DOI managed would be reading their work email. The news that the accounts were silenced, or as emails called it "paused," ran in national newspapers and magazines. That same afternoon, DC reporters were asking their contacts, both in the DOI and the park service, for comments. Reporter Tim Cama from *The Hill* reached out to Rebecca Matulka from the Department of the Interior with a request for information on the rogue tweets, with an offer for Signal or WhatsApp for privacy. She shared that email with other communications staff. It was quickly becoming evident that the social network on which the new president had built a reputation was going to be a first stress point between existing federal workers and their new leadership. After eleven o'clock that night, Tom Crosson, chief of Public Affairs for the park service, urged that all National Park Service Twitter account holders change account passwords and check over who had posting rights.

It quickly became evident that a wholesale Twitter ban was a problem, as DOI agencies used the platform as a conduit for important public safety messages such as those about earthquakes and volcanoes from the US Geological Survey and those concerning weather-related closings at national parks. In an email included in the records, Michael Quinn, who worked with communication at Grand Canyon National Park wrote, "Just to let you know—we're in the middle of a major winter storm and Twitter is an established way that we connect with travelers—and inform them of park road closures and deliver safety messages." The Women's March, scheduled for the next day in Washington, was also a concern because public safety messages needed to reach into a crowded event in as many ways as possible in case of problems. Waiting until Monday for guidance could put lives at risk. Because the new leadership was still being put into place, contacting the administration would be difficult on an evening filled with glittering inaugural balls and celebrations. Megan Bloomgren, an experienced government spokesperson, had worked with the transition team and was the point of contact. Frank Quimby emailed that Bloomgren was "working it, but seems disinclined to respond tonight." The official Mount Rainier National Park Twitter account tweeted that if you wanted to know what roads were closed, you'd have to look at Facebook instead.

Then there was the matter of who sent the tweets. After the rogue retweets from NPS's Twitter account, it updated its password and revoked app access. It tracked the last login to 4:16 p.m. in San Francisco. It concluded that someone inside, who had access to the account, had accidentally retweeted. But there were other concerns with the content of the tweets that were reshared, which made it look like the attendance at Trump's swearing in was less than that of Obama's. The size of the crowd was a real sore point with the president, to the point that the next day, Press Secretary Sean Spicer angrily told reporters at a media briefing, "This was the largest audience to ever witness an inauguration—period—both in person and around the globe," a statement that *Washington Post* fact checkers rated four Pinocchios. The park service hadn't calculated crowd size since their estimate of about four hundred thousand at the Million Man March in 1995, which drew legal threats from the Nation of Islam. But an

NPS photographer took photos of the event that showed the crowd size and *The Guardian* (Swaine 2018) reported that Spicer called several times the next day requesting photos that were a more flattering version of the crowd. The *Washington Post* reported that Trump himself had called the acting NPS director, Michael Reynolds, angry about the retweet and seeking photos he would like better. *The Guardian* article indicated that the photographer complied and cropped the photo to make the crowd look larger. This was an early sign for government employees that there would be pressure to depict reality in terms of things that made the president look popular, which adviser Kellyanne Conway deemed "alternative facts" in an interview with *Meet the Press* on Sunday. On Tuesday, another official account from the NPS spoke up:

@BadlandsNPS—Burning one gallon of gasoline puts nearly 20lbs of carbon dioxide into our atmosphere

@BadlandsNPS—Flipside of the atmosphere; ocean acidity has increased 30% since the Industrial Revolution. "Ocean Acidification"

@BadlandsNPS—Today the amount of carbon dioxide in the atmosphere is higher than at any point in the last 650,000 years

@BadlandsNPS—The pre-industrial concentration of carbon dioxide in the atmosphere was 280 parts per million (ppm). As of December 2016, 404.93 ppm.

Four tweets about the climate, sent over about two hours. They briefly became a Twitter Moment—a group of tweets held together to tell a story that Twitter staff set for automated promotion on the site. And then, a few hours later, those tweets were deleted. It was too late—they had definitely gotten a lot of attention. The Weather Channel noticed, bringing in climate experts to attest that the facts the account shared were true. Other journalists also published stories. Twitter users were paying attention, too. Badlands National Park's account exploded in popularity. It had fewer than eight thousand followers before the tweets, and more than one hundred thousand after. Less than an hour later, @BadHombreLandsNPS was online tweeting, "Hey, friends. Here to support @BadlandsNPS with the science facts they can no longer share." That one tweet was liked more than eleven thousand times. It looked like employees from other government agencies noticed, too. In the 147 replies were messages from other Twitter accounts saying they were other government employees, supportive and ready to act. @realUSDOE tweeted, "We here at the (Alternative) totally legit department of energy are with y'all." @realusedgov chimed in,

"Sharing education is an important thing!" And more than one hundred others, mostly small individual accounts, responded with encouraging messages like, "YOU ROCK" and "In Dark Times, heroes always appear. YOU ARE OUR HERO!!!" The next day, Sam's account from NASA tweeted, "Rogue Twitter accounts are fun, but gov't employees and scientists are very afraid of being fired if they speak out & share facts. #resist." By the end of that month, Alt accounts for several national parks, several for the EPA, the Department of Justice, the Department of Defense, branches of the Department of Homeland Security, the White House, and the Department of Labor had sprung up. And some had begun calling themselves AltGov.

Ning said he didn't know much about Twitter when he started his first account, @ginasarmyFTW, which had a tagline "Gagged but Unbowed. Our mission is STILL protecting human health and the environment." Gina referred to EPA administrator Gina McCarthy, who was an early casualty of the new administration. After a few weeks "in the wilderness," Ning said he felt he had to act. But, like other government employees, he had seen the reaction to leaks. Numerous press accounts quote former EPA employees as being told to keep a low profile and to not make waves, in order to survive. A go-getter, Ning found himself without much to do at work. During that mostly idle time, suspicions were taking over. According to the *New York Times*, America Rising, a Republican campaign research group, requested emails of employees who criticized the policies of the new administration. They asked for files that mentioned former EPA Administrator Scott Pruitt, the president, or were exchanged with democratic members of Congress. It was a troubling time.

For Ning, being an Alt didn't start as a political thing. He said he is not a political purist. "My personal perspective is that compromise is not a four-letter word," he said. He said he wasn't originally concerned about the change in administration, as he had previously worked with people on both sides of the aisle. His thinking was that "I can have opinions, but my job is to do what I am told to do. I feel really comfortable leaving my personal opinions away from my job." The transition between presidents was a sobering moment, he said, when he realized that the appointees really wanted to see the work of the agency fail. The existing career staff were in a bind, he said. "I felt sidelined by the new administration's appointees, even in my areas of greatest expertise and even when I was trying my hardest to be of use to them." He knew other staff felt the same way and reached out to some people from other EPA regions about a group account. It was such a scary step. He did find others who agreed to join, and added them to a group account, but they ended up never posting. He worried about the implications of others knowing about the account and knowing the password, so that first account didn't last. He went to the public library so that nothing could be traced to his home internet. He created a more secure ProtonMail account, so he could start fresh on Twitter in the interests of a solution that was more secure. It was a hard decision, and he said he felt very alone. Even posting anonymously was a big personal leap. "The fact that I did decide to do something like this . . . it speaks volumes," he said. "I thought it was not just the right thing to do, but an important thing to do."

Some accounts were run by people who weren't employed by the government but were familiar with the inner workings, either because they worked as contractors or because they worked in a heavily regulated industry. On January 25, 2017, Dallas's account tweeted "@Alt_fda 2 days without a post on our main social accounts. We would like to bring you great news about food & drugs but . . ." The tweet got a large response, with more than a thousand likes and comments like "Glad to have you here uncensored! Thank you!" and "Keep it up, folks! You work for America, not for Trump!" and "We are listening here now. Post away and educate. We will spread the word." Even famous people offered endorsements of the AltGov accounts.

At other federal agencies, employees worked together to start Alt accounts. For example, as a callback to Trump's calling his competitor, Hillary Clinton, a "nasty woman," a group of female park rangers from multiple different areas worked together to form @NastyWomenoftheNPS. Multiple voices on the account represented some of the spread of the park service. Being staff at a national park can mean quite remote living, at times in areas where, when visitor season ends, you are only seeing a handful of locals and the other park staff who stay throughout the winter, but Colby's account let far-flung staff have a voice together. Sam's account, likewise, came about when employees and contractors, concerned about what would happen to the extensive climate data that NASA collects, organized to create a group account. Morgan continues in the same position in the Department of Justice that he held on that dyspeptic election night. "I really struggled with whether or not I could continue working in the government, knowing that I would be working for Trump. I eventually decided that I needed to stay and try to be a voice of reason from within the government," he said. Though his initial foray into social media on Reddit didn't get a strong response, he decided to try again with Twitter. He posted a long Twitter thread describing his fears that the new president lacked a conscience and would hurt the country—a thread that was retweeted more than four thousand times. His fiancée was very confused when his phone started lighting up with notifications from new followers and people who had liked his post as they were trying to have a dinner date. "What did you do!?!" she asked.

For Asher, it was more about the job. His entire career had been in public service, with a strong desire to have the best outcomes by having smart processes and being prepared for the future as he worked for the American people. As he watched the transition, he thought it became clear that the new administration's goal wasn't the same. Serving the public and protecting geographical and cultural resources were in tension with enabling business and reducing the size of government. It started at the top of agencies. As a member of Congress, secretary of the interior nominee Ryan Zinke had supported removing protections from federal lands and repealing environmental regulations. Much of government takes place in the shadows—bureaucracy is complicated and just not very interesting. Asher was worried that people wouldn't know what was going on with their government because reporters wouldn't know to ask the right questions. He knew several parks had Alt accounts associated with their names. With Asher's place in the Washington Area Support Office, he could provide context from a higher level, reaching across all park facilities. He had a chance to bring public information to light that could help preserve what he saw as the American people's land and heritage.

Rest assured, we're still here for facts and science. We will keep in close contact with our NASA friends and update you when necessary.

A lot of good people are very afraid of losing their jobs. And for them, keeping food on the table trumps running a Twitter account.

We're going to use this account for science & political news + calls to action. We hope you stick with us. Facts matter now more than ever.

@RogueNASA (Sam)

3

LET'S TALK

Though government interactions with the media are tightly controlled, there have always been leaks. Sometimes they're deliberate. If the government is developing a new policy or program, letting a particular journalist know about it early can help the news outlet, as the audience will flock to the station or newspaper with the "exclusive." It could be part of a deal that involves sitting on a different story for an additional day. This gives bureaucrats some more time to prepare a response. Bureaucrats and politicians will also sometimes offer exclusive news as a strategy to set up a journalist to perhaps owe a small favor in the future. For journalists, it's not always a good idea to publish leaked information, though. Sometimes it is a trap. Journalists can be used to make leaks a part of a political process or even as revenge. If a proposed policy might be unpopular, a trusted source can leak its existence, asking to be attributed as "an unnamed government source" or "a source close to the deliberations." Later, if there is a lot of backlash, the government can always disavow the story and blame the journalist for getting it wrong.

Regardless, leaks are a consistent part of government reporting. In the case of the Trump administration, an unprecedented volume of upsetting stories on matters great and small, credited to unnamed sources, started early and continued throughout the entire term. Reports about campaign collaboration with Russia began leaking in early January 2021. A story about an executive order focused on possibly removing restrictions on "black site" prisons, little-known facilities that might use torture as a method of interrogation, leaked the Tuesday after the inauguration. A trickle of truly sensational stories, sourced from leaks, was a regular feature on front pages, with their release timed to create a "breaking news" moment on the various news commentary shows on cable TV.

The leaks were immensely frustrating to the president and other officials in the newly forming administration. There were attempts at crackdowns. Government documents show 120 leak incidents were referred to the Department of Justice for criminal investigation in 2017 alone—more than three times the number in the previous year. Efforts to track leaks continued throughout the presidency. At work, Asher found himself in the awkward position of being asked to report on anyone that knew had social media accounts like the one he, himself, was running. Even though he wasn't doing anything wrong according to government policy, it still felt weird, and he was glad the account was anonymous. He kept his tweeting to evenings or work breaks, and always used his own personal cell phone.

Information generated by the government, from meeting records to scientific data to the content of employee emails, belongs to the public and can usually be freely shared. Some are published openly, either online or in the government document repositories located in libraries around the country. Sometimes the public is denied access, usually because it has been determined that releasing the information would be hazardous to national security. Much of it, however, falls into a middle ground. It's not pushed out to media in press releases, but it's not a secret either. It is available upon request. The Freedom of Information Act, or FOIA, proscribes the process for getting that information. It's possible, but it's not easy. Some nonprofits help. For example, Investigative Reporters and Editors, a professional group for watchdog reporters in a variety of media, offers its members regular training and multiple tip sheets on how to work through the process. Each government entity has its own procedure to learn, and nonprofit groups like American Oversight employ attorneys to make requests, then publishes records online. But for most federal records, the process of accessing them is difficult. Each agency has its own process and it's typical to wait months or sometimes years to get the information sought.

Leaking classified information would mean termination or even jail time for government employees. That doesn't mean government employees can't play a role in keeping the public informed. Those with deep understanding about what the government is doing can also have a lot of influence simply by pointing out things that are OK for the public to know, but that the public and journalists wouldn't know to ask about. An example would be highlighting public comment periods. These are times when a government agency or commission must, under federal law, accept open comments from the public as a part of a decision-making process. A comment period must be published in the *Federal Register* for a few reasons: it creates a mechanism for the public to participate without relying on contacting their representatives and also helps ensure that if the government is spending money, different companies will have an equal chance to submit a bid for a contract. If you are a contractor, you might follow the *Federal Register* closely, but for average citizens, it's not exactly bedside reading.

As the Alt accounts tried to keep the government working well, it helped to get public information on the radar. They were developing a good platform from which to do that. The audience for content from the AltGov increased rapidly, with some accounts showing more than fifty thousand followers before they sent their tenth tweet. Just @RogueNASA grew to more than four hundred thousand followers in the first forty-eight hours of the account coming online. The initial messaging was about climate change, and other scientific topics hit home for followers eager to see information preserved. Prominent personalities joined the media in taking notice. For example, actor George Takei tweeted,

> @GeorgeTakei "I am following this group and encourage others to as well. Science, fact and reason must be heard, must win out over politics and power."

One of the early actions that AltGov accounts took was making people aware of comment periods for issues including changing automotive emissions standards. Some of the accounts like @RogueEPAStaff had gathered large numbers of followers in the initial flurry of interest in the days after the inauguration. Others remained small, such as several accounts that represented branches of the Environmental Protection Agency (EPA) from particular regions of the country. They began to realize that there was power in working together. Twitter uses rules called algorithms that help to determine what people will see in their feed. When more people engage with a tweet, the algorithm assumes it must be something people want to see, and it shows that tweet to still more users. If Charlie saw Drew's tweet about new efficiency standards and shared it himself, the combined power of their followers and favor from the algorithm would mean that more people took the chance to weigh in against a policy change that could increase pollution from cars. The different accounts from different parts of the EPA found each other quickly—some already knew each other in real life, others just developed a tight, but anonymous Twitter relationship.

For other accounts, it was Twitter interactions that let them start to form a group. Tweeting at someone, or tagging, is using someone's handle, like @AltEPA, in the body of a tweet. This mention is a way of getting that account's attention, as it triggers a notification, which they will see as a little blue dot over a bell at the bottom of the app. This kind of tagging happened from the very first moments after the initial tweet from the @BadlandsNPS account, and it continued. However, as accounts with tens or hundreds of thousands of followers were getting tagged by those followers and others who wanted to comment on what they were doing or saying, the number of notifications became too much. Twitter caps the number of notifications symbolized in the blue dot at ninety-nine-plus, but trying to scroll through hundreds of messages to read them becomes impossible. Here, a private conversation feature that Twitter supplies comes in handy. The feature is called direct messaging (DM) and people can communicate while on the app, but in messages that others can't view. Up to fifty accounts can participate in one of these private chats, which they call DM rooms. Accounts that said they were "alt" or "rogue" government employees began messaging each other, seeking to work together. The idea isn't unique to the AltGov: state political organizing groups in the United States, and general organizing and resistance groups around the world, have used the feature as well. Groups like Heroes Resist, which had account names referencing comic book characters among others, and Geeks Resist, which had science fiction references and sometimes engaged with geeky celebrities like Mark Hamill and Mythbusters's Adam Savage, use them as well.

As the weeks began to pass following the inauguration, the mission began to evolve, and the Alts began to see results from their efforts. The accounts that would form the AltGov began to coalesce. One of the first actions a new president must take is staffing the department heads that become his cabinet and filling lots of other roles in the administrative branch of the government—as many as four thousand positions, which NBC News wryly noted was "a particularly daunting task for a president-elect who was reportedly surprised to find out that he would have to replace the White House staff." Once the new president took office, it was time for those new department heads to face congressional approval. As the fears about disappearing data seemed to be realized, the new president's proposed cabinet members had backgrounds that were concerning. Several of the suggested administrative officials appeared unqualified to lead their agencies— sometimes badly. There were conflicts of interest, lack of knowledge in the area, and in some cases, an existing outspoken opposition to the agency the nominee was to head. For example, Scott Pruitt was picked to head the EPA despite his background of suing the agency repeatedly as the Oklahoma attorney general. Pruitt even described himself as "leading advocate against the EPA's activist agenda." Ning said that inside the agency, the crackdown on information began to be a problem. "Once the appointees came in, people got a lot more nervous."

There was a flurry of tweeting about the proposed cabinet, and some nominees seemed especially problematic. The president's nomination of Betsy DeVos as secretary of education raised some eyebrows. The former chair of the Michigan Republican Party, DeVos described herself as a national leader in the fight to reform education, primarily through school choice. Her family has been listed as one of the hundred most wealthy in America, and was active in supporting Republican political candidates, to the tune of millions of dollars. Her nomination was contentious from the beginning, with some liking the strong support of school choice and others worrying that it was an attempt to weaken the US public school system, which she called "badly broken," redirecting education dollars to charter and private, in some cases faith-based, educational institutions. There was concern that though she would administer policy on public education, she herself did not have direct experience with it. She attended private school herself, as did her four children. The @Alt_DeptofED account was active in opposing DeVos, sharing links to articles about the nominee and inspiring other Alt accounts and followers to do the same.

Aggressive humor marked some of the attempts. For example, when Tanner was concerned with potential policy priorities for new labor secretary Alex Acosta, he encouraged his followers to send the nominee bags of candy penises. Prior to that, Tanner fought hard against the first nominee, Andrew Puzder, the CEO of the parent company of Carl's Jr. and Hardees restaurants. Puzder was first floated as a nominee in December, and it became official on Inauguration Day. The *Washington Post* reported that "as the head of a fast-food company, Puzder is a supporter of the approach touted by Trump on the campaign trail that lowering taxes for corporations and the wealthy and loosening regulations for businesses can boost job creation." He also opposed raising the minimum wage, opposed making employees like those in his restaurants eligible for overtime pay, and noted that if workers become more expensive, employers would be more likely to turn to automation. He opposed the Affordable Care Act because it raised expenses for businesses, and his businesses had been accused of violating labor laws. His nomination raised eyebrows with women's rights advocates as well, as he defended racy advertisements for his restaurants, telling CNN Money, "I don't think there's anything wrong with a beautiful woman in a bikini eating a burger and washing a Bentley or a pickup truck or being in a hot tub. I think there's probably nothing more American." These views were followed by a revelation that his ex-wife, Lisa Fierstein, had appeared on an episode of *Oprah* titled "High-Class Battered Women" and alleged that she had been physically abused in the marriage, allegations matched by a deposition in their divorce proceedings. It's an assertion Puzder denies, and Fierstein later recanted. Tanner didn't waste time sharing information about the nominee. "Even Puzder's managers were victims of his corporate greed: lawsuit alleges they were fired for age and longevity" he tweeted, with a link to a news article. He reshared a tweet from then Senate Minority Leader Chuck Schumer about why Puzder was not a good candidate. He became more assertive, tweeting pictures of an office full of rats, one with the furniture hanging from the ceiling and a welcome box of Krispy Kreme donuts that had been filled with broccoli, using hashtags like #Resist and #NotOurLaborSec. There were more serious efforts as well. He supplied a phone number and encouraged followers to call their senators to ask them to oppose the nomination. When Puzder withdrew from consideration, Tanner tweeted, "Our nominee dropped out, so does that mean we are the baddest damn alt_Gov account in this cyberspace?"

The nomination of Trump campaign aide Sam Clovis as an undersecretary of agriculture for research, education, and economics seemed like a personal affront to the career staff at the United States Department of Agriculture (USDA). Clovis was an Air Force veteran with decades of service including as an inspector general. He held a doctorate, but it was in public administration. The stalwart supporter of the president was also a climate change denier, telling Iowa Public Radio that "I am extremely skeptical. I have looked at the science and I have enough of a science background . . . and a lot of the science is junk science. It's not proven." Some of that science he called junk was created by the USDA's own cadre of staff scientists. Clovis himself seemed to lack the credentials for the job, which are actually spelled out in law, which reads, "The Under Secretary shall be appointed by the President, by and with the advice and consent of the Senate, from among distinguished scientists with specialized training or significant experience in agricultural research, education, and economics." Valentin was vocal in sharing reasons why Clovis was a bad choice including information from CNN articles and assertions that he was only backed by "giant agribusinesses." Noor created an image with Clovis's photo and the words, "Even if his anti-science record weren't enough cause for concern, the latest reporting suggesting that Mr. Clovis may have facilitated Russian collusion in our elections raises these concerns to an alarming level" quoting Vermont Senator Patrick Leahy, who served on the senate agriculture committee. The hashtag #NoToClovis began to trend as other AltGov accounts and followers began resharing the same image with that hashtag, working together behind the scenes to coordinate information.

There was a sense of urgency, for there seemed to be battles on every side. During the campaign, Trump had promised rapid action on a variety of issues, and he began keeping those promises within a week of his inauguration. He signed executive orders on the Affordable Care Act, environmental regulation, and immigration all within that first week. At the same time, for the nascent AltGov accounts, the need to serve the public by offering access to information about what the government was doing was matched by a sense of the risks they were taking and fear for their jobs. The same day that Trump was inaugurated, he filed papers with the Federal Elections Commission to assert that he was qualified as a candidate for president in 2020. His paperwork stated that "while this does not constitute a formal announcement of my candidacy for the 2020 election, because I have reached the legal threshold for filing FEC Form 2, please accept this letter as my Form 2 for the 2020 election in order to ensure compliance with the Federal Election Campaign Act." This meant that he could raise and spend funds on campaign-type activities. This included rallies that could serve to both promote a future candidacy and to bolster support for his administration's action. It also meant that under the federal Hatch Act, federal workers could not legally criticize him on government time or with government resources. Federal employees received memos reminding them of this, and some Alts who were managers were asked to keep an eye on their employees to ensure none of them were criticizing the president/candidate. Morgan said that he, like Asher, was extra careful. He said, "If I do tweet against Trump while at work, I try to do it over my lunch break when I'm physically out of the government building, so I could argue that I'm meeting the letter of the law."

The AltGov itself also grew, as many new accounts appeared, representing more federal agencies. Some were quite obscure—things that many Americans would not even know about, such as an account for tiny San Juan Isle National Park or for the National Institute of Standards and Technology. Media coverage and interest grew as well, with everyone from Mashable to The Weather Channel sharing about the movement on social media or in stories. Other resistance movements were paying attention as well. Defending Democracy Director Alice Stollmeyer noticed and began looking for important accounts to pay attention to. "I mostly looked at whether or not they were tweeting as if actually 'being' or representing the federal agency they represented irl [in real life]. For example: did an alt EPA tweet about EPA–related topics? Also, I tried to avoid adding duplicates.

I also looked at genuine, original and quality content—not just retweets. And coming from a place of being pro-science and pro-facts rather than being anti-Trump." Stollmeyer, who is listed as one of the most influential Europeans on Twitter, put together an early list she called Twistance, for a Twitter resistance movement. This list was then linked in multiple media accounts, giving the impression that AltGov accounts were, together, something larger than the individual feeds. The accounts also continued communicating with each other. Ning said, "I don't know where that catalyst moment came from. No idea where the original two were. Somebody reached out to me." It began with just replies and reshares of similar information on the public side of Twitter. "Someone tapped me and said 'Hey, come over here into a DM that had a few folks in it.'"

Some of the people with Alt accounts who aren't employees of the federal government, made their first connection on Twitter as well, moving from general activism to some taking on an Alt persona to be part of the group. Ning remembers, "I was supporting the March for Science accounts and interacting a lot . . . publicly." Reid ran one of those accounts. "I actually started Twitter right after Trump's inauguration under a different handle," he said. "We were terrified at how the removal of critical facts would harm citizens and put our earth at more risk than it already faced. We had thousands turn out. It was very successful." After the march, Reid kept the account going "to push back on regulation changes that would be harmful to the environment, scientists, citizens, and stunt innovation leading to the USA sliding down in ranks of world leaders." It was in that capacity that he started interacting with Ning, Gary, and others—commenting and sharing messages. Eventually, Reid said he and Ning developed "a closer friendship." "We started talking behind the scenes, and I encouraged him to go Alt," Ning said. Going Alt meant that Reid also gave up his original Twitter name in order to take the Alt Foreign Trade persona. He didn't work for the government but did work with the government in a heavily regulated industry closely linked to trade.

Noor started working on activism on his own. "I made the account—did my own thing, made a website," he said. "I was just putting up resources for government stuff. Mostly environmental things. That's close to my heart anyway." He noticed that the EPA had started putting up a bunch of comment pages, but they were not centralized, so it was hard to keep up. "I put guides on that website," he said. He was also following rogue insider accounts. "I was following E [@RogueEPAStaff] and I responded to something he said," Noor said. "We went back and forth a bit and started building a casual light friendship." Ning messaged him to say "we really need your help. He knew that was one of the things I do is graphic design." Noor also needed a name change. "I don't know if they will accept you, because they don't know who you are," Ning told him. The concerns about bad actors were growing as more information about Russian social media campaigns affecting the election appeared in the news. Not wanting to be seen as a troll, or infiltrator, Noor took on the name @ RogueGPO, which he used for several months, although he wasn't related to the Government Printing Office. He has used a variety of different Twitter handles since the early days.

That need for graphic design was a sign that the AltGov itself was beginning to work together more intentionally. The efforts to form a structure were a challenge from the beginning, as they were coordinating different interests, personalities, and outside commitments. They soon settled into something of a routine. Although some of the Alts were new to Twitter, others weren't, and they knew the best way to get a message to show up in a lot of feeds was to make it look popular. Large accounts make messages seem popular, and so does engagement—lots of likes and retweets. The Alts used the size of their following to their advantage in those early days. "Our drops were coordinated, our timing was 6:00 p.m. eastern time. We had Noor make three or four graphics to choose from, we all fired off in unison and then retweeted each other. Then our followers boosted us too; it was really targeted," Gary said. That ability to follow and participate by sharing posts was uplifting to those followers who were looking for information and a chance to feel like they could make a difference. "I had indirect contact with the accounts. I would retweet their posts and would comment now and then, but that was it. Sometimes they would respond back to my comment and wouldn't at others. Their posts were giving me an outlet for my sense of hopelessness and rage over what was going on in this country. It was a much-needed outlet for many, obviously," Rahel said.

There was power in numbers, but behind the scenes it took a lot of coordination, and it wasn't always easy. As accounts found each other, they established areas of agreement on cabinet appointments and on new policies from the government. The size of the group and the changing nature made it hard sometimes to figure out what people wanted, and anonymity made it hard to get to know people. One interesting thing they tried was having people in the DM (direct message) rooms for those becoming insiders to take personality tests as a way of learning a little bit about people for whom questions like "What do you do?" and "Where do you live" were not possibilities. The Myers-Briggs-type tests formed the basis of a spreadsheet that listed each Twitter handle and its personality types. "I imagine it like this," Gary said, "one hundred and fifty people, through a series of terrible events walk through one hundred and fifty doors into a room. The door closes behind us. The light goes on and you're all standing around wearing masks. Then what do you do? How do you figure each other out? We were all really green back then and somewhat naive (and easily frightened)." Some accounts had better knowledge of information security and they taught the others. Using a special cell phone, called a burner phone, just for AltGov work could make an account somewhat harder to trace. Using a service called a virtual private network would make it seem like the account's actions were coming from different cities or even countries and could help with security as well. Dallas explained that the stakes felt very high. He believes that the FDA maintains a blacklist of those who have aggrieved the agency in some way, and said he had evidence that there was an effort to find him out—"a bounty on my head," he said.

The need to feel safe conflicted with the need to act. The people who ran the accounts had a common thread of acting to ensure that the government could still serve its purposes, but their domains varied. Science was common, particularly relating to the environment. But civil rights, immigration, national lands, and health care competed for attention. The Alts created a set of DM rooms to keep things straight, with some focused on campaigns on particular issues and others more social. "We had DMs set up per topic and were only for that topic of action. People could join the ones that fell in line with their interests." Carter, a strong organizer, helped to keep actions focused and effective by making schedules and keeping track of what was done. At the same time, security was important. Sabah explained, "If you think of it in terms of classification, we have a few that would be 'code word' level that only certain accounts are in. Not necessarily probation, just no need to know. We also have call to action DMs that are for whoever is interested in that particular CTA [call to action]." This level of security was needed for protection, particularly for accounts whose holders still worked for the government. "Some of our larger accounts (myself included) are leery of new people. All of our accounts have varying levels of risk involved with what they do, so we try to break the DMs down to fit everyone's comfort level," he said.

Amadi, who has a professional background in national security, went outside of Twitter to write a lengthy article on security steps on the blogging site Medium.com at the end of January. He began, "As a privacy advocate/fanatic, here are the tools that I personally use and I suggest you use them too, especially my fellow #altgov accounts." He started with tool suggestions: programs that you could use to encrypt data on your computer's hard drive or your phone, stating that people needed to "secure yourself from prying eyes because this administration will more than likely expand surveillance powers." Some of the suggestions were simple, like enabling an encryption setting on a phone; some were more complicated, involving the installation of and use of a different computer operating system. The Alts differ quite a bit in their level of sophistication with technology. One told me he used these kinds of tools and more or less gave a digital shrug and said, "I'm terrible at OPSEC," or operation security.

Trust has turned out to matter quite a lot. As accounts began tagging each other and showing up in DMs, it became obvious that groups of all political interests were using Twitter features to organize, and some of them were unfriendly—seeking to identify and destroy what they saw as a "deep state" obstructionism that formed part of what they were told was "the swamp" in government. Amadi's article covered safety for this as well, talking about how sharing locales, names, and activities can threaten your privacy. Amadi suggested using different usernames on different accounts and avoiding revealing personal information. The AltGov account holders realized that there were risks in affiliating and sharing, particularly for those who had federal government jobs under an administration they had seen fire people who were disloyal. They were only as strong as the weakest link, privacy-wise, and it was hard because they didn't even know who the person was on the other side of the account.

A code of anonymity, even with each other, became the rule and they felt a need to have some idea of whom to trust. Journalist Brooke Binkowski, who served at the time as the managing editor of the fact checking site Snopes.com, was asked to help as a third-party secret keeper. She alone would know the identities of the account holders, and they would trust her to verify who was safe to include in the group. Binkowski, who left Snopes early in this project, used a variety of methods to check out the accounts. Some account holders were asked to provide photos of their government credentials along with dated items, like the day's newspaper. Others could send a picture of themselves at work. In some cases, Binkowski or an associate would call the agency where an AltGov worked, ask to be transferred to speak to them, and expect to be told a code phrase they had worked out on Twitter. In a few cases, Binkowski actually met with an account holder to verify them in person. The vetting is intense— Lee joked that Binkowski knows more about him than his spouse does. For many of the Alts, Binkowski is the only one who knows their real identity. Some Alts know each other in real life, but many others do not.

Carter, who ran @Alt_Mars, was on a mission in more ways than one. He believed in signs of a looming climate crisis—one that worried him a great deal, and his tweets had a drumbeat of environmental warning that mixed in with other topics:

- It's not your imagination. Summers are getting hotter.
- Lobby your representatives to protect your local resources! Make them care.
- Think climate change won't affect you personally? Think again.
- Your oceans are dying.
- Some days I wonder if you don't deserve your impending extinction.
- My sister Earth is the crown jewel of planets; for her, I #resist the forces that are devouring her bounty and condemning it to extinction. #IAmTheResistance.

He had degrees from Harvard and Yale and worked as a space architect. His job involved designing the human cabins for crewed missions for both spacecraft and the International Space Station, plans that were imitated in some well-known films about space travel. At the same time, he was burdened with the knowledge that inaction on climate change was likely to accelerate as the Trump administration removed climate change data and pulled out of the Paris Climate Agreement. One of his projects was designing an ark—a plan that could help preserve humanity if the planet became unlivable—with plants that could produce sufficient food and oxygen to sustain life. He felt deeply that his work with the AltGov was existential—a vital and sacred duty to try to stop or at least slow damage to science, exploration, and the planet he shared. Carter's sense of urgency and organization led him to being a leader behind the scenes in the early months. Ning described him as "a perfect example of Alt and real life combining." He helped to organize topics and information drops and "brought a good professional level," Gary said. His "ideas were incredible," Noor said. But as the coordination between accounts continued to grow, a rift developed.

Even with Binkowski's vetting, it was still a multistep process to get included in the most central message rooms—the ones where Alts might choose to share some personal information. A special room with a limited group of Alts was used to help socialize new accounts into the ethos of the group, which included coordination on projects and serious matters, but also a lot of sharing funny memes and joking around. The room was known as "The Gauntlet" and was almost a kind of hazing into the group, and Morgan found himself in there with "content heavy on puns, jokes, sexual innuendo, and off-color jokes." In late August, he joined in a conversation sparked by a GIF of a voluptuous woman who could hide bottles of liquor under her breasts, with some of his commentary suggested by his fiancée, with whom he was texting on the side. It was an immature, bawdy conversation about bra sizes and bottle sizes, and the messages and GIFs flew through quickly enough that it was hard to keep up with everything in the conversation. People who are inside a DM conversation have the ability to add other people to the room, and no one had noticed that someone had added Carter. He was not amused. He immediately left that room and sent incensed messages to some of the accounts he was used to interacting with, before unfollowing them and leaving several of the other rooms he participated in. Morgan tried to apologize, but Carter wouldn't hear it, admonishing Morgan for his "unspeakable display of sexism and vulgarity." Carter said Morgan was not respecting the "noble endeavor" of AltGov and that Morgan's entire generation had serious problems if he thought that kind of interaction was appropriate. An additional effort to apologize also failed, and confused and hurt, Morgan left The Gauntlet and some other smaller DMs and deleted Twitter from his phone for a while. He still had the account and could look at what was going on through the web browser version of Twitter. He still was a government employee, with a following and the ability to interpret government actions for those followers. Sabah and Ning reached out and urged him to come back.

I am in the mood to give you some behind the scene fun facts:
CBP tried to catphish me on Twitter twice in 2017, once in 2018.

In 2017, they used a "USCIS west coast employee" who was "very interested" in joining the #resistance & insisted I just give her the username & password.

2018, they created a twitter account & sat on it for a few months, collected followers and even commented on some tweets, then asked me to DM them because they had some "documents" they want to pass on by email. Sure, why not since a simple image search found a chive profile pic.

I got the email and sent back some notes on the same pdf with a harmless payload that initiated a blue screen of death. Since they never scrubbed the metadata off the pdf.

FYI: Tails OS and unlimited VM's are useful.

@Alt_USCIS (Wilder)

4

THREATS

Sometimes the president has the power to change how the government works through an executive order—a mandate for one of the divisions of the government that falls under the executive branch. President Trump took office with a plan to sign several, and one of the most controversial of these was Executive Order 13769, which, among other things, blocked people from Iran, Iraq, Libya, Somalia, Sudan, Syria, and Yemen from entering the United States. When it was announced, there was a mix of confusion and outrage, as some people were already in transit to the United States. What would happen to them? Was the move a smart act for national security, or illegal religious discrimination? Large numbers of Americans, including volunteer attorneys, went to US airports to protest or to offer services. The attorneys wanted to help people who were waiting on loved ones from those countries who were already in flight but had had their visas revoked, and to help arriving passengers who were detained at airports. AltGov accounts wanted to help as well. The @alt_uscbp account said, "When I first created this account, it was so I could counter the lies Trump was telling about Muslims and his Muslim ban." His first tweet was "POTUS immigration order is causing chaos everywhere." Several other Alt accounts tried various forms of online action, which included statements of support like @AltArmedForces tweeting, "I proudly serve aside countless Muslims in the US military. To make Islam the enemy is to also make those protecting YOU the enemy."

Wilder worked with immigration and knew there would be serious problems. He believed that the travel ban was a poorly implemented mess that was likely to cause real pain to people caught in the middle. "It was extremely clear that the whole goal was just to go on TV and say there's a travel ban," he said. He contacted some people he knew who worked in airports, and the news was alarming. The frontline civil servants in Homeland Security dealing with immigration did not have procedures in place. Across the government, other people who dealt with immigration as a part of their agency didn't either and the confusion went all the way to near the top. Acting Attorney General Sally Yates would later tell a crowd at an Aspen Ideas Festival that she was on the way to the airport after a White House meeting, when she got a call from her principal deputy. "Matt calls me and says, 'You're not going to believe this, but I was just on the *New York Times* website, and it looks like the president has instituted some sort of travel ban.'" She described using the plane's Wi-Fi trying to find a copy of the executive order to read.

Chris said it was chaotic for everyone who worked in immigration, calling it an "absolute disaster." He said, "There were people in all parts of the application process who were affected—midapplication, those who were approved who hadn't gotten on a plane yet." For people who already had a life in the United States as international students or workers, if they were renewing their visas to continue their education or their job, that process ceased and there was no way to know what their options were. Universities didn't know if their professors and students who were returning from visits home would even be allowed back in the country at all. "There was no plan, at all, other than: no more Muslims," Chris said.

Wilder was concerned about the immediate problem: planes were in the air with no clear plan for what to do when people arrived. Because the area between where you depart a flight and where you enter a country is something of a no-man's-land where the immigration apparatus essentially is the law, there was a great potential for abuse and there really wasn't a plan for oversight to keep that from happening. Wilder called it a "clear, clear, clear intent to confuse people." That lack of oversight meant confused new arrivals might face border officials who did improper things with serious consequences, Wilder said. He had heard that they were asking arriving passengers, jet-lagged and ignorant of what had happened, to sign waivers that would abandon their legal US residency, agreeing to return to their home countries—a move he called "completely illegal." The passengers were coerced by vague threats that family members already in the United States might get deported if the passenger didn't comply. Those volunteer attorneys were waiting at many airports, but the passengers didn't have a way to find out about it because the media coverage of the ban was about the political fallout and the protests outside, so the information passengers needed just wasn't getting through. "That did not help the traveler coming from Iran or Iraq" coming back home to family living in the United States "who would meet someone with a badge, a gun, and a passenger list that included lots of information about you—your job, your family in the states, and if you had a minor, nondeportable, crime." In group texts with others whom he knew from years of working in different aspects of immigration, he learned that they were "literally targeting people" for harassment and intimidation, hoping they would voluntarily abandon their green cards for what they thought was the sake of their families, and go try to deal with the US embassy at home.

Wilder describes himself as a hermit who dislikes attention, and said he waited a couple of days to see if anyone was going to start sharing needed information. He didn't know if his account could attract anyone, asking himself, "How do I do it? Why do I do it?" He decided it was up to him and started tweeting messages for families of what to tell their relatives when they arrived, jet-lagged and deeply confused. His direct message notifications started firing off, as befuddled relatives reached out to him trying to find answers, because the government was trying to match policy to a surprise executive order and not communicating about it. When he could, he directed them to online resources that answered their questions, and a few times even helped connect them to individuals who could maybe help.

At the same time, he was trying to use his account to redirect the media to information that would help them run public service stories about what was actually happening. "Sometimes it's not about finding the information," he said, "it's about asking the right questions." News media were tagging him in tweets asking him to verify information they had heard because the facts were hard to follow as the on-the-ground policies seemed to be changing. So he provided what he calls signal boosts, because "people are so overwhelmed with the new president—they are really missing out on the little things that are hurting small circles of people here and there," he said. "There was not one issue that was critical. Everything was critical," he said. During the travel bans, Wilder shared specific information on how to get help from those volunteer attorneys at airports, links to sites in Arabic and Farsi languages explaining what to do, and an image of a wallet card people could use. "I had no intent beyond telling a bunch of famous people this was happening and will you please spread it around, because people do not know." Wilder described his account as "virgin territory" at the time, as social media users and the traditional media covering national issues were struggling to make sense of the rapid changes from the new administration. The government was not communicating well, so Wilder was.

Yates was fired for refusing to enforce a ban she determined was not legal, and Wilder's virgin territory quickly became a familiar one. Over the next three months, the American Civil Liberties Union (ALCU) and other organizations began bringing lawsuits against the government, questioning the legality of the ban. On February 3, Seattle judge James Robard issued an order that blocked the ban. The Department of Justice appealed the next day, a Saturday. On February 9, the court refused to reinstate the ban. On March 6, the president signed a new executive order, fine-tuned to exclude people who already held visas and green cards, in an attempt to avoid the appearance of illegal religious discrimination. Ten days later, it was blocked by a Maryland court. The administration appealed the next day. While this was going on, Wilder continued tweeting, his tone sometimes becoming more strident—calling the president "King Cheeto" for example. He shared news updates on the court cases along with insight he had into the process of developing the successive bans like "For the second time around, no DHS personnel is being consulted on travel ban EO 2.0. DOJ is however." And "EXCLUSIVE: NEW EO TRAVEL BAN: NOW ordered to make more immediate changes to what was last draft. DHS [Department of Homeland Security] scrambling to re-write-internal fight." Wilder also published links to original sources like court filings and, in early March, a full DHS report, which had previously been leaked to the Associated Press, that concluded that citizenship alone was not enough to demonstrate that an individual might be a terrorism threat. At this point, his account had grown to about thirty-two thousand followers.

In April of 2017, Wilder, working from home, was standing in his kitchen waiting on the microwave to finish warming the leftovers he was planning for lunch, entertaining himself with his phone. He was talking in a DM room with a few other accounts that he had been in private messages with for about six weeks, when the blue dot indicating a notification popped up over the bell icon in the app.

Odd.

It was from Twitter Safety, and the message changed everything. It was short—a notice that there was some kind of legal request about the account and to look for an email. "Adrenaline imprints memories in your brain," he said.

On March 14, Twitter received a summons by fax that stated that the company was required to "produce for inspection" "[a]ll records regarding the Twitter account @Alt_USCIS to include, usernames, account login, phone numbers, mailing addressed and IP addresses." News reports around that time noted that the request seemed to be intended to find out who owned that account. If Twitter complied, Wilder's real identity would be revealed to the government and, through public records, eventually to the news media and the general public. The summons threatened court action if Twitter didn't comply and, inscrutably, ordered the records be supplied March 13—the day before Twitter actually received the summons. It was supposed to be a secret. The court filing states that the government requests the social media platform to not let the user know, but Twitter did not want to go along with that. The company told Customs and Border Patrol Special Agent Adam Hoffman that unless there was an actual court order forbidding it, they would let Wilder know.

Twitter fought the request from the beginning. They immediately replied that they would not comply with the directive and even gave Customs and Border Patrol a deadline by which they had to withdraw the summons in order to avoid being sued by the company. Twitter did file suit, and the filing against the government stated, "The public, user-provided description of the #ALT_USCIS account described its user or users as '[o]fficial inside resistance.' . . . Tweets from this account use hashtags such as "#altgov," expressing self-identifying as part of the broader alternative agency movement." The company shared the concern that if anonymous accounts could be identified, an important route of dissent could be suppressed.

As the news quickly spread to other accounts that claimed to be Alt-Gov, worry and fear spread as well. "We struck a nerve in the administration, and they didn't like it," Mickey said. "I was terrified that it was going to impact the original group of Alt accounts (including myself) and the administration was going to use all legal means to expose and charge us with frivolous charges." They described sleepless nights and fear that they would lose jobs or the opportunity to work as a government contractor. The fear was there, even for the ones who did not work with the government. Lawsuits, even frivolous ones, are expensive, time consuming, and carry risks. "Any of us could be next," Hunter said. There wasn't much most of the accounts could do to help, but Gerry had the idea of using Tee Spring, a company that will let you design T-shirts and donate the profits to the charity of your choice, to donate to the ACLU, and some immigration organizations. The dark colored shirts read "#WeAreAltGov" and the slogan "Tweet despite the heat" over an American flag with a zigzag pole based on the symbol for electrical resistance. They raised several hundred dollars.

It turned out that the summons was the end of a process rather than a start of one. A series of emails released to watchdog group American Oversight show that DHS officials were aware of other AltGov accounts like ALT_RAIO and alt_CBP and were monitoring them as far back as late January and suggested an organization trying to manage technology some members didn't really understand. One official noted, "I don't have access to Twitter. . . . I need to get with these modern times." On January 30, Andrew Onello, who worked as a chief information security officer for the DHS, sent a breakdown of several AltGov accounts, including mentioning looking through employees of the agency by combing lists of the accounts' followers. DHS was in chaos at the time because of executive orders and travel bans, and perhaps this kept them from doing much more than note that Alt accounts existed, and that they might become a concern.

When Twitter received the summons, it began its own lawsuit, but also acted to protect Wilder, Wilder said. "The first thing they did was contact the ACLU," Wilder said. Twitter asked the nonprofit if they would want to represent Wilder as an individual and the ACLU agreed, asking a team of several lawyers to help. The company defied the request to not notify Wilder about the summons. The communications were serious— "You need to contact an attorney"—along with a list of attorneys who were aware of the issue at the ACLU.

Wilder said one of his immediate worries was whether he slipped in the processes he used to keep his account reasonably private and anonymous. He racked his brain to remember if he had ever logged into the @Alt_USCIS account from his own phone, which would have made the address of his internet connection apparent. The rest of the information on the account was made up, he said, but the network address could be a problem if he had ever made a mistake. His second worry was a laptop he had only used for Twitter. He wanted to make sure it could not give away private information. He reformatted the hard drive twice, to make the information stored on it unrecoverable, then destroyed the drive itself. He took some chips from the main part of the computer that could possibly have identified information on it and live-tweeted himself baking it in the oven to destroy them. "I didn't sleep" he said, until the summons was rescinded, spending time looking at other ways he acted online and removing what he could. His fear wasn't just for himself, but for his family. He was separated from his spouse, and he had to reach out and ask the spouse to anonymize their social media a bit.

He called the lawyers at the ACLU that Twitter recommended and learned that Twitter was about to sue the government. Filing court papers makes the matter public, but, he said, the lawyers didn't feel like the suit would catch much attention. They were wrong. The summons quickly became public, with multiple news outlets running stories, even overseas. In a piece on her regular evening show, Rachel Maddow reported that the summons cited a portion of the US code relating to "inquiries relating to the importation of merchandise," adding "one: they don't have a sense of humor and two: they're not that awesome when it comes to the legal stuff." She described @Alt_USCIS as "this mean, parody Twitter account." But CBS justice reporter Paula Reid noted that although it wasn't clear why the agency wanted to unmask this account, "It does suggest that they believe it is legitimate and tweeting out legitimate information."

The lawyers helped him go through his past actions to check and see if he had shared any privileged information. He had not. They found that everything he had shared had been made public in some way prior to his sharing it. He said they became confident that "there was nothing legally they could do to me." At the same time, the exposure in the media caused his account to grow—moving from around thirty-two thousand to more than seventy thousand. Most people would celebrate their grow-ing influence, he said, but it was no party for him because he was already feeling exposed "That was my fear." He thought about alternative plans. The ACLU people he talked to told him that they could help arrange for him to hide if his information became public and he was threatened. He considered hiding out with extended family if he needed to. Wilder gives the ACLU a lot of credit. "They literally dropped everything" they had to make themselves available he said, offering their cell phone numbers and even taking a call at two o'clock in the morning. He said he felt "that they really cared about my well-being, and they really cared about the cause. . . . They cared about protecting free speech online."

The summons also brought up serious questions about citizen rights to privacy and corporate responsibility. Free speech was in play as well, as the threat of having your identity exposed could cause you to think twice about sharing your views—a matter that concerned some members of Congress. Ron Wyden, a Democratic senator from Oregon, asked the department for clarification in his role as ranking member on the Senate Finance Commit-tee. His inquiry described him as "gravely alarmed." He wanted to know why the subpoena happened. The department's response included a desire to see if the account owner, whom they suspected was a government em-ployee, had committed misconduct. The Inspector General for DHS, John Roth, told the senator that his office helped scrape the tweets from Wilder's account and then compared them to DHS information to see if any of it was classified. It was not, and in his report to Wyden, the inspector general said, "I'd like to make it clear that DHS OIG has not played any role in attempting to identify the owner of the @ALT_USCIS Twitter account, and only learned of the issuance of the March 14, 2017, summons when it was reported in the media." The response also shows some concern for the effects of investigations into people's social media. "Our investigation protocol includes controls for situations in which First Amendment activity is implicated," he wrote, "and we strive to ensure that our work does not have a chilling effect on individuals' free speech rights." Acting commissioner Kevin McAleenan also replied to Wyden's questions, framing it as a matter of internal misconduct.

Massachusetts Representative Katherine Clark asked as well, noting that the summons cited a part of the US code referring to importation of goods, but Clark's letter wryly notes that the summons "does not specify what merchandise @ALT_USICS was attempting to import into the United States." Clark requested an inspector general investigation because "it would appear that this summons was used for an unauthorized purpose to chill political speech." In other words, she was concerned that the administration was misusing the law to silence critics. Clark also noted that the summons instructs the recipient to not talk about the summons. "I am concerned that others may have been subjected to unlawful summons in the past but have not come forward." Clark's concerns may have been worthwhile. After Trump left office, it came out that the Department of Justice had, in fact, been asking for phone records and emails from various accounts belonging to multiple journalists around the same time.

It wasn't just members of Congress who felt the summons was problematic. On April 6, Twitter filed a complaint in the US District Court to block the subpoena. In the filing, Twitter stated that Alt accounts are a platform for current employees who disagree with the administration to exercise their First Amendment rights and that anonymity is crucial for that to work. "Such fears are likely to be especially great for users of 'alternative agency' accounts who are currently employed by the very agency that is a principal target of the commentary," the suit says, "in light of the retaliation, harassment, or even loss of livelihood that might occur if their real identities became known to their superiors." Ultimately, the issue with Wilder went quiet because Customs and Border Patrol withdrew the summons. But an April 7 email from Molly Groom described the agency as "working with DOJ on what steps to take."

Wilder was confident that because he had only shared information made public by other sources first, he had done nothing wrong. But he still worries. He wonders if the government withdrew the subpoena because they figured out who he was and decided he wasn't actually a threat. He worries about vigilantes. He said he figures that most people who might think of attacking him as defending the president would just choose to mock him online if his identity became public. Perhaps a few would go as far as to drive by his house. "There's always going to be that one crazy guy" who might do something stupid, he said, remembering back to when Edgar Maddison Welch drove from North Carolina to Washington, DC's, Comet Ping Pong Pizza and fired an AR-15 inside the restaurant, believing a conspiracy theory about child endangerment happening there. Welch was sentenced to prison, but Wilder said, "But it takes only one crazy guy with a gun to completely alter the direction of my life."

Threats were a part of life for AltGov accounts, and Wilder's notoriety attracted some unwanted attention. For example, Twitter user @AnthonyBartol15 tweeted a photo of someone wearing an FBI hat like the ones you can buy from the tourist kiosks in DC with the words "We are coming for you pal! Mr. Alt_USCIS." Wilder replied with snark, "Ok. Bring snacks. Don't forget your blood pressure meds." The account blocked Wilder after the reply, but followers took screenshots of the threat and circulated them so that others could report it to Twitter. The account was suspended. He got direct messages as well, some profane and one telling him to be careful because "U know in America we have the right to carry lord Jesus lead." Threats both on open Twitter and in direct message were a common part of being an Alt. Alex got several and also took a mocking approach, taking and posting screenshots of the menacing direct messages. He said he wasn't actually too worried about it. "I kind of think of them like bomb threats: unless it's a weird situation where some group is trying to minimize casualties, the threats just project weakness. The people who really want to blow you up won't ask permission first." Other Alts took it more seriously. When Noor was threatened with someone wanting to "teach you a lesson," he locked his account down for a few days.

As far as Twitter and social media in general in democracy: my perspective is that we kinda took a safety-critical domain (the political process, participatory representative democracy, governance, among other things) and allowed it to be driven by software that was written under a framework that simply did not believe it would ever operate in a safety-critical domain.

There's also a weird impulse to just write a Medium post titled "How My Joke Account Fooled Everyone And Why You Should Consider Yourselves Lucky I Wasn't Evil," because there is no way I should have ended up here. I'm a rando software developer. No political experience. Why did an anti-propaganda organization "vouch for me" before even vetting? Why did a CNN anchor call me? Why do a bunch of journalists and people who appear in boxes on CNN like Rick Wilson follow me? Like, this is farce. It's comedy. But it feels like the kind of comedy club where the guy's bombing with 99% of the audience, but you're there laughing your _ss off and can't understand why people don't see it.

@AltCyberCommand (Alex)

5

STRATEGY

Information has always been something of the major focus for the AltGov accounts—information they shared with each other in private messages, information from inside their agency that was publicly accessible but not known outside the agency because no one had thought to ask. Information that might shape conversations in the future. The Alts used a variety of strategies to make their information sharing effective, and those strategies take a variety of forms. Sometimes, it's a matter of careful planning and coordination. Knowing that people are more likely to share a message that makes them feel something strong like rage or joy, maybe an account will create more of those kinds of messages. Sometimes it's a more seat-of-the-pants strategy, where an Alt comes up with a message for an event that's happening right now. There are advantages to both.

Some of the Alt accounts had strategic training in other parts of their lives, whether for business, for government work, or for contracting work for national security. One of those lessons was that the ability to influence someone doesn't have to come from an actual position of power. Even AltGov accounts that held powerful positions in their agencies were not doing the kinds of things that anyone outside their agency was likely to know about. But what they did have was information and the willingness to share it. Even though the information wasn't classified or even kept out of public view by some departmental policy, just listening to what followers were worried about and sharing information that helped them understand could make a big difference. In some cases, it was even possible to set the agenda: to shape the conversations by telling people what was important to think about.

They had to be quite strategic. Booker had a thoroughly developed strategy, enriched by the lessons he had learned on the job. There's a normalcy bias, he explained. Events that should be alarming are presented as if they are part of things that could normally happen, and because people don't like uncertainty, they will come to believe it is typical. A story about spying or foreign influence is treated as if that kind of thing happens all the time. People are likely to accept a mundane explanation for extraordinary events because it's easier to understand that way. When there is information to which you want to attract attention, you have to choose your method. He said, "How to release the information is dependent upon desired impact 1. Stories with high potential to spread virally are released through social media. 2. Stories likely to be ignored by media outlets, based on news cycle dynamics or inherent normalcy bias, are released through social media. 3. Stories with high impact, which fit traditional media standards of evidence and vetting, fit the current news cycle, or require in-person legwork are generally worked jointly with a member of the print or television press."

This collaboration implies that the media are a part of investigating some information before it is released. Truly, US laws governing media and expectations from the readers and viewers of news do help to make this happen. But when little-known information about an embarrassing administration action or policy would show up in the news, with some news articles crediting upward of twenty unnamed sources, the government was concerned. There was a government-wide effort to encourage employees to avoid leaks. It went a step further at the Environmental Protection Agency, where employees were required to attend antileak training sessions, both for classified information but also for what news articles described as "controlled unclassified information," with the admonition that even if information is not classified, it could still affect national security. According to news reports, a document used in the training warned "Enemies of the United States are relentless in their pursuit of information which they can exploit to harm US interests." Employees were also reminded that there were official channels where they could report wrongdoing through inspector general offices. This was both true and something that persisted across presidential administrations. However, AltGov account holders had a relatively high level of distrust that useful information was being preserved or released. The subpoena against Wilder meant that the government was specifically going after them. They even had collected evidence from studying the internet protocol addresses that interacted with their accounts that the government was continuing to try to monitor and gather information from many of the Alt accounts.

It was safer to share information with a journalist, perhaps using encrypted message tools like Wire and Signal, that were harder to monitor. Many journalists who covered the Trump administration had contact information for these apps right in their online profiles. "I have discovered that everyone has at least one reporter they work with," Gary said. Some reporters who worked with Alt accounts were from new media outlets like Buzzfeed, and others were from cable outlets. On the reporter side, some of them followed AltGov accounts as well. For example, CNN's Jake Tapper followed Charlie, and Jim Acosta followed Sabah. In fact, more than 130 journalists from outlets as big as MSNBC and as small as local television stations followed at least one of the AltGov accounts. Of them, thirty-seven specialized in covering environmental issues—not surprising, given the movement's origins in keeping science data public.

The journalists were helpful in both getting information out and for adding credibility as they verified things. But they worked on their own stories, only sometimes choosing to follow leads from or get help from AltGov accounts. From their side, the accounts sometimes saw that it was important to get a piece of information out to the public that maybe wouldn't seem newsworthy on the surface. In other words, it's more than working with the press to try to ensure that information that's released to the public is verified. There's also a need to help the information spread. Booker made an analogy to medicine. Rapidly spreading information has been described as "going viral." He described how in gene therapy an HIV virus that causes disease can be altered so that the harmful part is replaced with something helpful. So it is with his message strategy. "If other countries' propaganda attacks are virtual viruses, we've replaced the payload with civics and media literacy. Just as rapidly spreading. . . . But not a disease: a virtual vaccine."

That's where emotion comes in. "Eliciting emotional response is an effective tool, if used correctly," Booker said. Strong emotions like anger can help get a message across effectively. Users are more likely to reshare bits of information that incite outrage. "They spread rapidly," Booker said. The spread, the likes, and the reshares, in themselves help the information get selected by social media algorithms to be presented to more people. Popular pieces of information are also more likely to be believed. The wisdom of the crowd can lead to some pretty inaccurate beliefs—this even forms its own logical fallacy. It's also effective in getting a story seen while lowering risk. "The anger would serve to divorce any resulting story from my initial tip, increasing its credibility and preserving our ability to operate [with] less scrutiny from hostile entities," Booker said.

Another strategy was humor. For a long time, Sam signed off every night with an outer space-themed GIF. Sometimes they were semiserious, like an astronaut planting a flag or Sally Ride spelling the word "astronaut." Others were silly, for example cats chasing flying saucers or planets. "Snark and humor and silliness are the Trojan horse to get people's attention," Ning said. Although some accounts are more comfortable with in-your-face humor than others, they recognize that it works. "Regrettably, Twitter users are less likely to reward for civil and polite language; snark baits engagements," Taylor said. Reid put it more directly saying, "Trade is boring, so I do a great thread on trade, I get four likes. I say, 'Did I remind you that I hate Trump?' I get one hundred likes, lol." For Asher, it is like the strategy of taking the wind out of the sails of the KKK by having Superman battle them in a comic. Instead of arguing facts or explaining why something is bad, just make fun of it. It then becomes silly. "In my personal experience the best way to counter bad information or disinformation isn't to try to explain why it is bad, it's to completely dismiss it," he said. The humor was sometimes in the service of schadenfreude: when someone enjoys another's pain. Humor didn't always have the desired effect for everyone. A recurring campaign hashtagged #AltsAfterDark is an example of this: a designated time when Alts and followers would share a series of funny GIFs. Some people thought it was hilarious, but others thought it was childish or diminished the gravitas of AltGov. Still, once in a while, an Alt account will ask for feedback from followers, and humor is one of the things followers say that they appreciate the most.

Part of the strategy is knowing how effective you are, and some of the Alts are very attentive to the success of their messages. Most keep track of followers, either on Twitter or using other apps like SocialBlade, which can show changes in the numbers of people following over time. Using an analytics feature that Twitter offers, some track impressions—the number of people who have had access to a particular tweet in their feed, in addition to the number of those who like or reshare a particular post. When there are coordinated campaigns where everyone shares something about the same issue at the same time, they will track and discuss those kinds of measures. Some track things like engagement rate—the number of likes or shares they get divided by the number of tweets. Someone told me his goal was a 5 percent engagement over twenty-eight days, and that he knew that tweets with images, GIFs, and other multimedia perform better, so he tried to do that wherever possible.

That procedure extends to interaction with others too. One Alt described a process of trying to be the first to reply to a tweet from a high-profile account, like the US Press Secretary (at the time, Sean Spicer). By being the first to reply and forming a tweet that said in a few words something that many people would agree with, it meant high visibility for his account. He also mentioned that he would sometimes respond to someone's tweets with a detail or piece of context to help add to what the tweet said. When he does that, he makes sure that what he says can stand on its own so that it's something that the followers of the original tweet might want to share. With other AltGov accounts, his strategy is a little different. He'll ask a question that gets responses or makes an engaging joke. This, too, is planned out. This kind of interaction helps the tweet do better, but also builds good will, which might mean someone will be more likely to share something for him later.

Strategy also helps win followers. Taylor said he likes all replies to his tweets so that his followers know it is a conversation. It's possible to close off the direct messaging features, but he keeps it open, though he ignores most messages, which include strangers asking him to support things that have nothing to do with his account. He also ignores the death threats that show up in his message box. Further, he tries to like posts for other Alts if they don't have any likes, figuring that getting the ball rolling will lead to other likes. It's easier to do something you know is already popular than to take the risk first yourself. This Alt also said he would sometimes remove tweets that weren't doing well. His reasoning is that as he engages with other Alt-Gov accounts or with high-profile accounts like the actual presidential press secretary, some followers check out his profile to see if they would like to follow him (he can see this happening in the analytics as well). By keeping only tweets that do well, he's leveraging something called social proof—the idea that if a lot of people approve of something, it must be good.

Strategy can mean temporary alliances with people you ordinarily wouldn't trust. Some of the AltGov have significant technical skills and use them to battle people they think are bad actors. You can find fingerprints of AltGov action showing up later in news stories and even in congressional proceedings and more. For example, in February 2018, Special Counsel Robert Mueller indicted multiple Russian citizens for interfering in the US election, and several news organizations noted a specific reference to the Twitter account @TEN_GOP. The account, purporting to represent the Tennessee Republican Party, was notable for its more than one hundred thousand followers, for its resharing of a great deal of pro-Trump stories, and for its claims of election fraud that somehow the Trump campaign overcame to win. Mueller's indictment suggests that it was an account that was run from a Russian "troll farm"—groups of people paid to post decep-tive and meddlesome information on social media in order to sow chaos. The indictment surprised journalists, but it was welcome news for some AltGov members who had a hand in exposing the deception behind the account. Alex had found an online source that said when you try to do a password recovery on Twitter, the service will fill in information it knew, in this case the country code of the phone to which the account was registered. The source tried it with the @TEN_GOP account. The country code that prefilled was from Russia. Unfortunately, the account that originally found it had a very small number of followers. It was unlikely that this news would find much of an audience. Alex knew it was in the public's interest to know that Russian trolls were creating US-focused social media. Alex had a somewhat larger audience than the original account, but decided "intentionally, and with forethought" to get the Russia connection to a very large audience by getting the account of Louise Mensch to share it.

@LouiseMensch

So, @Ten_GOP is Russian. Not a good look for those boosting it. At all. Thanks @AltCyberCommand

Mensch, who has written some romance novels, was a controversial figure in the world of social media information. As a former British member of Parliament, she sometimes had accurate information, but was also known to freely share unvalidated conspiracy theories. Her shares of unvetted, negative information about conservatives may delight frustrated liberals, but spreading potential misinformation could hurt when people need to make informed decisions. Alex thought the additional size of the audience was worth the risk of associating with an account he saw as having questionable credibility. "Louise Mensch wrote an editorial in *The New York Times* that proved that asking the right questions was way easier than answering them and went off into confirmation bias land. You'd get hit up three times per week to 'call her out,' which in my evaluation was stupid because I had little to gain and a huge network effect to use," he told me. "So yeah, fully premeditated." Booker also amplified the evidence against @TEN_GOP. He told me, "I sent the video to a Senator's staffer," adding that the senator was on the Senate Select Committee on Intelligence. Alex enjoys a bit of schadenfreude, having moved a minor explanation on Twitter to higher recognition and ultimately the permanent public record. "Like, here is a guy from Twitter explaining what a f_ckup this was, on camera, and entered into federal record for all eternity," he said. Although Alex and Booker were able to make a difference, Alex felt a little awkward working with a figure like Mensch. "It's an odd thing to have social media advocacy make you feel like a sociopath. . . . I recall the Mensch association made a few of us wary at first, but it was well-played."

I think I've always told my kids, find your people. Be good, be kind. Find people. It doesn't matter if you're popular—just find people you get along with and love you the way you are. The Twitter world, I don't even know why I entered it. Starting it, and at the time starting what I thought might be a business. I didn't know how to do it. I didn't know what I was doing. There started to be this barrage of negativity about the country and all that. I think I felt a little bit of relief about the belonging. There was always a part of me that wondered—are these people all good? Are there people in this DM who aren't who they say they are? It was a mix of feeling a sense of belonging and still not being able to share who I really was, because I am not sure who they were.

@TheNationalGood. (Noor)

6

STORMS

The National Weather Service had been tracking Hurricane Harvey since it formed on August 17, 2017, starting as a tropical wave off the coast of Africa. Though it hit parts of the Caribbean as a minimal tropical storm and weakened, the waters of the US Gulf Coast were very warm, and forecasters feared that the storm could reorganize. On August 23, it did, and by the next day, forecasters grew increasingly confident that a major storm could hit the Texas coast. The storm fed off the warm water and got stronger fast, reaching a dangerous Category 4 by Friday evening. Winds of 130 miles per hour swirled over the ocean, slowly drawing closer and closer to the more than two million people living in Houston, America's fourth largest city. Sam lived nearby, so he stayed close to the weather reports—stunning radar images showing a monster with winds so high they earned a rare "extreme wind warning" stretching nearly the entire coast of the state of Texas. The storm came ashore in Rockwall, more than 180 miles from Johnson Space Center, but insult slowly met injury as the winds and rain held together and meandered over the state and the Gulf of Mexico, dropping day after day of record-breaking rain over south and mid-Texas.

Houston has several nicknames: Space City (referring to NASA), the Big Heart (for its aid to more than one hundred thousand evacuees from Hurricane Katrina), and the Bayou City (named for the serpentine waterways that cross its downtown). Although the city is fifty miles inland from the Gulf of Mexico, it sits at only about one hundred feet above sea level and is prone to flooding. And flood it did. Parts of the Houston area received more than fifty inches of rain in a week and at its peak on September 1, one-third of the city was underwater, with more than thirty-nine thousand people forced from their homes. Though the governor had preemptively declared thirty counties disaster areas, this declaration wasn't accompanied with mandatory evacuation orders everywhere, in part because previous hurricanes had shown how difficult it was to clear out such a high population from the coast. Harvey was a slow-moving disaster that played out, in part, on social media.

As the floodwaters continued to rise in parts of Texas, desperate families called 911 hoping for a rescue, in some cases from a house where water was pouring in and rising as high as their attic. Some panicked callers were put on hold. The city's 911 system, on a normal day, processed around three thousand calls, and even with that, residents sometimes complained about slow responses. For Harvey, the city beefed up staff taking 911 calls. Normally, there were about twenty-five people, but during Harvey, more than two hundred were deployed, processing seventy-five thousand calls in a single weekend. The 911 center itself flooded. Residents waited on hold, sometimes more than twenty minutes, watching the waters rise around them. Local help was not forthcoming, so they turned to their cell phones, posting pleas for help on social media or texting friends and family who sometimes posted on their behalf.

Halfway across the country, Ning was watching Twitter and seeing these pleas: "Cancer patient with feeding tube"; "My Mom, elderly and disabled and have my nephew"; "Need rescue at Park Dale Mall read just south of Rose Hill Acre"; "(1 adult, 8 year old w/autism) on top of car in garage." The appeals kept coming, and they were heartbreaking. Watching from afar, he saw people's worry turn to fear and then to terror. Emergency services were overwhelmed so volunteers stepped in to help. Ning knew one thing—AltGov accounts had an audience. Was there a way to get the information about who needed help into the hands of the people who were offering it?

Gerry didn't work for the government but had a trusted account. He was able to talk to others in some of the DM rooms, a process that still mystifies him. "They were joking around, and then I was joking around with them. And I don't know who it was that plopped me into a DM, but I ended up in a DM just randomly, and I don't know, it felt kind of like I was . . . I'm trying not to sound lame here, but like, well, I'm cool. You know, like, I joined like, some secret club or something," he said. Gerry was online, too, and keeping an eye on the storm. By Sunday, August 27, Ning was talking with Suuad, Gerry, Noor, and Morgan in the main AltGov message room. Between them, they had a good understanding of how federal agencies such as the US Coast Guard and FEMA would work alongside local agencies like fire and sheriff's departments to help those in need. One of the issues was with information problems: they could see people seeking help outside the overwhelmed 911 system and at the same time they could see people with boats wanting to help, but not knowing where or how. Could they call on their followers to help them with a fix? The tagging features on Twitter—searchable usernames and hashtags—could make it easier to catalog all the calls for help. It's possible for one person to have multiple Twitter accounts, so Suuad registered a Twitter account called @HarveyRescue and Noor created a graphic for the AltGov accounts to share. Followers could reshare it in hopes that a #HarveyRescue hashtag would trend and people in need could use it to make their tweets easier to find, which followers, local media, and Twitter influencers did.

Gerry had never used Google Sheets before, but he felt like the need to help was urgent. "At that time, we understood that, you know, Trump and the administration was just so dysfunctional. There wasn't any faith that they were going to actually move quickly enough. It really felt like we were the only ones doing something." They started to see the work begin to pan out. Suuad, Gerry, and Morgan searched Twitter for requests using the hashtag as others entered the requests into a Google spreadsheet so that multiple people could access it. Five hours of feverish searching and typing went by as row after row of the spreadsheet filled, but the tweets needing to be keyed in kept piling up. Morgan started feeling like he was hours behind.

Meanwhile, Noor tried to reach volunteers who posted that they had boats and to contact existing rescue organizations. He soon contacted a group called the Cajun Navy. There are several groups that have "Cajun Navy" as part of their name that do charitable work, including search and rescue. Cajun Navy volunteers first became famous in the aftermath of Hurricane Katrina, where volunteer locals, using their own fishing boats, conducted high-water rescues in residential areas or plucked people walking chest-deep out of the flood waters and transported them to shelters. After Katrina, Lt. Gen. Russel Honoré told CBS News, "In reality, most people are saved by neighbors and volunteers after a disaster than are saved by organized rescue people." Noor was hoping to find those neighbors and volunteers and match them up with the calls for help, which were overwhelming Morgan and Suuad and coming in faster than they could type.

It was a risk, but they knew they needed help. Via tweets, they asked their followers to help out by sending direct messages (DMs) offering aid. Rahel, who had been following AltGov accounts since they first came online, said, "I wasn't sure how they were going to help, or what I had to offer but I was willing to give it a shot. I was watching it unfold both on Twitter and the news and couldn't just sit by and do nothing. If there was something I could do to help, I had to do it. I responded to the tweet and let them know I was willing to help if they still needed it." Messages began to come in with followers offering help. In a DM room, they received instructions and access to the spreadsheet, now configured so that anyone with the link could add to it. It was a powerful moment for some of the followers. Rahel said, "My first reaction to what I was seeing was a sense of being overwhelmed and awestruck all at the same time. I was now included in a group DM with the very people I looked up to and came to regard as heroes. It was very intimidating to say the least. I wanted so badly to help and not mess something up. I was amazed at what I was seeing. The Alt-gov accounts had taken all their knowledge and experience and had come up with a way to help the people of Texas." These first volunteers, found through the follower network the AltGov had already built, became the start of the data entry team.

Twitter DM rooms turned out to have numerous problems. Anyone can participate in a conversation, and messages are loaded as soon as they are written, which means that threads of conversations get mixed up together in a way that can be very hard to follow. But it was the only thing they had. "It was incredibly inefficient," Gerry said. "Obviously. Everybody was anonymous, right? Nobody knew anybody's phone number or anything. We literally just had Twitter to communicate with each other." New people continued to volunteer and were added. The effect was like being dropped into a crowded space where there were multiple conversations, and it was hard to pick out any coherent messages. Additionally, as the hours stretched on, people didn't want to take breaks because of the life-or-death situations that were unfolding, resulting in sleep deprivation making matters worse. Suuad retweeted requests in real time adding searchable hashtags so that someone could look at his Twitter timeline for a collection of curated tweets. "I jumped in doing that and didn't lift my head up for three days," he said. His spouse, who didn't really understand what was happening, was tasked with running their household as he stayed glued to the internet.

It became obvious that running things from Twitter was not working, and the project moved to the business communication tool Slack. Slack allows conversations in multiple channels, keeps records, and allows links to important files, like the spreadsheet, be placed in an easily accessible location on the home page. Some channels can be created for public access, while others can remain private and by invitation-only. The move made it easier to keep up with needs and responses, but it also initiated the first crisis regarding leadership. At some point, a new private channel called Admin raised some hackles. "We understood what was going on," Gerry said, "not entirely, because we never obviously had done this before." In retrospect, Gerry said the discomfort was understandable. "We're all volunteers. But as somebody who, you know, could have put in just as many hours as somebody else who ended up in administration felt like they understood what was going on, and they felt like they should be in a higher position." Gerry said he wasn't trying to be anybody's boss, but he knew that organization was the only way they would be able to keep up with their promises of help that were being conveyed through Twitter.

While the drama over who could get things organized roiled, other problems cropped up. With multiple groups following online requests for help, some volunteers with boats or high-water vehicles fighting through the flooded streets were arriving at homes to find them abandoned. Someone had been rescued already or found their own way out. AltGov's out-of-town followers were having trouble finding locations in a city with addresses such as Cherokee Circle, Cherokee Drive, and Cherokee Lane as well as County Roads 2210, 2120, 2130, 2140, and 2170, among other confusable names. As local news and online influencers saw and shared the hashtag, requests kept pouring in faster than the new volunteers could handle. And the water didn't stop rising when the sun went down. Flood waters became more hazardous after dark with floating debris, rafts of fire ants, and even alligators.

The number of volunteers grew, making it easier for some to take breaks. By the wee hours of Monday morning, enough fresh volunteers were available and agreed to take an overnight shift. Asher had joined later, so he stayed up with them. Once there was enough help finding and entering data, some Alts were able to move on and find bigger solutions to the problems at hand, which included keeping data ordered and consistent. Some volunteers were tasked with geocoding, which is a process of taking addresses, or sometimes just descriptions of locations, and figuring out their latitude and longitude—information that a software program could use to create maps for volunteer rescuers to follow. Multiple people editing in a single shared spreadsheet caused problems with duplicated information. At the same time, the work got more attention from the media and as a result, companies began offering solutions. The data visualization company Tableau offered help by converting addresses into helpful maps that allowed volunteers with medical training assign priority requests—a process called "triage." For example, a person who relied on dialysis and needed rescue would receive higher priority than a person with small children and no medical issues. When volunteers verified that a rescue was concluded, they could mark it as complete.

Bringing in new people began to cause other problems internally as well. Asher was involved at the beginning and had issues with people "trying to carve out their piece of the pie" on the rescue effort, which made it difficult to maintain anonymity or even good processes. He was already working on things related to the hurricane as a part of his actual job with the government, and he became "just flat out overworked and stressed." He was complaining about it in a different DM room and someone, whom he still doesn't know, temporarily used Twitter's block feature against him. This feature lets a user keep his or her posts secret from particular other accounts, but it also has the effect of kicking the blocked account out of any shared DM rooms. "I left one night talking to everyone. I came back a bit later and it's all gone. I didn't want to deal with the stress or the drama, so I wiped the account," he said, figuring there were other ways for him to help preserve public resources and data in the face of the Trump administration. He started a new @AltWASONPS account a few months later when another account, who knew who he was in real life, asked him to come back.

Verifying rescues meant talking to people who needed them—a sobering reality volunteers were poorly prepared for. Volunteer Kathryn Taylor told NowThis news that "I was literally tweeting to people who were trapped in their car and people were saying it was life or death and no one could get into 911." It was important work. It helped ensure that rescuers went where they were still needed and helped terrified people realize they were not alone. In some cases, as the 911 system was struggling, it was also the only positive contact that desperate people could make. The emotional cost for the volunteers was brutal. Noor said, "The highs are really high and the lows are really low, but if a person believes that the highs will exist at some point, you can get through the lows. Although, I will tell you, that the lows were really super-duper low." The team that worked on the phones nicknamed themselves "Rainbows and Unicorns." The true nature of the work, talking with drowning people, was too horrible to say out loud.

Requests kept coming in around the clock. More than two hundred volunteers had joined in the effort, some creating elaborate setups including multiple screens and devices. Their work was passed along to volunteer boaters and the US Coast Guard, who used the new maps to identify stranded people growing increasingly desperate as water continued to rise and the sun started setting once again. Morgan had taken time off work so that he could focus on keeping a rapidly growing organization functional. More volunteers meant more hands to type in requests and more voices to make calls to boaters and those in need of rescue. It also meant more chances for misunderstanding and chaos. Time was an enemy, as volunteers needed to leave to go to their regular jobs, to take care of their children, or even just to sleep. As procedures changed to match the number of people doing the rescuing and those needing to be rescued, it was tough to pass along new information consistently as jobs were being handed off. Morgan stepped back to learn each job and wrote them down into a common format that made it easier for people to step into.

The 911 system was still there of course and there was concern over whether volunteer rescue could or should take the place of official emergency rescue. At the same time, the number of people needing help continued to grow, and morale was becoming a problem. Although volunteers were working long hours of tedious and disheartening duties, it was hard to see if their efforts were really making a difference. One bright spot was when the US Coast Guard, which had asked the volunteers if they could provide map data in a different format, reached out to say that it was working and helping them help others. This news was a moment of joy for the volunteers—their efforts were working. The HarveyRescue Twitter account shared the news. That joy soon soured, though, when the Coast Guard tweeted, "*This is NOT true. If in need of a rescue, please contact 911 or use the official USCG numbers pinned to the CG official Facebook and Twitter.*" The volunteers were crushed, and one tweeted back, "I will do the same. I know you don't have cell power. I'm actively helping others. @uscg you rock, but some folks can't stay on dying phones." The reply was immediately followed by requests for help like "S.O.S. Mentally disabled senior & wife stuck 2nd floor: 5735 South Braeswood Blvd, Houston, TX 77096. Please call the coast guard. Thank you." AltGov members still don't know why the agency told people to not post. Perhaps it was because they were talking to the local Coast Guard and national headquarters, which controlled the Twitter account, didn't know. It's also possible that in the political climate, admitting working with an AltGov effort would be too risky for an official government agency. Morgan and Suuad took to Twitter in reply, one response containing more obscenities than the other. Later research found that some government agencies see social media as a useful tool in disasters, but that while they monitor social media, they don't try to use volunteers to collect information. Morgan said he tried to remind people of the good that they were doing—they could see it at the top of the maps, which tracked listings in the database of rescues needed, which was growing rapidly. It also tracked rescues completed, which moved more slowly, but did continue to grow. A new boost came soon after when Houston's official emergency service Twitter account thanked HarveyRescue.

It was Wednesday, and pleas for help were still coming in. Not all of the rescues were from government groups or even from organized volunteers like the Cajun Navy. Individual good Samaritans who had boats and the will wanted to help too. A boating team was working, reaching out to people who posted messages offering to help. The team would call and find out what kind of equipment they had, exactly where they were, and how much they were able to help. Boating team members would talk to these volunteers and use the map to find nearby people who could use that kind of help. It was never clear why, or how, it happened, but as the boating team reached out to boaters, people needing help started calling some of the volunteers on their personal cell numbers. For a while, it was OK and volunteers who received the calls were able to update the map and sometimes notify nearby boaters. For efficiency, HarveyRescue got their own phone number and birthed another team for phone rescue. Volunteers who manned that number would pass along data to the entry team for inclusion on the map. They also were on the other end of calls with panicked people, stranded and watching waters rise around them. Fortunately, help was continuing to show up.

By this time, more than seven hundred people were helping to find and log requests, to update maps, to dispatch boaters and other rescuers, and to talk to the desperate. The volunteer base had expanded geographically as well, with teams in Australia and Europe working day time hours in their part of the world, making it possible for US workers to rest during their evenings. As Alice Stollmeyer, executive director of Defending Democracy, a European nonprofit that works against the threat of autocracy, told American National Public Radio, "The beautiful thing of this initiative is the location of the volunteers becomes irrelevant." At the same time, more than a week in, the continuous churn in people and mission-caused stress that began to boil over.

Some of it was the work itself, which felt relentless. Suuad had the early job of looking for tweets seeking help and then retweeting them so that others looking to enter data would just have to follow one timeline—his. The tweets kept coming, with only a bit of a slowdown at 1:00 a.m. "I would pass out in my bed with my phone next to me. I set my alarm for 5:00 a.m. every day and I would just go through my mentions. It was one hundred 100 percent, no breaks every day." It meant giving up everything else in life. Suuad said that it was up to his spouse to do "one hundred percent of the parenting" while he was working on HarveyRescue. As Suuad said, "It wasn't like we said, 'let's emotionally and psychologically prepare ourselves to watch hundreds of people die.'" He said he really didn't want to talk about it. His spouse "to this day doesn't know what I did, or why." It was hard for the group working on the rescues to talk about the trauma too. "I haven't really heard anyone acknowledge it," Suuad said. "I wasn't really going to process it in that group. They're not my family." As new volunteers were coming in droves, others were facing burnout after a few days. Suuad noted, "Not to process through that degrades our effectiveness. We become a little less strong for other people."

There were frequent arguments on Thursday, Morgan said, and it became obvious that the self-organizing team run from people's couches all over the globe needed some organization. "Even this grassroots, on-the-fly org really needed leadership. Someone to say 'yes' or 'no,' or give direction," Tai said. Morgan took advantage of the respite that the growing volunteer base allowed and wrote a set of operating procedures that worked, sort of. They made sense to the people who had been involved the entire time but were confusing for newcomers, and new issues came up, which meant that some parts became useless. Leadership was a fluid idea. When someone had to log off, it was a matter of who was available and willing to step up to take charge, but the rest didn't always agree. When Morgan and Ning, who had experience in large bureaucracy from their government work, proposed a hierarchy with team leads, it was taken badly by some of the volunteers who had been with them from the beginning. There were accusations of behind-the-scenes deal-making, and no one was at their best to think about the need for organization, instead feeling like they were being cut out. Some of the people who had been with them almost from the beginning, close followers who had even felt like family before this, logged off and walked away. Twitter influencer @AynRandPaulRyan worked with developing a process for bringing in and training new team volunteers, which helped get the work done, but the damage to relationships was irreparable for some.

At the same time, the growing need for resources like spreadsheets and publicly accessible mapping was pushing against the capabilities from free versions of software. There were cases when the list of needed rescues, kept in a Google spreadsheet, simply crashed, appearing to erase not only hours of work, but the real needs of families in peril. As the project became more publicly known, Google reached out to help, as Tableau had earlier. The company allocated some business-class servers to the project and assigned some of its staff to work on modifying Google sheets to meet the complex need of hundreds of people hitting an online spreadsheet from all over the world. The free version of Slack hit its limit, and the company helped by adding capacity to the account so that they could still use it. Engineers from competing companies were working with AltGov members with technical abilities to solve some of these problems, which had grown to include other areas of the Gulf Coast beyond Houston itself.

Within the HarveyRescue organization, issues continued to crop up. Sometimes, the work straddled the line between good, necessary actions, and ethically risky ones. For example, one group was trying to help by essentially triaging people's medical needs. This could be good and necessary for someone on medical oxygen or running out of needed insulin. But on the other hand, understanding someone's situation didn't mean they could guarantee that help would be timely. A volunteer on the phone halfway across the world had limited control over what a volunteer with a boat might do near the person to whom they were talking. Could they essentially be offering false hope? Could it even be dangerous? The volunteers worked on this in a private medical channel on the Slack, one that even the administrators couldn't see. As issues like this were discussed, people in the channel became upset.

The fall of 2017 was an active one meteorologically speaking. The lessons learned from Harvey were quickly brought back to life when Category 4 Hurricane Irma came ashore on Cudjoe Key, Florida, on September 10, after devastating numerous Caribbean islands. More than six million Floridians were ordered to evacuate. It would become the costliest hurricane in the state's history. It took eighty-four lives. HarveyRescue, now known as CrowdSource Rescue, facilitated more than 250 rescues in that storm. The number of rescues was smaller, in part because of dangerous water conditions, which made ground and amateur boat rescue dangerous or impossible in many cases. The psychological toll of talking to desperate victims continued. "We tried bringing in crisis counselors and holding self-care meetings throughout, but it wasn't enough," Morgan said. "Folks were breaking down, and it caused lasting damage to some."

Once again, the effort shifted focus in the face of changing needs, serving as a source of information about on-the-ground conditions and as a connection between people in need of resources and people who had them. Volunteers mined Twitter for first-hand reports in places too remote for media to cover and talked to people in need on the phone, flagging about fifty critical medical requests that were then handled by local emergency services. They called community businesses and organizations, collecting information about what places were open and available to help. They published that information and shared it on social media, which was the only link some citizens had in a time when roads were blocked and the power grid down.

Internally, things worsened. "The same exhausted people who really needed like a good debrief, and like some actual rest went on to do Irma," Suuad said. "I know that we helped," he said, but the cost was high. Competent volunteers from Harvey stepped away, not able to handle a round-the-clock schedule and talking to victims. New volunteers stepped in but fighting broke out. "They thought that the way they wanted to do things were the only way to do things. And they wanted to assert more control over decision making, and how things were done," Suuad said.

Another storm, Hurricane Maria, was churning its way across the Gulf of Mexico. Once again, they wanted to help. CrowdRescue, in collaboration with technology companies, combined new expertise in data collection and newly developed mapping tools. Maria was a Category 4 hurricane when it hit and was the worst natural disaster to affect Puerto Rico in recorded history. The territory was hardly prepared. Years earlier, news reports announced that the island's power company, the Puerto Rico Electric Power Authority, was not up to the job. It had failing infrastructure and a dependence on oil that made cost control difficult. Clean water was also a challenge, even before Maria. The territory was deeply in debt—about $20,000 per person, on an island where household income was less than that. Roads, bridges, ports, and dams were also in poor repair. Maria, with its twelve-hour lashing of winds up to 174 miles per hour, destroyed the feeble power grid as well as thousands of homes, agricultural fields, water systems, cell phone service, and more.

There was concern from the beginning about the quality of federal response to help the island. As a semiautonomous territory of the United States, most residents speak Spanish, the island competes in the Olympics under its own flag, and residents don't pay personal income taxes. They don't vote for US presidents and their only congressional representation is a nonvoting member of the House of Representatives. San Juan's mayor at the time, Carmen Yulín Cruz, was outspoken about what she called a lack of federal support, appearing on numerous TV news and public affairs shows. In the face of criticism, President Donald Trump noted that rescue was complicated by the fact that Puerto Rico is an island. "This is an island surrounded by water, big water, ocean water," he said in a speech that gained international news coverage. A poll conducted at the time showed that half of Americans who responded didn't know that Puerto Ricans are American citizens, and some commentators also wondered if the president knew this as well. Puerto Rico's governor, Ricardo Roselló, issued a statement with an implicit reminder, urging that "we ask the Trump Administration and the U.S. Congress to take swift action to help Puerto Rico rebuild. This is a game-changer. We need to prevent a humanitarian crisis occurring in America." When the US government made decisions like awarding a tiny energy company, Montana-based Whitefish Energy, which at the time had only two full-time employees, a $300 million contract to reconstruct large portions of the power grid, this did not boost the confidence for the Alts and their followers. The firm was alleged to have ties to Secretary of the Interior Ryan Zinke. The inept and slow response to the storm meant that some of the AltGov found another opportunity to use their knowledge to fill the gaps that the government was leaving open.

Though CrowdSource rescue had originally expected to help in Florida with Hurricane Maria, the storm took a different path and so did the AltGov-led actions. "Most boat owners there were impacted by Maria themselves, and outside volunteer groups like Cajun Navy couldn't get there," Morgan said. Cell towers were damaged, and so were utility poles, so without communications or electricity, information itself was a huge need. Where were roads impassable? Where could residents access clean water? Some companies tried innovative ways to help, like cellular service access points suspended from balloons, where residents could get a signal and send messages to worried friends and family. Lessons learned from the previous storms were helpful, but in some ways, Hurricane Maria was a new learning experience. Tai used his knowledge as a business analyst to work with processes in a way that was helpful for a self-organizing team. "I was on alert if there were problems and sometimes got alert notices at night and joined in to fix . . . things. Handled people. Helped maintain our membership lists and also who we had banned," because they were causing more drama then helping. "Although most people stayed within a single or a few channels, I floated across all of them and dealt with issues as they arose, or reported stuff up the chain. Everything from we need more staff to arguments happening in a channel."

Some of CrowdSource's volunteers had family in Puerto Rico and knew that accurate information would be a regular problem. CrowdSource had started using the push-to-talk phone app Zello, which works with either cell signal or WiFi, to talk to the Cajun Navy during Hurricane Harvey, and it found it was helpful in Maria as well. They made more than ninety broadcasts, produced in English and Spanish, that shared updates on what was open and how to get help. Working with technologies mastered in previous storms, CrowdSource created interactive ground condition maps that showed where roads and bridges were passable and where to get fuel. As the maps evolved, more information was added such as where to get water, what health-care facilities were open, and more. Statistics on map use show that the app was opened more than two million times in just three weeks.

Hurricane Maria was also a chance for AltGov to continue its information-sharing mission. For example, Dallas had worked in disaster relief. Maria was a staggeringly strong storm that hit already vulnerable islands. Dallas had a moment of insight that became almost prescient of the government's struggle to mount a recovery effort in Puerto Rico. Disaster cleanup is a major and complicated process, but he had experience to share. In a long thread that fall, he shared tips on everything from what respirator to buy to how to make a Tyvek suit out of a building material used to wrap houses for insulation underneath the facing and duct tape. "Unless it's another live human, nothing is worth sickness or your life," he wrote. "U must protect yourself first."

Many of the seven hundred volunteers dropped away after the 2017 hurricane season, but not all of them. Ning and Morgan had an interest in doing more, and so did Gerry and some others. They began working toward developing a persistent nonprofit that would pool volunteer labor to provide support during disasters. As they worked, it became apparent that they would not be able to do direct rescue like that during Hurricane Harvey. "Our volunteers were not trained in disaster response," Morgan explained, "and we were afraid that continuing to use volunteers like that for direct victim assistance would cause more harm." For the short time the project was active in the 2017 hurricane season, the fact that they were not experts in rescue wasn't a legal problem because good Samaritan exceptions to laws protected them from liability. "But if we continued doing those kinds of services indefinitely, we would be at significant legal liability." To continue to facilitate rescues when 911 was overloaded would have required insurance, and the cost was "far, far beyond what we could manage as a start-up nonprofit." So the new organization worked to find other ways to help the first responders and victims by using volunteers to locate and share information.

Tai and two others created a nomination board that would elect the first board of directors for a permanent nonprofit that grew out of the AltGov's work. Gerry said he feels a sense of pride in what was accomplished. "I know we were definitely helpful," he said. "I just got goosebumps thinking about how cool that was, that we were able to do stuff like that. It wasn't my idea. I can't take credit for it. But just very cool. Like, we definitely were useful, doing a lot of really, really good, cool things during that time."

For Suaad, the trauma of dealing with victims, and the pressures of a constantly changing organization with infighting, were the beginning of his disengagement with parts of AltGov, though he stays in contact with some of the people. Although he describes his experience with Hurricane Harvey as trauma, he also said that "it's changed my life." He's directed his energy into projects that better his own community, which he describes as "very, very, very, very, very poor" with a median income for a family of four under $25,000. "I got to be a part of something like this," he said. "What I was searching for and helping do in Harvey, I could dive in here and have that immediately affect my community."

Tai also described his work with hurricane rescue as life-changing. "It was amazing how much support we could provide—from home. I learned about how disaster support works, volunteer orgs, a lot about ops, leadership, management. It was my first real use of social media," he said. Tai declined to participate in the nonprofit, and he moved on becoming involved with a community emergency response team in his area, which are groups of volunteers who are trained for the types of disasters that might impact their locale: tornado response or earthquakes or wildfires, for example. He has also used some of the lessons about data mining and how information flows on social media to work on what he calls "data for good" projects.

Imagine you're seeking asylum from a nation throwing chemical weapons at your children. Imagine what you must have experienced to be this desperate.

For the people in the back:

SEEKING ASYLUM IS NOT ILLEGAL

@NastyWomenofNPS. (Colby)

7

WHERE ARE THE CHILDREN?

Immigration from Central America and Mexico was a hot-button issue from the very beginning of the Trump campaign. The president, launching his bid for the White House in a speech, said, "They're sending people that have lots of problems, and they're bringing those problems with us. They're bringing drugs. They're bringing crime. They're rapists. And some, I assume, are good people." Immigration through the southern border was far from a new problem, but it made for a great talking point in a presidency for which a "great, great wall" on the southern border was a significant campaign promise. Things became more heated early in the Trump years, when news of migrant caravans coming from Central America to the United States dominated conservative networks and some mainstream media as well. In 2018, BuzzFeed had a reporter travel with a caravan of more than one thousand migrants who were coming on foot and on other transportation hoping to go through Mexico. Some of them would try to stay in Mexico, and some of them would try to enter the United States. Migrant caravans help these travelers make the journey and avoid some of the dangers they may encounter. For example, criminal gangs will try to steal things from the migrants or in some cases assault them, sexually or in other ways. But there was a sticky point: the migrants in the caravan told the reporter that they were seeking refuge from violence in their home countries. As such, they would be able to seek asylum if they crossed into the United States under US law. If they didn't have a legitimate asylum claim, they could be deported, sometimes even the very same day. In April 2018, via multiple tweets, President Trump asked other countries to help the United States keep migrants from coming to the US southern border. He mentioned NAFTA, the important trade agreement with Mexico and Canada, as well as the status of foreign aid that the US gave to Honduras and other countries that are allowing migrants to leave. He asked in a tweet for Mexico to stop the people and drugs, ending with "NEED WALL!" He then talked about how border patrol agents could not do their jobs because of the liberal "catch-and-release" policy. As president, Trump had taken several steps on his own to try to suppress immigration, for example signing an executive order asking his administration to end catch-and-release and putting in place a controversial plan to send up to four thousand National Guard troops to patrol the border.

The administration's tough actions on the border had started even earlier. As soon as March 2017, John Kelly, then the secretary of the Department of Homeland Security, told CNN that the administration was considering separating parents from children as a way of deterring people from coming to the United States and seeking asylum. In a meeting later that month, he reassured Senate Democrats that such a policy was not actually being considered, but later media reports and congressional transcripts show that some children were separated from their parents. For example, there was a trial separation program in El Paso, Texas, in 2017, affecting around 175 families. It was later revealed that because the administration did not effectively track family members, it was going to be difficult to reunite them in the future. Conservative pundits and organizations like the Center for Immigration Studies stated that potential immigrants were being coached on what to say regarding them receiving asylum, which put considerable pressure on the government.

Even though the trial family separation program had been controversial, discussions on a family separation project continued into 2018, with a draft zero tolerance policy circulating by April 4. Attorney General Jeff Sessions ordered that policy on April 6 and said that all people who cross the southwest border illegally must be prosecuted, which was complicated for those traveling with their children, as parents would be put into detention facilities that didn't accommodate children. By May 4, the new Department of Homeland Security secretary Kirstjen Nielsen had signed a memo requiring that adults traveling with children must be referred to the Department of Justice to be prosecuted. Zero tolerance. Sessions then gave a speech saying, "If you are smuggling a child, we will prosecute you and that child will be separated from you as required by law," which left the question of what was going to happen to the children who were taken from their parents.

When those children's mothers and fathers went to jail under the zero tolerance policy, the children were reclassified as "unaccompanied," which meant that they went into a network of shelters run by the Department of Health and Human Services. The administration argued that this was a way to keep children out of the hands of traffickers and safe in the custody of the US government. The look was bad, though. Media shared images of tent cities full of teenagers close to the Mexican border in Texas. A CNN report stated that a Honduran woman told an attorney that authorities took her daughter while she was breastfeeding her and handcuffed the mother when she objected. At the same time, parents appearing in immigration court were telling judges that they had no idea where their children were. There were even examples of young children appearing in immigration court without their families. The American Academy of Pediatrics issued a condemnation, stating "We need to treat children with compassion and respect. This means not separating them from their parents. This means not keeping them in detention. This means having pediatric guidance and medical professionals to care for them when they are in United States custody." Even the United Nations Human Rights Council issued a condemnation of the administration's policy, saying it might "amount to torture." The UN's condemnation came just a few days after the United States pulled out of that same Human Rights Council.

For some of the Alts, the issue of child separation was deeply personal. Noor was an immigrant, coming to the United States as a child with his parents. But back in his home country, his parents had seen child separation first-hand when missionaries arrived in their country and took native children from their families, forcing them into boarding schools—a pattern that has been repeated in many countries. Wilder also felt personally close to the issue. Also an immigrant, he said his parents instilled in him the obligation to "stand up for something that you're thinking wrong. You can do that even while you're hungry . . . no one can take it away from you." He shared tweets about people who were exploiting corruption in the immigration system to profit off housing the children and detaining the adults. For example, he tweeted, "The Supreme Court validating indefinite detention of immigrants by ICE. Money for private prisons," letting followers know that there was a financial element behind the political news. Wilder said he saw the AltGov, working with others, as a group that could make a difference through information and advocacy.

For Chris, it was a work issue. He said that the impact on the Department of Justice (DOJ) staff was really different depending on where they worked. "By the time someone would reach the nondetained court in another state, it was pretty removed from the sheer horror of incarceration and separation. But if you were at a court in Texas . . . it was a lot closer." In Texas, "people are seeing parents asking where their kids are or are getting reports of people not coming to court because they were murdered while waiting in Mexico." But even though he didn't live in a border state at the time, Chris said, "We were still horrified at what [was] going on." He described it as cruel and inhumane, and said he couldn't understand how DOJ headquarters could approve of this policy, asking "how are you ok with snatching children from their parents after they've already been through such a horrendous ordeal to get to the US? And they didn't just up and decide to come—they were already suffering before, so to take someone who has already suffered so much and steal their child?"

The important legal issue was that many of the arrivals were seeking asylum. "Asylum is not illegal. At all. Going to the border and presenting yourself and requesting asylum is exactly what people are supposed to do. This act was taking a legal, internationally recognized humanitarian act and criminalizing it in such a degrading, cruel way," Chris said. He also said that some of the immigration court staff started implementing small acts of resistance like leaking information to the media and pointing out how decisions on removal varied in different venues. Judges in California might be more lenient than judges in Georgia, for example, because there are more advocates for immigrant rights in California. Chris said the disorganized way the plan was put together caused a lot of harm, because if they didn't keep up with tracking children and the children were too young to identify their parents, it was going to be very difficult to reunite them.

Ning said that for him, it was also a work issue, but more from a policy perspective. He said that it seemed like the goal was more to divide the public than to have beneficial impacts. "When you're the federal government," he said, "you have care for the people who we impact. And the child separation policy was a great example of perhaps lack of planning, or lack of caring for the impacts that would have on real people at every turn." Beyond this, he said, he is just interested in child welfare, so solving a political problem by causing trauma made him sad.

Noor wanted to try to make a difference. He knew that one of the big questions that needed to be answered was what was happening to the children who were in care. He reasoned that bad things happen to people when they are out of the public eye. It was a reasonable fear. Health and Human Services data released a few years later showed more than two thousand allegations of sexual abuse of unaccompanied minors in government care were made in 2016 and 2017 alone. Those were allegations. Department of Justice reports indicate that they confirmed that there were more than one hundred cases where the government caregivers themselves were reported to be the abusers. Because of the volume of children who were separated, they ended up being sent to facilities around the country.

News programs had video of school buses equipped with toddler safety seats and stories of children being flown around the country. Where were the children?

Noor had been an elementary school teacher and worked with scouts. He said he was drawn to the issue by the "power that place holds in our emotional and mental well-being. And that if we're separated from place, which to me, includes not just physical land, but family and that whole connection to our natal beginnings, you know, when that gets ripped apart the fallout is just enormous."

The news was heartrending. ProPublica published an audio recording of children screaming as they were being taken from their parents. Binkowski, who was involved in central AltGov DM groups, visited and actually crossed over the border to take photos and shared them in messages. She also passed along front-line information. Noor found it all horrifying. He reached out to some of the former hurricane volunteers who had worked on building the database of needed rescues to see if they would help look through public information and create a broad view of where separated children were being held. ProPublica already had a crowdsourced effort underway to figure out locations. Noor and his team were able to add a lot. There weren't enough federal facilities to hold everyone at the border, and some other states agreed to take some of the children. Noor's team figured out that if you called the administration at the state-run centers, they had to disclose who they were keeping. "So through making these personal phone calls, the information that we got from the detention center administrators was enormous," Noor said.

The Alts felt disquieted and angry. So did other Americans and dozens of groups, including the National Domestic Workers Alliance and MoveOn, which organized a series of protests in about seven hundred places on June 30. Noor was on the phone talking to ProPublica about adding AltGov data to their site while sitting at a Delta Air Lines gate in his city's airport, on his way to join other Alts to meet in person and join the march in Washington, DC. It cost him time and money to take this trip, but Noor believed in the cause. He knew that his mother-in-law had made the journey to DC three times. "I know she didn't have any money," Noor said, "so it must have been a sacrifice to do that." Noor wanted to be able to tell his children about it, just as his mother-in-law had.

As an added incentive, "I wanted to meet some of the people I had worked with over Twitter, face-to-face." A few hours earlier, Reid had boarded an Amtrak train, his first train ride ever, headed the same way. That evening, they shared a ride from their hotel over to Ning's brick-faced house, and knocked on the door. "I already knew enough about people that nothing surprised me," Noor said, comparing it to seeing a friend for the first time in years "and you just carry on where you left off." Ning opened a bottle of wine and the three of them sat in lawn chairs in the front yard, enjoying the evening breezes, watching the stars, and talking until late at night.

The next morning, two more Alts who lived near DC, Asher and Morgan, rang the bell. Ning answered, clad in her blue Rogue NASA T-shirt. The five had breakfast: bagels, quiche, orange juice, and coffee. As Ning put out the food, he was overwhelmed. "Just love and respect and relief and gratitude for each other." He said it was fun to see that the other Alts had the same personalities in real life as they did when online: Reid's quick, irreverent jokes, Noor's warmth, Morgan's slightly nerdy sense of humor. When it came to the march itself, Asher waxed poetic, tweeting,

> Earlier today, before the march, there was a secret #AltGov gathering.
>
> We stepped out from the shadows and marched together for #FamiliesBelongTogether
>
> This isn't to say that we are special or important. Like you, we are just people.
>
> It's to say that, we are not just a group of anonymous people on the internet. We are real and #WeAreAltGov
>
> We stand together and we stand for what's right.
>
> So the next time you are out just remember, that person next to you, that group of people across the street . . .
>
> They might just be the #Resistance, they might just be #AltGov.
>
> And this is important, because you are not alone. We are not alone. And together we are strong.

March organizers estimate thirty thousand people attended the DC march in Lafayette Square on that scorching hot, 104-degree day. There were speakers: Alicia Keys and America Ferrera among them. Signs read "only a coward cages babies" and "Jesus was an immigrant." Actor Lin-Manuel Miranda, creator of *Hamilton*, sang "Dear Theodosia" from the musical—a song that Aaron Burr sings to his daughter in the play. Miranda said that the song was the calm point in the musical. He told the crowd at the march, "There's parents right now that can't sing lullabies to their kids. And, well, I'm just going to sing a lullaby that I wrote, and this is for those parents. We're not going to stop until they can sing them to their kids again."

When the march was over, the five Alts weren't ready to say goodbye. They went to a downtown restaurant, Rosa Mexicano, to refresh and cool off. It was mobbed, so they sat at the bar. Ning had brought his child with him to the protest—it was the child's chance to see history in the making, but it was also a lot, and the child was "completely overwhelmed" and overheated. Asher asked for a washcloth and ice water and gently draped it around Ning's child's neck to help them cool down. The Alts munched on chips and guacamole, relived the day, and tweeted a few pictures for their followers: Ning's wooden front door and a circle of the feet of those who marched. Ning described Asher's actions as "a wonderful touch of friendship. Solidarity. Kindness and thoughtfulness."

You can see the friendship among the Alts in what they post. In fact, for a few of them, a substantial majority of their posts are relational, showing support for each other. Reid, Ning, and Noor use this as a strategy, frequently retweeting and @mentioning other accounts when they post. One of the ways that the Alts sometimes show solidarity for each other is through silly threads, often with multiple animated GIFs that they will hashtag as #AltsAfterDark, or calling it a Happy Hour thread. Alt accounts, resistance followers who interact a lot and consider themselves #AltFam and other followers will rapidly share funny images or contribute to silly conversations like which Alt would deserve which theme song or who would play them in a movie (many of them say they would want Mark Hamill). But the friendships between Alts themselves are strong and reach beyond DM rooms into social groups who say they trust each other implicitly.

For example, Hansa works for a state government, not the federal one, but he has a close friendship with some of the Alts who do get a federal paycheck. Lee, who is his good friend, said, "I mean . . . most of us . . . the Alt/gov types . . . we're really there to bond, offer hope and not feel alone right?" Lee was a later addition to the AltGov DMs, not making his account until 2018. He had trouble fitting in, and Hansa tried to help. "He helped guide me in that realm and helped me process all kinds of things. Challenged my assumptions, pushed back when I was out of line, etc.," he said. But mostly, they had common interests, starting with Hansa narrating an experience in the world's slowest checkout line and moving to many inside jokes. "Probably my most jaw-dropping 'I know we are in some strange way cut from the same cloth' moment was discovering we both a) love the movie *Last of the Mohicans* and an extreme furthermore to that, b) we both have the main movie title musical theme in our music collection, and each have it on exercise playlists of sorts." Hansa was close to Gary, too, at first because they both shared interest in geology. Hansa tweeted a picture of a rock core from work and tagged Gary, getting an interested DM back.

Hansa was an early addition to core AltGov message groups, but the friendship was bigger than that. When Hansa had a series of life events that left him hurt and very alone in a strange state where he didn't know anyone, Gary was there. "For six months, I talked to him every night," Gary said.

Ever since the first meeting for the Families Together march, Ning, Morgan, Asher, and Gary have been close. They've used Zoom for virtual meetings and chatted on other social media platforms. Gary explained, "We didn't want to lose each other, like if we got banned or something else happened. . . . We need to keep our resistance chain strong for the future—stay embedded, stay connected." Gary didn't live near the others, so their interactions were always over technology, but Asher, Morgan, and Ning continued to meet up in person, visiting each other's homes, eating at a restaurant in a DC suburb, and touring vineyards in northwestern Virginia. Ning said AltGov is a precious and rare chance for community. "When you're in federal service," he said, "people tend to not talk about politics," because their careers span multiple governments, and their oaths are to the constitution. Discussions with other Alts were a chance to speak freely. "A chance to be a human, rather than just someone in public service."

Quick review of the zombie variant of Twitter puppet.
Zombies are old accounts. A real person opened an account, never really used it, and never deactivated/deleted. The account sat around. Maybe the profile has some real seeming info, a photo. Maybe a banner, maybe not.

The number of tweets can be all over. Very few tweets all the way to tens of thousands.
The keys are followers, follows, and content.
Followers are often small #s. Some, get into the 1000s. This is mostly due to FBRs. Look at the followers, are they mainly FBRs?

Then, check who they follow. Usually, they won't follow many. More active zombie accounts, they will follow each other, bots and maybe some big accounts, not for interest, they are for amplification and algorithm building.
They want to look real, so they interact with each other.

# of tweets related mainly to if they are automated or not. Non automated zombies sleep and stay inactive for periods. Get active when certain disinfo or propaganda is being pushed.
Multiple accounts being run by one person, talking to themself, basically. To amp a message.

As they go along, they feed off any real accounts they can snare. But, zombies on Twitter are slow moving and not very . . . smart. Easy to notice and escape, if you stay alert.

@OldTenahu. (Gefen)

8

FINDING FAKES

Tate became interested in automated Twitter accounts right at the beginning of AltGov. "I got obsessed with finding these patterns of accounts that were just tweeting the same exact information," he said. His obsession led him to teach himself Python, a computer coding language, and use it to find tweets and the accounts that sent them. He could then classify those tweets to find automated ones that were trying to spread disinformation. He wasn't alone—other AltGov accounts with similar skills saw the problem too.

Bots are a part of life on Twitter, and some are friendly. For example, a bot called ThreadReader will take a group of related Tweets and turn them into an easier-to-read narrative on a web page. Handy. All bots are automated accounts—programmed code causes the actions that the account performs, such as searching for the name of an airline and lost luggage so as to automatically send the URL to register for help. It can also be more sinister, like to boost bad ideas and kill good ones. As social media platforms encourage their users to connect with many people, individuals who use those platforms are set up to see messages from large numbers of people. All these messages are just too much to read, so social media companies began helping by using automation rules, called algorithms, to determine what people are most interested in seeing. Out of all the posts from the accounts a user follows, the algorithms only include the most interesting stuff in the user's feed. One of the ways these algorithms decide what posts are interesting is by noticing which ideas are liked or shared. The logic is that people like or share things that are significant to them. Sinister bots can short-circuit that process. If a bot is programmed to reshare or like a particular phrase or hashtag, that idea starts looking more popular, and it's then more likely to show up in someone's news feed.

Almost from the beginning of the AltGov, Gary, Booker, and Tate recognized that bots were a continuing problem on social media. They all had some expertise in computer programming, and each wanted to use their skills to help with the bot problem. Each of them took a different path to learning how to identify bots, and they both worked alone as well as helped each other learn. They pulled in a few followers, too, one with connections to software development and another who didn't have technical skills but could do things like keep track of screen names that they were investigating. When they worked together, they found a coordinated campaign to spread a message related to the February 14, 2018, shooting at Marjory Stoneman Douglas High School in Parkland, Florida, where a student at the school killed seventeen classmates and wounded fourteen others. In the midst of this horrific event that captured the attention of Americans, the message sent was, "HIGH SCHOOL SHOOTER CONFIRMED #DACA RECIPIENT #q #QAnon," which was shared and reshared by many Twitter accounts, along with a link and a badly cropped photo of TV coverage. This was intended to make it look like a TV story about the shooter's immigration status, but it actually wasn't. Using tools they had written, the Alt team was able to figure out that the message was shared from about fifty accounts every twenty-four minutes for more than half a day: automated blasts of information intended to encourage existing racial division in American society. The Alt group, calling themselves the AltGov Information Restoration Division, wrote a lengthy article on Medium about the origin of the article, the botnet, and possible sources. They also wrote about links between bot campaigns like these and Russian disinformation campaigns. The article was long and complicated, but it did get some interest. When Tate messaged a link to Twitter founder Jack Dorsey's @Jack account, he actually received a reply: "Just something like, 'Oh, this is great,' which I thought was kind of interesting to even have read it and responded," Tate said. Heartened, the team, with some involvement by Asher, continued to work. Their main goal was to educate followers, including those on Twitter and Tate's more than one thousand subscribers on Medium, and to broaden the education when followers shared the information with their own networks. Tate said it wasn't his goal to change the way the social network itself operated with regard to bots, since that was something they really didn't have the ability to do. Instead, they would inoculate the public against these malicious messages.

In the early days, Booker said there was a very specific set of goals. First, identify the sock puppet network of pro-Trump propaganda. In the context of the internet, sock puppets are accounts where someone is pretending to be something that they are not. It could be that someone was very religious but ran an online account where they pretended to be an atheist in order to say unkind things that made people who saw the posts think bad things about atheists as a whole. The anonymity that allowed AltGov members to make accounts also comes with a great deal of risk, because it's not possible to easily know who is behind the accounts. Sock puppet accounts are one of the tactics of cyberwarfare between countries, and they were believed to have significant involvement in the 2016 election. A Russian "troll farm," an organized group of workers who operate as sock puppets to cause disruption in other countries, was indicted as part of Robert Mueller's special counsel investigation. For example, sock puppet accounts befriended US activists and asked them to organize events on divisive issues like race and religion—real rallies and protests that did actually happen. In 2016, before the election, comedienne Samantha Bee visited Russia and interviewed troll farm workers, one of whom told her, "I don't identify myself as Russian online. I identify as an American. I'm a housewife from Nebraska." One of her interviewees, who said they had one hundred Twitter accounts, had goals to make people angry, change their minds, or cause them to just give up and walk away.

The second goal was to find the networks of bots that were built to amplify the messages from the trolls. This included searching for copies of the text of a troll's tweet and then looking at their patterns. It could be the exact content being shared many times or it might be sharing particular hashtags to get them trending. People have to sleep, but computer programs don't, so an account that tweets around the clock might be automated. Inauthentic accounts often have either stolen or automatically generated profile pictures, so that needs to be looked into. Networks of bots will show patterns in the times of their tweets as well, maybe with some retweeting at 1:00 p.m. and others at 1:00 p.m. plus five seconds, the next 1:00 p.m. plus ten seconds and so on.

The third goal was to make sure the trolls and boosting networks were actually Russian and then report them to Twitter. This might mean using Alex's technique of password recovery. It could mean looking for tweets with the Russian alphabet's Cyrillic characters. It could mean using the Internet Archive to find tweets from years ago that were in Russian, followed by a recent reactivation and switch. When they could make that user report, Twitter would start a process where an account gets reviewed and hopefully suspended.

They were lofty goals. Booker hoped to eventually use things that he learned to develop what he called "shield applications." He was inspired by the social media abuse targeted at David Hogg, a seventeen-year-old survivor of the Parkland shooting. Hogg and other students became vocal activists in favor of gun control and in turn, were battered online by anonymous accounts falsely claiming, among other things, that Hogg was a crisis actor and not actually a student. The apps Booker was working on would automatically screen out posts from bots and trolls, making it so certain Twitter users could use the platform freely, without having to see the abusive posts. Hogg said, in interviews, that he didn't favor social media censorship, so this app could be a possible tool to help Hogg and other trauma victims.

The problem was time. For those with the skills, it's relatively straightforward to write bots. For those with the money, trolls can be hired—some media outlets even ran stories on public want ads in Russia listing needed skills. For Alts, money was a personal investment and time was after a busy day job. Gary wondered if there might be a better way. Would it be possible to train large numbers of followers as amateur bot hunters? There would be some challenges. To sort through large numbers of accounts required some adeptness with computer coding. It wasn't very much, but it did require installing a statistical computing language called R and then running commands to get data from Twitter and put it through existing programs that could detect timing and repetition issues that suggested an account might be a bot. Bot hunters would also have to understand what a bot might look like versus a bad actor who spreads bad or inflammatory information to distract from important issues. And to be efficient, the whole thing would have to be coordinated. Tate preferred to work on his own. He had reached out to @conspirator0, a data scientist who did extensive work on identifying bots and posting informational threads and asked if he would share tools. "They've respectfully declined," Tate said, so he continued on his own path.

Gary thought he could do the training, and he got to work on an eight-page guide to the technical bits as well as definitions and general information on the types of bots and which ones cause problems. Other Alts like Asher and Cameron worked on recruiting volunteers to help with a variety of tasks. There was help from others including @ZellaQuixote who, along with @conspirator0, maintained an extensive Twitter feed about bots and bot networks and had tens of thousands of followers. @ZellaQuixote tweeted, "Folks, if you've been wanting to join the fight against disinformation and propaganda bots in social media, this is a great opportunity. @AltGS_rocks has done a fantastic job of making the tools and techniques for doing so very accessible. (Nice work, @altGS_rocks!! You rock.)" while sharing Gary's original tweet. Asher posted a thread on how to get the technical knowledge. People started volunteering right way, with eventually more than one hundred contributing.

The lessons learned from creating Harvey Rescue came in handy. Gary, and eventually Asher, who came to take on more of a leading role over time, knew that organization and consistency were the keys to success. Initially, the efforts were a collaboration with @AltYelloNatPark, an account that was originally vetted by Binkowski. That account, which was one of the ones formed immediately after the inauguration, was a heavy hitter with hundreds of thousands of followers. When they asked for help, sharing Gary's original tweet, dozens offered. @AltYelloNatPark was working on two projects at once: trying to start a citizen bot spotting group and recruiting followers to organize for political action against what the account called "The Anti Parks Caucus," which he told a magazine was "a group of ultra right-wing, white supremacist, ultra-nationalist republicans who want to remove federal protections from public lands and sell them to the highest bidder. Basically they are oil and gas industry front men in the party and would sell their own mothers if it made them a buck." @AltYelloNatPark and Gary's group tried to work together, but trouble began almost immediately.

As Asher tells it, there was a difference of opinion about the role of a bot-spotting project. Gary felt that training citizen bot spotters was both important and enough. @AltYelloNatPark wanted it as a part of a bigger effort including establishing his nonprofit "Defend Our Parks." Because of the fast growth, Gary and Asher had established an organizing group in a separate direct message room and on Slack, including several volunteers who had had a significant organizing role in the hurricanes—particularly Tai, a professional project manager who had shown great people and project-organizing skills during the hurricanes. Gary suggested in a direct message to that group that they split up so that people who were interested in the bigger-picture items that @AltYelloNatPark wanted went with @AltYelloNatPark and those who wanted to focus specifically on bot-spotting could stay with Project Bot Spotter. @AltYelloNatPark had many volunteers that he had placed in their own DM rooms, and he exhorted them to avoid Gary and Asher, directly accusing them of being "opposition forces" and of pretending to offer training while actually taking away technically savvy people. He also tagged both @conspirator0 and @ZellaQuixote along with others in a tweet saying, "You folks are our Bot Busting training and expertise consultants. Our team coordinators will be available for training almost immediately," which @conspirator0 said he found confusing, as he had never made such an agreement. "It made me more skeptical of that particular account (I already had some skepticism as they seemed to have a lot of gofundmes for random things and nothing indicating any expertise in spotting bots or studying disinfo)."

Eventually, people did split off and some stayed with @AltYelloNatPark, and more than one hundred were left in the AltGov effort.

The organization was extensive. Roles included spotting likely bot accounts by observing their behavior and looking for particular hashtags or posts that seemed to be automatically boosted. Volunteers at this level might look at trending topics or checklists they created of Twitter influencers whose postings were likely to be getting a lot of boosts from likes and retweets from automated accounts. A few volunteers made new anonymous accounts so they could observe and interact with people who used disinformation-prone hashtags. One volunteer described it as his time with the "crazy-Qs," which were accounts pushing and analyzing posts related to the QAnon conspiracy theories. He would spend time observing those accounts and then report back to the administrators' DM group, called Deep Thought, about what he saw, usually ending with a shower emoji to symbolize the need for a bleach shower to remove the contamination he felt after being immersed in the disinformation. He'd come back with ideas for hashtag campaigns that real people were planning and that bots would later pick up and amplify. Looking for those hashtags was a good way to find bots. Deep Thought initially had thirty-two members, ten of whom were Alts. Tate was in that DM, but rarely participated.

The project had two major foci: find and report bots and pushing positive messages on social media to educate and counteract malicious narratives from bots and trolls, which they called "slyjacking" the conversation. New volunteers got admitted to an introductory Slack channel where someone from Deep Thought would introduce the project and a tour of how Slack was used to manage things. Volunteers could then pick a place to put their efforts. They might work on the bot spotting team: a technical job. Some volunteers like Stacy and Greer, who had worked in IT, already had the technical skills to get started right away. For others, they'd read the tutorial, then the volunteers would meet online at a prearranged time for "Coding with Rocks" to learn how to automatically pull groups of Twitter accounts and to highlight ones that had suspicious characteristics. They would then go to work, using a combination of the Botometer tool, some data visualizations, and human assessment to categorize suspicious accounts as likely to be bots or not. Other volunteers would report the bots to Twitter and keep track of the results, which were strong. Many false accounts were suspended. They celebrated their successes and worked at getting better. As the project grew, resources became a problem. A continuing concern was managing things in Slack because the account was rapidly reaching the storage capacity for a free account. Other volunteers tried to figure out a way to come under the umbrella of an existing nonprofit so that they could apply for a grant to keep the technology running.

At the same time, another group of volunteers was working on fighting the negative narrative that bots were pushing as a part of Team PAM, which stood for Positive Active Measures. This group tried a lot of different things. A few volunteers made new accounts that made them look like ultra-conservative Americans and tried having conversations with other outspoken people on Twitter about issues like immigration and gun control—acting like supporters but asking questions like, "How do you know that?" when people made wild claims. Others took ideas for topics that were trending, spotted by the bot-finding team, and created counter messages that were posted and shared, using the same coordinated liking and resharing that worked for misinformation accounts. For example, at the time a #WalkAway hashtag was trending as a way to encourage exasperated users some incentive to give up on a clearly broken political process. Team PAM tried to "slyjack" that message by composing, tweeting, and retweeting messages that encouraged readers to #WalkToward positive values like fixing problems in America, rather than just being angry about them. Another consistent hashtag they tried to get to trend was #WeCanAllAgree, to "slyjack" the conversation by educating the public. For example, one message was, "Bots are everywhere, even in YOUR feed. #WeCanAllAgree that we'd rather talk to humans."

One of the most successful PAM efforts was attached to the Second Civil War Letters campaign that followed Alex Jones and Infowars assertion trending in bot/troll circles that liberals were planning some kind of incitement to civil war. Alt accounts started tweeting ridiculous #LettersFromLaborDayBBQAssault in the style of war-time letters back home. For example, from Asher:

> Attention all Resisters, this is a Code Coquelicot Alert. The enemy has found out about Project Backyard Grill. By word of the great General Maddow, all forces should redirect efforts to Project Corn Hole. #LettersFromLaborDayBBQAssault

Or from Taylor:

> Dearest #DeepStateWarriors, Alex has discovered the plan. But worry not, you must keep the grills fired up. Simply keep Alex away from the food. . . . And the dogs. #LettersFromLaborDayBBQAssault.

This campaign and others where the Alts were involved, tended to be the most successful. But time and attention from the Alts was sometimes sporadic, especially on the PAM side. Gary got a new job during that time, and he had to bow out. Asher worked to keep things going, but in the end some aspects of the project, especially PAM, never got a whole lot of momentum. One perpetual concern was the motivations of people who were participating, particularly since some of the volunteers used Slack with their real names and because anonymity was always an essential with the Alts. One of the training channels related to safety, and it was easy to see the differences between the volunteers in terms of attitudes toward security, with some volunteers stating that they weren't doing illegal things, so they didn't worry about it in this project, and others posting detailed suggestions about ways to obscure identity in a project like this, since, as one volunteer posted, "We're all only as secure as our weakest link." Ultimately, security ended up being the demise of the project.

As more people volunteered to participate, security concerns grew. Volunteers were asked to sign a volunteer agreement, that read, in part,

> We are non-partisan. We have members from across the political spectrum and this is not the place to discuss politics. Don't assume because we work together that we have the same opinions.

> We are here because we want to support informed and inclusive democracy, free from propaganda, disinformation and automated methods intended to disrupt calm, civil, fact-based discourse between human beings. We don't judge other people's opinions or their right to have them. We do fight against artificially causing topics to "trend" through using bots, repeaters or other systematic means that aren't real people talking with each other. We also oppose provoking dissension and divisiveness in order to disrupt; disseminating falsehoods and hate speech; falsely undermining trust in our media and institutions; and having foreign powers interfere with local affairs for nefarious ends.

> Volunteers are here at the will of the project leadership. The leadership may remove any volunteer at any time, without notice or discussion.

The successes grew. You could log in in the morning and see the list of "killed bots," those who Twitter had suspended. At the same time, the Alts who were part of the Deep Thought room became more and more scarce, with the exception of Asher, who stayed active until the end. In Slack, some people let their guard down and shared their real identities and personal information. One morning, there was a message from Asher stating that the project was over. The reason was security. Some of the volunteers had connections to other organizations that did things on the illegal side of hacking as resistance. The risk was too great. Asher directly messaged some of the team leaders, which resulted in a brief split of effort from some who tried to keep things going. However, it quickly fell apart. Without the star power of the AltGov accounts, people weren't energized. And some volunteers were deeply hurt. One follower who worked on the project tweeted a screenshot from Slack and said,

> I understand how difficult this has been. I've been here from the begin-ning. Over all these months, it has become worse, but never so bad as now. And our support is gone. WHAT is more important than our de-mocracy? If we lose that, there is nothing left. It will take generations to try to find everything we lost. I probably won't be here. However you, your families, your children, your grandchildren, will have to struggle and suffer, because we weren't here to fight. My tears are profound. As yours should be. I'm sorry. This is who I am. It's why I came. IT's why I stayed. What is more important than our democracy? The bots have been unleashed in these last weeks. How do we fight them? If not us, how? If not now, when? . . . I see you are already gone.

The end of Project Bot Spotter wasn't the end of efforts against bots. Greer ended up getting a job with a technology company that mapped social net-works, and his work included identifying malevolent actors online. The Alts who were bot-spotting from the beginning continued their work, in some cases expanding it, pulling in a few of the original volunteers and building secret bridges with other individuals and organizations doing similar work.

Dallas ran his own campaign called Six Clicks. It was targeted spe-cifically at bots that boosted the president's influence. He tweeted, "The idea behind #SixClicks is that with six clicks you can remove 2 twitter bots from trumps follower count. There by [sic] reducing trump's mes-sage reach and influence. It's also really satisfying to take something from trump that he really values, his Twitter followers." The campaign went on for more than a year and got some noticeable results. He tweeted that Trump's followers decreased by two hundred thousand in the first days of the campaign. He shared a screenshot of the president's profile, highlight-ing the reduced number of followers. Dallas encouraged followers to share and retweet the hashtag and to post how many they reported that day. Long chains of replies followed a video he made that demonstrated how to use Twitter's report feature, which got more than one hundred thousand views. Followers retweeted it along with still photos to make it simpler, or with other articles or graphics that showed how to report. Dallas tweeted at influencers like actress/activist Alyssa Milano and resistance podcaster Mueller She Wrote to try to get boosts but didn't succeed. His followers tried as well, tagging Twitter resistance figures like @TheRealHoarse and @MikeFarb1 without luck. Still, he encouraged his followers,

> Most importantly you cannot become discouraged if you do not see immediate results in trumps follower counts. We are like the river water that created the Grand Canyon.—Dallas #SixClicks

Tate moved on in his own way. He left his contractor job and began working for a private research center where he did much the same kind of work while also pursuing bot hunting on his own. He and a collaborator found evidence that the app Power10, built by Roger Stone's protege Jason Sullivan, let some pro-Trump activists turn their accounts into bots that automatically reshared posts, giving them more visibility due to Twitter's algorithm. It was deceptive because the app used real accounts temporarily to do the sharing. The automatic bot detection processes Twitter had been using were not able to catch it, so it went on for three years. When *Business Insider* asked Sullivan if he was deliberately trying to get around Twitter's rules, he responded, "It was a deliberate attempt to make sure Americans could actually get their word out. Censorship is REAL. THAT should be your story." That "word" included messages from Trump and supporters as well as posts from QAnon conspiracists, with a particular target of Representatives Ilhan Omar and Rashida Tlaib, the first congressional representatives who were both Muslim and female. Several citizen data scientists including @conspirator0 shared their evidence about the bot network on Twitter as well as in a documentary about QAnon called *Q: Into the Storm*.

@AltYelloNatPark stopped talking about bot-spotting work, but regularly tweeted about infiltrators, sometimes naming Asher and Gary, sometimes not, though it was not easy for them to see these messages, as @AltYelloNatPark used Twitter's block feature to shut them out. Asher believed he had proof that the @AltYelloNatPark account wasn't being authentic, and shared that on Twitter, including a link to an article from National Parks Traveler, an award-winning nonprofit website that covers park and protected land issues. The article stated, among other things, that the people behind @AltYelloNatPark weren't affiliated with the Defend Our Parks organization for which the account was fundraising on GoFundMe. The @AltYelloNatPark had several GoFundMe campaigns that said they were for expenses for funding a research project in the park. Those campaigns seemed to raise tens of thousands of dollars over several years.

Here is what keeps me up at night. My alt account is the only way to speak broadly to people about what's going on in our federal space. I've angered Trump enough to be blocked, and my systemic rebukes hit closer and closer to my home. Who will take the flag when I go silent?

I <3 all of the ?s of how folks can help. We need you to vote someone into office who cares about having an ethical, functional government, doesn't remove employee protections or shut us down for political reasons, gives a workable budget, and lets us hire. We need your help.

@AltUSDA_ARS. (Valentin)

9

MAKING A DIFFERENCE

In November 2017, national news reports circulated about a veteran named Johnny Bobbitt who gave his last twenty dollars to a stranger who had run out of gas. A couple, Kate McClure and Mark D'Amico, started a GoFundMe purporting to raise money to help Bobbitt get his life in order. The campaign was a huge success, eventually raising more than $400,000. Then, in August 2018, the *Washington Post* reported that Bobbitt didn't actually get all the money. It looked as if the couple had stolen most of the proceeds. Several AltGov accounts were outraged and intervened. Booker took the lead. He shared on his Twitter feed portions of multiple media stories about the alleged fraud, and then revealed that he, another Alt, and a closely-tied follower were working with groups to try to get Bobbitt more support.

@AltUSPressSec

We (a few other alts and I), reached out to everyone from state, local, Federal, VA via Homeless Vets hotline. Informed it's being treated as a high priority case so he'll receive all the help he's willing to accept. I'll also follow up on the immediate result tmrw and Tues. DM4Details

At the time, a follower tweeted,

@IDESS_HaloStar

THIS is why I don't donate to GoFundMe. I've seen many people in my area set up an account at a bank for the person/cause they are raising money for . . . and donations can be made online.

Booker, who later credited Reid and accounts @JeffBFish and veteran advocacy group @commondefense for helping, followed up two days later with,

@AltUSPressSec

Pleased to relay report that Private Johnny Bobbitt, USMC (Ret) has retained pro bono legal counsel, entered a new rehabilitation program, and is currently OFF THE STREETS in a hotel. Details remain non-public for his privacy. We will keep you updated as more develops.

What seemed like a happy ending wound up turning sour. One year later, in November 2018, it was revealed that prior news reports had missed a substantial element to the fraud: Bobbitt may have been in on it. A prosecutor from New Jersey told reporters that the entire thing, from the twenty dollars in gas money to the GoFundMe, was a scam that McClure, D'Amico, and Bobbitt created together in order to raise money from good-hearted, unsuspecting donors. The Alts' effort to help was complicated by lack of information. There were multiple layers to the anonymity and unknowns in this case—unknown people requesting donations and anonymous accounts trying to help make a difference in a sympathetic case. Mirroring the follower's earlier suspicions, Asher later tweeted,

@AltWASONPS

This is exactly why I don't get involved in any donations, fundraisers, sales, etc. This is despicable.

Often, though, efforts to help did work out well. Some AltGov accounts were known for working privately to help out followers, with long-standing, consistent efforts. In particular, the accounts associated with the Veterans Administration (VA), Lee and Parker, regularly assisted veterans. Lee said that being able to help others was part of his inspiration for creating his account. A veteran himself, he said, "I hate the VA. I don't go here for sh_t. I pay money I don't need to, to go elsewhere BUT I also want to make it better and many people don't have the options I do. It's a massive bureaucracy, it's scary . . . sometimes the smallest direction pointing can help people." He said he spends much more time helping people behind the scenes, in fact, than he does engaging with followers on the public side of Twitter. It was his plan from the start.

"I expected it and hoped for it as did VBA [Veterans Benefits Admin-istration]," Lee said, adding that he saw his online help as an extension of his day-to-day work in a VA medical center. The daily work can be frus-trating, he said. "We are both vets who hear soooo many bullsh_t stories and whiners all f_cking day, so we are both fairly quick to sniff out the bullsh_t here. And I don't know what he does, but I just mute and move on, usually. If someone is really being a f_ck I'll flame them." Tough words aside, Lee did try to help when he could. He said the biggest thing that people who reach out to him required was help navigating a complex sys-tem to get what they needed. "Sometimes I've actually looked for locations of vet centers (a benefit almost no one knows about) close to them," he said. "I've also called bullsh_t on some stated treatment plan BS. Example: 'the VA told me I cannot request a female therapist for MST [Military Sexual Trauma] issues.'"

Lee said he had to be careful with how he helps. "It's hard for me to help specifically many times, because it would mean opening up their chart . . . which, in theory, I could easily do, BUT I'm blatantly violating HIPAA at that point, much less risking exposure to myself," he said. "The most tangible things I've done is find numbers for people. It's somewhat risky but not really. . . . The public sees a wall of general info numbers. . . . I am able to generally look up any VA employee or office given enough time and get a person behind the iron curtain." Lee said he was glad when he could help, but it's also full of frustration at times. "Honestly though . . . much of my time with that is spent investigating people's situations that are complete bullsh_t or they've made worse themselves and I don't have time for that."

In the end, Lee said he used Twitter to help people in several ways. Through his job, he helped to start a veteran orientation program, and suggested a social media-based help system. "That got shot down," Lee said, "but it gave me the idea that it would be useful." The real-life work involves both efforts inside and outside the system. "I actually hate the god_mn VA." He said,

> It's such a monolithic, imposing situation. . . . The VA is full of good people and great services . . . sometimes people just need a helping hand to get in the door and get pointed to the "start" block. Soooo many veterans encounter the VA and just say "f_ck this."

But others tried to scam the system. Lee described finding a GoFundMe page of someone claiming to be a veteran who was denied treatment. He forwarded the information to the official VA GoFundMe account, which quickly took the post down. He said he had relationships with accounts for VA facilities in several states, but "none of them know I run this account. They'd be stunned." He said a "main factor" in keeping the account is because he feels like he is helping on both sides.

For Parker, it was similar. He worked with the VBA, which coordinates a large number of tasks ranging from pensions to education funding to home loans and more. The process of working with this sector of the VA is mystifying as well, he said. "Veterans reach out with questions about their claims. Answering their questions about how to proceed is a big part, telling them what to really expect, how claims are reviewed, pitfalls to avoid. I also tell them what to say to ensure their inquiry to the VA is not lost in the bureaucracy." It happens all the time, he said. Parker's account was set up so anyone could message him, and his pinned tweet said he would help any veteran. He estimated that he received messages three or four times a week.

In a leaky administration that threatens to fire those who share information, helping others becomes tricky. Sometimes, Parker could help right in a Twitter direct message by explaining a process or procedure. In other cases, he used other forums as a way to be more directly involved. He would direct those with questions to visit different social media sites that have pages that engage a lot of veterans, or to use official places to ask questions about claims. "I have to do that in a very careful way though to remain anonymous," he said. "From the other forums I can either provide my actual contact info or refer them to a network of trusted colleagues that can help." It took a variety of ways to help, including dealing with procedures and identifying and helping to get mistakes fixed. Parker said, "We know how to maximize benefits the ways that Joe Schmoe doesn't." He said he's helped someone get more than $20,000 that the agency had improperly withheld, helped people add dependents to benefits, and more. "It's a highly complex system," he said, that even has its own court system. Sometimes, a veteran will win an appeal and get compensation in a lump sum that was owed for more than thirty years. He added that he doesn't mind the drain on his time. "I love it," he said. "I'm an odd thing in government . . . I truly believe in the mission. It's not the job security (I don't have any in my position) nor the money (private sector pays people in my role much more)."

Sharing information can also spur real-world action. Sam said that the entire @RogueNASA account was created in order to hold a space for sharing accurate scientific information in the event that NASA became silenced. This was a real concern, even prior to the Environmental Protection Agency (EPA) delisting climate change data—a move that spurred groups of scientists and hackers to band together to pull down and make copies of the data, store it out of the country, and therefore out of the reach of the US government. Several of the AltGov accounts have a special interest in climate and other environmental data—ones with EPA personas like Ning, Charlie, and Dana for sure, but other ones like Gary as well. But the issue of data preservation has come up in other areas too.

Asher said, "My entire focus, both in my career, and as an Alt is making change and making things better." Once, he noted a message from a follower that the Agency for Healthcare Research and Quality guidelines was being defunded, and consequently, the public was going to lose access. These guidelines are a list of practices in medicine that were vetted and qualified under a rigorous set of criteria as the best in evidence-based medicine, Asher said.

"I spent a few minutes scrolling through the site and looking at conversations and quickly realized two things. One—that this was big, the guidelines that were available were covering a broad range of things. And two—just about everyone that I saw talking about it was in the medical community." Like the climate data that inspired some of the very first AltGov accounts, this was information important to human health and that might go away. Asher's interest took several vectors. First, he said, the large followership of AltGov accounts could bring quick awareness. "I knew that even just a few of us pushing messages on it would get quite a bit of attention," he said. There were bigger issues as well. The clearinghouse website made the guidelines available and easy to find at no cost to those who searched for them. Like climate data, studies that originally collected the data housed on the website were done with public funding and therefore, the public deserved access to the data it had paid for. "I saw the removal of this resource as just another way to hide things so that you have to pay to access them," Asher said. So, he acted. He posted,

@AltWASONPS

HHS is planning to take the National Guideline Clearing house down on July 16, 2018. It's a critical resource for doctors researchers & others in the medical community. #AltGov #AltFam #GeeksResist #Resistance Let's use our skills to back this whole thing up and prop up a copy.

The tweet got more than four hundred likes and retweets. It was almost too successful. "We had a few complications," he said. "While I did expect to get some exposure by tweeting about it, it was more than expected. . . . So much so that we almost DDoS'd the guidelines server," basically sending the server so many requests that it could fail. He sent messages of clarification, asking followers to shift efforts and contact congresspersons and to take other actions as he worked on coordinating downloading the data and making it available another way. Asher said, "I jumped off and took a nap for a two to three hours and got back on around eight o'clock. And then, after getting back on, I was working on it until like 2:00 a.m. that morning. I called in sick so that I could finish up with everything."

Ultimately, people that Asher brought in on the effort began a conversation with federal employees about coming up with an alternative way to make the guidelines available, which he described as, "Not just a working copy of what was on http://guidelines.gov but something better, based on actual feedback and suggestions from the medical community, researchers, and people in the tech field." These discussions caused Asher to have a bit of an identity crisis. He was invited to be included in the conversations, which was a natural fit given his interest in smarter processes. To do so, however, would have meant possibly sacrificing his anonymity as an Alt-Gov. Eventually, he decided the risk was too great, so he let others join in while he passed. Missed opportunity aside, he felt it was worth it. "I feel great about it," he said. "We ensured that there is a copy of the data that will remain publicly available and can be used as a resource until other resources can be brought online. We increased exposure to something that, as we found out, had been known about for months, but very few people outside of the medical community actually knew about it." As seems to be typical with AltGov projects, Asher was instrumental in identifying a problem, coordinating a response, and doing a lot of the work, yet the person behind the account got none of the credit. He doesn't regret that. "I feel that we helped to facilitate things that may not have happened otherwise . . . and that makes everything worthwhile to me," he said.

One of the most prominent, and more controversial, ways that accounts take direct action is in fundraising. This happens with both vetted accounts and others. @RogueFirstLady, whom Binkowski said she has not vetted, published two minibooks in the run-up to the 2018 midterm elections. They were priced at $1.99 and downloadable, promising "informed perspective" on the goings on in the government, with proceeds donated to Beto O'Rourke's campaign against what the account called "Ted Gooze." The account suggested it gave more than $500 to the campaign but didn't provide receipts or evidence. It had an introduction written in the characteristic flawed English style of the Twitter account and then a long narrative in standard English describing Russian influence in the campaign written in memoir-style, mostly stuff a careful watcher of the news would know, along with personal details, like a statement in a prenuptial agreement that the president would get custody of Barron if the marriage ended and that the first lady had bought her own apartment in Trump Tower with her own money. The download was still available even after the midterms, as was a link to a Café Press store selling T-shirts and stickers with a promise that profits would be donated to the 2020 democratic presidential candidate. The account @RoguePotusStaff also sold a book—through Amazon—purporting to give insider information on events in the White House. Most of the vetted accounts have said they believe this eight hundred thousand-follower Twitter account was a fraud, in terms of misrepresenting itself as a resistance account. The book itself, which sold for $2.99, reads like something written by someone educated, although it was not carefully edited into a coherent book. The aspects that read as behind-the-scenes tend to focus on people and their motivations. The account used the Twitter bio page to include links to buy the book and a link to a short website that also promotes it. The bio implies that the writers are the same as the authors of a *New York Times* editorial that claimed, essentially, that staffers were managing presidential power. The account does not make claims about where the funds from the book go.

Several of the vetted accounts raise funds and other donations to expressly benefit others. For example, Sam's feed periodically would have a burst of retweets of pictures of followers wearing shirts that say "Rogue NASA" with various types of art. Sam shared the pictures of the followers in their logo shirts because "I love it. It makes me feel really good, like we're important enough in people's lives that they buy our stuff. It's a really cool feeling. And I'm happy it all goes to a good cause." The good cause has varied over time. At first, the account raised money for Girls who Code, which provides advocacy and resources to teach computer coding to girls, and for the National Math and Science Initiative. Over time, it shifted to funding scholarships to Space Camp through a nonprofit called The Mars Generation. The scholarships, which were available through an application process for students whose families qualify for free or reduced lunch at school, cover both the camp and the transportation to get there. A Texas-based producer designed art for the shirts as well as patches, caps, and other items and managed the sales as well, sending all profits as donations directly to the charity. Sam promotes the sales on the @RogueNASA account. He said the account continued fundraising, in part, because followers request having merchandise they can wear to show support for the resistance. It's personal as well. "It was a great feeling to see the additional people they were able to send to Space Camp last year because of our sales. . . . I think it was seven extra students." Sam said the students have classes in science and math that relate to space, learn to work together in teams, build a rocket, and do actual space simulations as both crew and Mission Control. In addition to education and experience, Sam said, "For a lot of kids who are maybe nerdy or bullied in school, it's a chance to meet other kids like them." For the NASA team, who already have STEM careers, enabling others is personal. Sam said, "I teared up when the winners were announced. I hope they had the best time."

The account Sam helps run has, on occasion, supported other causes as well. He was really excited when Discovery Channel star Adam Savage wore a T-shirt Sam's account created in a video Savage made as part of an effort to encourage voting in the 2018 midterm elections. "It's like we're all a part of the same team. It's really cool," Sam said. Sam amused himself with an effort to appropriate the hashtag #SpaceForce, encouraging followers to use it to show they were fans of open science discovery and knowledge who hang out with resistance. To Sam, this seemed more useful than describing the expansion to the armed forces that occurred during the Trump years. The shirt Savage wore, a Rogue NASA design, read "Space Force Cadet" and featured the @RogueNASA logo. Funds raised from this T-shirt went to RAICES, a group that provides support to reunited migrant families. Sam also teamed up with Tate, Dallas, and @BadHombreNPS on the sale of a set of patches. Funds from those sales were sent to the Government Accountability Project. Dallas was very clear on his account about the financials of the sales.

@alt_fda

Patches #Thread: As you know we sold patches to help support http:// www.whistleblower.org Those patches are starting to ship. What follows is the financials of your donations-

We sold $19398

total Cost of production

Patches—$2658.50

Shirts—$281.50

852 total items $5 per item sold to Nakatomi for labor and supplies= $4260

3.25% paypal fees—$630.43

Total production cost—$7,830.43

Sales—19398

costs—7830.43

profit/donation—$11567.57

Thank You everyone for your support of this cause. If you missed this round of patches and shirts, we are working on another round of donations with more patches.

The same accounts did another run of sales, with the ACLU as the beneficiary.

@alt_fda

#OffTopicbut @RogueNASA has requested that all profits from #AltGov (Includes our Patch!) merch sold this month be donated to the @ACLU! We also brought back their long-sold-out embroidered cap for the occasion! Check all the merch out at this link! http://store .nakatomiinc.com/roguenasa.aspx

At the end, Dallas shared a similar breakdown as well as a note from the ACLU to the badge merchant thanking them for the donation.

Some fundraising is related to particular, timely crises. In the summer and fall of 2018, massive forest fires devoured public lands in the western United States. The people behind Colby's account had experience in the area, knew people who were affected, and decided to help. The account said, "We had been posting about the California wildfires, and particularly the Carr Fire due to its impact on the park." The first help was just encouragement. "One of the park employee's spouses, who wishes to remain anonymous, came directly to us asking for postcards and letters of support," he said. Tangible support followed for firefighters and other workers who saw their own homes and possessions going up in the smoke. At "the prompting of our followers, we asked our contact to create an Amazon Wishlist. The list included all sorts of everyday household items, from plates to coffee mugs to dog toys. Basics to help them get back on their feet," Colby said. Other Alts helped share the need.

@RogueEPAFacts

Retweeted NastyWomenofNPS

We trust @NastyWomenofNPS and encourage you to consider pitching in even a small amount to help the Park rangers who lost their homes in the CA fires.

The followers really came through. "We had astounding success with both letters of encouragement reaching the base of operations and every single item on the wish list being purchased," Colby said, estimating that when you added up all the contributions and care packages it had a value of several thousand dollars. He said, "We posted photos and thank you letters from rangers as accountability." Like NASA's affinity for Space Camp, supporting rangers in need was personal. Colby said, "I feel proud and thankful to every single person who took the time to write a note or donate what they could to help complete strangers.

"As someone who has lost everything to a natural disaster, recovery and rebuilding is a long, arduous process. You never really get over the loss. The first days and weeks after the tragedy are critical though, when food, clothing, and shelter are at a premium. I'm glad that we could be part of the answer. I hope that we can continue to use our voice on this platform to support victims of natural disasters, especially when they are connected to a national park," Colby said.

Some accounts were raising money for their own personal funds. It caused a lot of controversy because some accounts like Asher, Morgan, Dallas, and Sam were very outspoken both in public and in private about any money being donated to causes. For example, immediately prior to the midterm elections, several AltGov supporters were encouraged to adopt a profile picture frame that either said "I am Voting" or "I Voted." At the time, the download page for the picture modifier went to a page that also let users purchase stickers, with a promise that some, not all, of the proceeds would go to charity. Some of the AltGov accounts adopted the frame and kept it. Others, concerned that it represented a link to an unwanted type of fundraising, adopted and then dropped it.

Dallas explained it to his followers like this:

@alt_fda

#DallasThoughts#Thread Hey peeps over the weekend you may have noticed that we changed our avatar and tweeted about how you could change yours as well. This is what we changed our avatar to:

This is the tweet we tweeted and then deleted.

We deleted this tweet and changed our avatar back to its "normal" look for a few reasons which we will talk about now.

When the original "I'm voting" ring was offered, it was given as an engagement tool to get ppl to vote. We were more than happy to support that as voting is important, now more than ever.

Buy [*sic*] the time we got to the tweet that we deleted, the avatar rings were attached to a charity we were not aware of or affiliated with.

We thought the rings were still free to use as an engagement tool with no back-end profit motive. After it was pointed out to us that they no longer were what we thought they were, we cut our ties.

We do not think the rings are bad or shouldn't be used for their intended purpose but because we cannot see the finances behind them, we cannot say to you that everything is on the up and up.

More

Therefore we will not be using them. Sorry for the confusion and for promoting something we didn't full [*sic*] understand.—Dallas

One group of Alts was especially sensitive to asking followers to solve one's own financial problems. "I'm not ok with the money thing in general," Suuad said. Even when it's clear what the money is going for, he felt the ask was "shifty." Another Alt noted that it's disturbing to see followers post that they would like to help, but just don't have the resources. When Booker announced a GoFundMe to pay for a trip to Hawaii to investigate presidential candidate Tulsi Gabbard, it got a mixed response from the public, with some questioning why this would be needed, and others wanting to help. The GoFundMe said, "We're going to travel to her district, talk to locals, find out the truth about Tulsi, and report back to the American People," while asking for $5,000. At least seventy-three people donated a sum of more than $2,000, but other followers posted pointed questions about whether it was actually funding a vacation. It got negative responses from the other Alts as well. "All these people felt guilty because they couldn't help, and aired all their financial shortcomings as proof," Sabah said. Booker ended up withdrawing from the GoFundMe and asked Asher to look at the transactions and attest that Booker never received any money. Asher complied. It's not clear that one anonymous account sticking up for another has much of an impact. Some AltGov followers posted with a thank-you to Asher, while other Twitter commentators continued to harp on the fundraiser for years afterward.

The amount of explanations of where money goes varies for different accounts. For example, in November, Sabah pinned a post about a book he gave to his nephew that was so inspirational, the nephew decided to enlist in the military. The post was fairly popular, with 224 likes and some comments from followers about intentions to buy the book. The link that Sabah shared was an affiliate link, meaning that the owner of the link makes a commission on the sales. The account has shared a few other books with those kinds of links as well. He doesn't share regular updates about how the money is spent, but has tweeted general statements about types of charitable support.

Sometimes the requests are even more personal. The parody account @alt_kellyanne_ was close with several Alt accounts, having grown attached during the hurricanes. The owner of the @alt_kellyanne_ account tweeted that she was having trouble finding a roommate and was in such bad financial straits that she was not going to be able to pay her rent that month without help.

@alt_kellyanne_

Feeling pretty f_cking sorry for myself today. I can't even fake the lolz. I'm sad, angry, and just super over the struggle. If the economy is so great why tf am I in this position?

Ning helped him get a message out about needing help, sharing

@RogueEPAFacts

Dear friends. @alt_kellyanne_ has been here since rogues went rogue. She led pet and wildlife rescues during Harvey. She works behind the scenes to keep us all safe. She's a fighter. If you've ever hit hard times, you know even a small amount of $ can help. Let's fight for KA.

That crowdfunding request for help made the difference.

@alt_kellyanne_

Thank you so much. The outpouring of donations & the msgs of have been amazing & I am humbled by your generosity. I cannot thank you enough for everything. Helping me make my rent $—literally made me tear up with feels. Thank you for everything. Also, F*ck Tяump

@educatorsresist, a vetted account, also raised personal money for supplementing college tuition. The account created a crowdfunding request on the site fundrazr.com that stated that although the holder had GI Bill support, it was not enough to pay all expenses to finish a four-year degree. The crowdfund site had evidence, like tuition receipts, and had raised $926 by November 2018. Hunter also raised money for educational expenses with AltGov help. Hunter wanted to go back to law school and finish his degree, saying he wanted to eventually enter politics and resist from the inside. Other accounts reshared his requests, particularly @bartenderResist, which is another vetted account, who fielded this exchange:

@56blackcat

Replying to @bartenderResist @alt_jabroni

Is this a real person?

@bartenderResist

Yes he is a real live person

@56blackcat

Good!

Hunter's campaign originally started on GoFundMe and was terminated for a reason that isn't clear. The campaign was restarted on a different platform—thrinacia.com—and ultimately raised $2,340. Hunter tweeted about taking his LSATs and getting his score, about his application and acceptance processes, and about his expectation to begin classes in spring 2019, which he did, earning his degree in the fall of 2021.

I want to return to normal. I want to go back to arguing about the second amendment, fiscal responsibility, and *gasp* TAN SUITS; I don't want to spend my time worrying that the very fabric of our democracy is unraveling before our eyes. I grow tired of watching this President burn anything and everything to the ground to hide his own culpability, but until this chaos stops, I will resist.

@AngryStaffer (Sabah)

10

WAR ROOM

One of the major accomplishments that the Trump administration claimed was judicial appointments. In some ways, Trump's appointments reshaped the federal bench in a more conservative direction, with younger judges whose influence would last for years. When he left office, almost one-quarter of active federal judges were his appointees, and some were more notable than others. In particular, when Supreme Court Associate Justice Antonin Scalia died unexpectedly in February 2016, then President Barack Obama did not succeed in getting a successor on the bench. Senate Majority Leader Mitch McConnell and Senate Judiciary Committee Chairman Chuck Grassley, both Republicans, argued that because the country was divided, and it was an election year, the seat should be kept open for the next president to fill. This controversial view stuck, and the Senate never voted on Obama's nominee, moderate appeals court judge Merrick Garland. The seat remained open for the rest of Obama's term. When Trump ran for office, he released a list of potential judicial nominees as a part of his campaign—a list created in collaboration with the conservative Federalist Society and Heritage Foundation, perhaps designed to encourage conservatives to vote for Trump because of the chance to control the courts. After Trump's election, one from that list, appeals court judge Neil Gorsuch, was nominated. He received a hearing, and the Senate sent him to the court with a 54–45 vote that included all Republicans and a few Democrats. Getting the vote required overcoming a filibuster and even changing a Senate rule to put Gorsuch in place. Some of the AltGov accounts had tweets about Gorsuch's candidacy, but it was around the same time as the subpoena to unmask Wilder, so their interest was divided. In the government, at the time, McConnell said. "As I look back in my career, I think the most consequential decision I've ever been involved in was the decision to let the president being elected last year pick the Supreme Court nominee." As it turned out, the highest court in the land was the focus of much attention and turmoil several times during Trump's presidency.

In June of 2018, Supreme Court Justice Anthony Kennedy, then eighty-one, made a surprise announcement that he was stepping down from his seat on the court, thus giving Trump an additional nominee. Kennedy was appointed by President Ronald Reagan, but he was something of a swing vote—siding with conservatives around 57 percent of the time. The next month, Trump announced that DC court of appeals judge Brett Kavanaugh, a 2017 addition to the list of potential justices from during his campaign, would be the nominee. Midterm elections were drawing close. Senate confirmation was ugly, including efforts to slow down the confirmation process until closer to the midterm elections. Members of Congress accused each other of rushing the nomination process, and the posturing took a great deal of time, even as members were complaining that they didn't even have time to review Kavanaugh's background materials before they were expected to vote. Vice President Mike Pence tweeted that previous justices like Scalia and Ruth Bader Ginsburg were confirmed with votes from more than ninety senators. "If we lived in a more respectful time, Judge Brett Kavanaugh would be overwhelmingly confirmed by the United States Senate. #ConfirmKavanaugh." Morgan reacted with an appeal to hypocrisy, tweeting, "The ABSURD posturing around blocking Merrick Garland's nomination and refusing to even let a vote happen has left your party with ZERO moral high ground to complain about lack of cooperation with Supreme Court nominations, you jackass." Name-calling tends to get emotional reactions, which was the case for this tweet. Morgan noticed, and was angry. He became interested in trying to get more engagement, likes, and retweets on his tweet than the vice president would have on his. He tweeted twice asking for people to like and reshare his tweet, and then twice tagged actress and activist Alyssa Milano, asking her to share. Colby, Chris, Ning, Reid, Jelani, and Asher did, along with some other AltGov accounts, but Milano did not.

It wasn't clear whether looking at Kavanaugh's background materials would have mattered. With a Republican majority in the Senate, his confirmation looked like a sure thing. But it became a lot less certain when California Senator Dianne Feinstein reported that a constituent had contacted her office and accused Kavanaugh of sexually assaulting her as a teenager. The constituent said it happened when they both attended a house party in the Washington, DC, suburbs in the early 1980s. Dr. Christine Blasey Ford, a college professor of psychology, was eventually identified as the person who contacted Feinstein. She passed a polygraph test given by a retired FBI investigator. Soon, a few other women also accused Kavanaugh of similar acts. This was taking place during the #MeToo era, with its heightened focus on sexual misconduct. A rapid series of events ensued. The first was an additional hearing on September 27 in front of the Senate Judiciary Committee with only two witnesses—Ford and Kavanaugh—something that @BadHombreNPS called "a pivotal moment in American history, methinks." The hearing was broadcast live and had two notable elements. First was Christine Blasey Ford's testimony, which was seen as sympathetic by liberals and conservatives alike. The second was Kavanaugh's, which was in turns wounded and indignant, with a bizarre moment when he asked Senator Amy Klobuchar if she had a drinking problem before denying that he, himself, had one. AltGov accounts had a lot more to say about the hearing. For example, Morgan tweeted, "Judge Kavanaugh's testimony was disgraceful for any judge, and should disqualify him from his previous job, much less the Supreme Court."

It didn't matter. The Judiciary Committee went on to advance Kavanaugh to the full Senate the next day. Republican Senator Jeff Flake, along with some other Republicans and Democrats alike, called for a one-week delay to allow for a follow-up FBI investigation into the misconduct allegations against Kavanaugh. The president approved a limited investigation that proscribed who could be interviewed and, to an extent, what could be asked. In the summer of 2021, *The Guardian* reported that a group of Democratic senators were still concerned about the matter and that a letter they received from the FBI Director Chris Wray indicated there were more than 4,500 tips about Kavanaugh that were never investigated.

Kavanaugh also faced opposition from former Chief Justice John Paul Stevens, the National Council of Churches, some of his college friends, the American Civil Liberties Union, and many accounts with the #AltGov. As Americans were trying to read the tea leaves of how undecided members of Congress might vote—Republicans Jeff Flake, Lisa Murkowski, and Susan Collins and Democrats Joe Manchin and Heidi Heitkamp—Sabah was trying to give some insight into what he said he was learning from conversations with congressional staff members. It mattered to his followers. While he was live-tweeting his conversations, his follower numbers passed one hundred thousand.

His tweeting was a combination of sharing public articles and inside information:

@AngrierWHStaff Sep 28 This article confirms much of what I've been told and reported here for the past two days. So, I guess I owe my source an apology for doubting them. Collins, Murkowski, and Flake have indeed been planning this. And they fear more to come.

Ultimately, Sabah's predictions proved incorrect, and Kavanaugh was confirmed. Sabah did keep his followers along for some of the cycle of prediction.

@AngrierWHStaff Sep 30

I'm not guaranteeing anything in this town. But I'm officially saying I would be *shocked* if he doesn't withdraw this week.

@AngrierWHStaff Oct 1

Also, I really don't predict anything TBH. I just tell you guys what little birdies tell me

@AngrierWHStaff Oct 4

I'm watching these Senators talk and I'm losing faith in my source again. More so, I'm struck by the fact that very few of them are actually going to read it, and the fact that they seem fine with Kavanaugh not being interviewed.

@AngrierWHStaff Oct 4

Guys—we'll see what comes out of this after the Democrats finish reading, but at this point this appears to be a pipe dream at best, unless the GOP is lying their ass off. Never gotten bad info from this person before, but I do apologize if this turns out to be garbage.

@AngrierWHStaff Oct 4

After Justice Steven's comments today, we might actually see all 5 vote NO. That's not my expectation, but his condemnation will carry some weight in the Beltway.

@AngrierWHStaff Oct 5

I would expect Murkowski and Collins to vote together, but everyone is being very quiet this morning.

@AngrierWHStaff Oct 5

For those of you that think it's over already, have some faith. I said from the beginning that cloture would probably pass and ending the debate to downvote is a good thing. Think McCain ACA.

@AngrierWHStaff Oct 5

Manchin, Collins, and Murkowski were always rumored to be voting together. We'll see.

Angry WH Staffer added,

Final prediction: Murkowski—NO Collins—NO Flake—NO Manchin—YES

But either way, I think vote fails 49-51

While the Alts were sharing information, they also tried to get the attention of legislators with things like Ning's Twitter poll: "Dems and Independents: If they vote NO on Kavanaugh, would you donate to Collins, Murkowski, Manchin or Flake?" They were also repeatedly exhorting their followers to get involved, mostly by asking them to call or email their senators. The day of the vote moved closer. On the actual day of voting, some of the Alts went to protests at the capital and tried to use their feeds to get followers to join them. Asher tweeted:

@AltWASONPS Oct. 5

If you are within a couple of hours of DC, come to the capital. Join us in protest. I'll be there. Will you?

Eventually, Kavanaugh was confirmed to the court, while protesters, including some from AltGov, raged outside. Sabah took his failure lightly:

@AngrierWHStaff Oct 5

Well, my prediction was totally wrong, so there's that.

@AngrierWHStaff Oct. 5

Definitely not beating myself up—anyone who tries to predict DC knows what a risky business it usually is—I'm just in a state of shock more than anything. Particularly at the R's that bill themselves as "moderates"—this was the time to prove it, and they sh_t the bed.

Other Alts were less sanguine, and the next day, they opened the War Room DM room. It was a combination of trusted followers—some from the hurricanes and some from Project Bot Spotter—and several of the Alts. The mission was to encourage registration and fight voter suppression in the midterm elections. As Cameron put it, "A concerted response is coming from the Alts & Rogues of #AltGov Stand by for the greatest counter offensive in the Twittersphere!"

The Alts were planning on using some of the strategies that had worked before. Timed drops of information could earn particular tweets favor from the Twitter algorithm, making them more likely to show up in people's feeds. Followers who had access to the Alts in DM rooms would spend substantial time and effort to help in different ways, and they had useful skills from graphic design to making websites to composing music. The Alts themselves had some famous followers, and they tried to use this as well. Getting a well-followed person, a Twitter-famous influencer, to share their message would put it in front of a much larger audience. This might let them get followers mobilized to vote themselves and to help make sure others voted. The goal was to encourage voters to turn out who would elect representatives and senators who would vote for what the Alts and their followers saw as good government: protections for science and the environment, civil rights, and rights for immigrants, and more.

The Alts who worked for the government had to steer clear of endorsing particular candidates, so there was some division of work. People who never worked for the government, or no longer did, felt free to post information in support of state or local candidates whom they supported. People who received a federal paycheck kept their messaging to basic civics like how to vote because of restrictions under the federal Hatch Act. The Hatch Act, which first passed in 1939, intended to reduce corruption by restricting how government employees could participate in political activities. It makes sense—if those already in government positions can use government resources to influence the political process, it makes it harder for outsiders to win elections. The Hatch Act forbids government employees from doing this with a lot of specific restrictions. For example, while they are at work, defined as "on duty, in any federal room or building, while wearing a uniform or official insignia, or using any federally owned or leased vehicle," they can't participate in campaigning. They can't distribute or display campaign materials, work for a campaign, wear badges or T-shirts, or use electronic communication like email or social media to talk about partisan things or people. Though leaders in the Trump administration were sometimes accused of or even found in violation of the Hatch Act (presidential adviser Kellyanne Conway was found to violate the act more than fifty times), Alts who worked for the government were careful. This meant not doing things publicly on social media at work, on work time, or on work equipment, but also sometimes restricting themselves from posting things at all. The War Room campaign, which focused expressly on an election, with risk of violating the Hatch Act.

For some of the Alts, there were more restrictions. When it comes to the Hatch Act, those who work in national security—for the Department of Justice, the Secret Service, or the Defense Intelligence Agency, for example—have special restrictions that forbid any partisan political activity, even on their own time. This applies to those who work in the elections apparatus as well, for example, the Federal Election Commission. This also applies to some judges as well as career holders of some of the highest government positions in what's called the Senior Executive Service. Conflicts of interest between government jobs and political activity seem pretty apparent: Can you administrate a fair election if you have a stake in who wins? The Uniform Code of Military Justice comes into play as well. Military service members can join a political party, but they can't be a leader in one. They can donate to campaigns, but they can't raise funds. And, importantly, they are not allowed to use "contemptuous speech" against the president and other leaders. The First Amendment rights of service members are held secondary to the interests of the military. The consequences can be severe including losing pay, being dismissed from the military, or even being imprisoned, even if they are off-duty and out of uniform. This matters to some Alts who have shared that they are active duty military members. One told me that although most of his life wasn't in the military, his service in his state's National Guard meant he really valued the privacy of an anonymous account.

So, some Alts were comfortable with asserting party or candidate preferences because either they didn't work for the government or they restricted their activities online to those outside of work. Tanner described taking a break, leaving the building, and walking far enough away to not be on work WiFi before using Twitter on his burner phone used for AltGov things. Another talked about telework days, where government employees are able to work from their home, when he could use his lunch break to get his phone out and check out what was happening in the DM rooms and maybe reply to a few posts that tagged him during the day. Some of the accounts worked with activist and musician Holly Figueroa O'Reilly's @BlueWaveCrowdSource on promoting candidates for Congress, hoping to get the accounts more followers, which would help those appear more often in Twitter feeds. Sometimes O'Reilly's organization would encourage resharing tweets on behalf of candidates, to help those candidates raise funds for their campaigns. O'Reilly had been involved with AltGov since the hurricanes where she was an important contributor. She participated in some of the most closely held DM rooms.

Most of the messages from the War Room were around citizenship—registering to vote and following through by actually casting their ballot. The power of celebrity was one of the ways the Alts tried to get the message spread as widely as possible. The Alts already had some celebrity followers, and Asher knew that they could get some celebrities they didn't interact with to help them. He had some luck directly reaching out to celebrities, either by tagging them in tweets or, if their account was configured correctly, sending them a direct message. "Sometimes people think that that other person (the celebrity or what have you) is too important for them to be able to have a conversation. And as a result, they never even attempt to reach out," he said. He encouraged some of the accounts in the War Room, both Alts and followers, to reach out. "Many will engage with you as long as you aren't like going super crazy or whatever," he said, remembering that at one point, an actress with multiple Emmy Awards was helping him with date night restaurant recommendations for when he was visiting her city. They had some luck. Accounts from actors like Debra Messing, Bradley Whitford, and Selenis Leyva reshared one or more tweets. Leyva had been a public advocate of Latino voting throughout the Trump years. Some of the posts created as a part of the #YouCanChangeThis campaign were in Spanish, with a follower who was a professional Spanish-English interpreter helping with translations. For example, "Borrado? No. Haga clic aquí. Verifica tu estatus ahora y #VOTA. #TuPuedesCambiarlo." The message suggested readers take care to not be "erased" by going ahead and verifying eligibility, and it included a video showing a series of tweets of people who were surprised that they had disappeared from voter rolls. A real celebrity highlight was when @DontTryThis, Mythbusters star Adam Savage, did a pro-voting video wearing a shirt that was part of a Rogue NASA campaign to raise money for less privileged teens to go to Space Camp.

One of the main messages was for people to check their voter registrations. Election officials may need to clean up voter rolls to improve efficiency, for example, when a voter moves between elections and should be removed from their registration at the old address so they are not registered twice. In 2018, a series of news stories, accompanied by some influencer posts on social media, were indicating that people were being improperly deregistered as voters. Advocacy groups like the Brennan Center for Justice were warning, early on, that there were risks, citing cases in Arkansas, where county clerks were told to decertify more than fifty thousand people because they were felons. In that case, there were many issues including listing names that had no such conviction and others that had had voting rights restored. By the time clerks were notified of the errors, it was impossible to fix some of the issues before the election. The group warned about tactics like challenging new citizens, those recently naturalized, about using an unreliable crosscheck system to track voters who move, and about legal threats from groups like Judicial Watch on local elections officials. In some states those tactics happened more in counties where most residents were minorities, which seemed like an effort to suppress democratic votes. The previous January, the Supreme Court had ruled that states could use lack of voting to deregister someone, which meant that people who hadn't voted before and wanted to vote in this election could find they weren't actually registered when they showed up to vote.

News reports around the country showed this was a problem. Even New York's Mayor de Blasio's son was unexpectedly deleted from the rolls and so was *Roots, Reading Rainbow,* and *Star Trek: The Next Generation* actor LeVar Burton. Sam had one of the largest followings—still more than eight hundred thousand—and was active in encouraging followers to check their status, even creating a guide of state-by-state information with links that followers could follow called the RogueNASA Voting One Stop Shop. When he tweeted simply, "CHECK. YOUR. VOTER. REGISTRATION." shortly after midnight one night, along with a link to an article about Indiana deleting half a million voters, the replies to the tweet included several instances of followers who checked and found that they were unexpectedly removed as well, some even despite having recently voted in a primary election.

A very interesting aspect of the campaign was using social media to encourage on-the-ground action. Taylor tweeted that Ohio's 12th congressional district was lost because people didn't get out the vote, with a link for followers to sign up to knock on doors. He retweeted a message from then MoveOn head Ben Wikler that showed data with what could happen if Gen Z voters could be mobilized to turn out in large numbers, Taylor shared how he, himself, asked twenty-somethings in his life if they were interested in registering and handed them application forms if they wanted one. Almost all took a form so they could register, he said. In the War Room, conversation focused on how followers might reach out to potential voters. Inspired, Gefen printed out registration forms and took them to a university near where he lived. War Room accounts shared a social media video that offered tips on how to register others. "Democracy rocks when everyone participates. You can help people register to vote in your free time," the video said, with suggestions like learning the process yourself, bringing charged devices and extra batteries so people could register online, and encouraging people to "be brave and approach people," and then sharing a photo of the person with their registration so it could be shared with others on social media.

Other parts of the War Room campaign included following up on registration by making a plan to vote. A different video encouraged followers to decide when and how they were going to vote, including details like figuring out when they could be off work and how they were going to get to the polling place. After they had the plan, they were encouraged to share it with others in order to be more accountable. Followers were also encouraged to vote early with a series of silly memes with the benefits of voting early. For example, a meme of an elderly woman delightedly looking at a computer and saying, "Voted early. More time for Fortnite" and a meme of the Morpheus character from *The Matrix* saying, "What if I told you folks who vote early get to ignore campaign ads."

One follower, a music producer who tweets at @dreamwithfaith, wanted to do more to encourage people to vote. Because of her job, she had access to some of the posh parties that followed the Grammy Awards and tickets to professional sporting events and wanted to use that access to get as many voters as possible. She worked with Cameron and Chris to set up a follower contest. The two of them were both still somewhat tangential to AltGov as a whole—they were included in the War Room but didn't have access to the central StratComm DM. They mostly worked with @dreamwithfaith on their own, setting up rules for the contest. "Help get out the vote. Win Cool Prizes. Save Democracy," the contest materials read. The rules were somewhat convoluted, but basically entrants could rack up points by tweeting about voting with particular hashtags, and then getting others to both like their tweet and post evidence of themselves voting, such as wearing an "I Voted" sticker or putting an absentee ballot in a mailbox. There were five prizes: first, an invitation to a Grammy-week party; second, swag from that year's Grammy Awards; third, an AltGov item like a RogueNASA T-shirt; and fourth and fifth, a thirty minute DM conversation with AltGov accounts. "Voting is important and a privilege Americans enjoy. Make a difference. Make some voters," the contest description concluded. A judge kept track of the entries and Dallas helped by making a promotional video and a video announcing the winners.

The articles after the hearings were focusing on the wrong element.

I reached out to some reporters and told them where they should really be looking.

But, of course, they were ignored, so I changed approach and verified my position with a few. Funny how things change.

@RogueVBA (Parker)

11

SHUTDOWN

Asher had been through government shutdowns a few times. In 2013, disagreement over funding the Affordable Care Act led to a sixteen-day closure. At the beginning of 2018 there was a brief shutdown largely due to disagreement about immigration. These closures were always a nuisance. Maybe government staff aren't working. Maybe they are essential, so they are still working. But for most of them, they don't know when they will get paid again. Alts who worked for the national parks were particularly affected—they were non-essential, but not working meant its own worries. The closing down and starting back up creates complicated work. Even more so for a manager.

The shutdown at the end of 2018, which stretched into 2019, was the longest in US history. Dark clouds had been on the horizon for weeks. Ning tweeted before Christmas that instead of enjoying the holiday with his family, he was figuring out ways to stretch leftovers for when he wouldn't have an income. The news stayed bad. Congress didn't want to fund a project to build a wall on the US southern border. The president wanted it. The impasse meant that Asher, having been with the government for long enough to be a manager, had even more to worry about. Lack of funding meant that more than four hundred thousand federal employees with essential jobs like air traffic controllers and law enforcement officers were expected to keep working, just with no idea when they might get paid. Others in less essential positions were furloughed, which meant that they were not expected or allowed to work and had no idea when they would receive a paycheck. In a particularly demoralizing turn of events, being furloughed required a trip to the office to get furlough paperwork. Many of the staff Asher managed were in this circumstance: lower-level employees who often lived far from work in the exurbs where the cost of living is lower. They spent gas money and time fighting the notorious capitol-area traffic to come in, get their papers, and turn around and go home. Asher, and several other Washington D.C. Area Support Office managers, put together care packages including basic groceries that they paid for and handed out with the paperwork as a kind, if futile, gesture to help with the pain of the shutdown. No civil servant goes into government work to get rich—in fact, Morgan took a substantial pay cut to return to federal work after a stretch in private industry. The lower-level employees didn't earn enough to have much of a cushion to ride out a shutdown.

The shutdown also meant that many of the staff at the parks themselves were furloughed. This was devastating for many of them. If they worked at remote facilities in the mountains or in the desert, the only nearby jobs in the area were with the park or the park concessions so staff were out of luck for finding other options. Surrounding businesses like hotels and restaurants supported tourists visiting Yellowstone, Arches, or Joshua Tree, but closed parks meant no tourists. Without those tourists, there wasn't a chance to pick up a side job. The money to support yourself simply evaporated. Asher's job with the Washington Area Support Office meant that he was involved with all the parks. About 3,200 employees were doing unpaid work and tasked with managing eighty million acres of park lands while the 21,000 others were furloughed. Communications staff are often furloughed as well, so one of the needs during the shutdown was getting information to federal workers and members of the public, who were largely in the dark. The news media did cover the shutdown, but primarily as a political story with a focus on actions and negotiations between the president and members of Congress. But it was a lot more than that. A government shutdown affects employees, of course, but it also affects citizens who need services from their government. AltGov accounts tried to fill both gaps, as well as advocate for federal employees.

Colby had a lot to say to enhance public understanding of the shutdown. NastyWomenofNPS really is a group account, and different posters told their own stories of how the shutdown affected them and their communities. For example, "What happens when the government shuts down? 'Non-essential' employees report to work, close down their office, and sign a notice of furlough 'Essential' employees (more than half of government) continue working without getting paid." Coming into the shutdown, "I've filled my pantry as best I could and have one full paycheck in my bank account. I really don't want a repeat of last time," Colby's account tweeted. Another tweet noted that one full paycheck wasn't that much, as he only earned $40,000. The shutdown affected contractors, too. "Contractors are even more impacted. With the bill Congress passed, fed workers may well get back pay whenever the shutdown ends. Many, many contractors are not getting paid either, and most ★won't★ get retroactive pay. Resentment and fear is far broader than just the feds," Morgan tweeted.

The shutdown didn't just affect the government—loss of government function also affects the public. The people behind Colby's account lived around national parks in some of the areas of the country that were remote and poor, where both the government investment in public lands and the income from park visitors constituted a large portion of the area's economy. Across the country, national parks generate tens of billions of dollars in visitor spending, a ten-fold return on investment. The last normal year, 2019, parks contributed more than a billion dollars just to the economy of Utah, where the parks are so important that visits are a part of an annual economic report to the state. When those visits dry up, it doesn't just hurt government employees and contractors, but citizens as well. Colby tried to help, sharing posts like, "Indian country has been significantly impacted by the shutdown. Check out this awesome beadwork by Ani, a Navajo woman, and enter the raffle for a chance to win and help support her family #NativeMade." Other careers were impacted too. Asher noted, "Think about this, over 300,000 feds are on furlough and not getting paid. The average cost of daycare in the US is $200 a week. If just 10% of feds have kids, the childcare industry is losing $6 million a week in revenue."

The costs to Americans were about more than jobs. "Food stamps and tax refunds will very soon be affected by the government shutdown . . . this may be the moment his base wakes up. Maybe but I doubt it," Charlie tweeted. And a shutdown actually brings extra cost, Colby said tweeting,

> Mail, disability checks, veteran's benefits, etc. are delayed Public lands are vandalized Non-essential employees anxiously wait at home, unable to seek another job or pay bills. Every. Single. American. is impacted by the shutdown. Same Americans claim the shutdown is proof feds are worthless. Eventually, we return to work We waste even more money trying to return everything to order than if we had been paid to do our job from the start #TrumpShutDown.

While federal employees, like the TSA, are apparent in places like airports, a shutdown affects other, little-known processes that affect daily lives too. "Trade Related: The USITC (United States International Trade Commission) website is completely offline now. Expect Imports to slow down dramatically as there is no way to classify goods for Customs/PGA (Participating Government Agencies)," Reid tweeted. Some of the impacts on trade were especially concerning. Dallas noted, "Good morning America! As the shutdown continues on, inspection needed items are starting to pile up at our ports. Things like acetaminophen API. Your food is being inspected by unpaid workers with reduced staff on reduced sample rates as well. #TrumpResign."

Some of the education seemed to extend to the president himself. *The Hill*, a web publication that covers politics, published an article about the president sharing an anonymous op-ed from a conservative opinion site, The Daily Caller, that said, "If the shutdown is just about "rhetorical bickering," it is a loss. "But if it proves that government is better when smaller, focusing only on essential functions that serve Americans, then President Trump will achieve something great that Reagan was only bold enough to dream." Morgan had a reaction of frustration. "Hey dumbass, you don't know what 'essential' means. During a furlough it is focused on life & safety, & just keeping critical systems running. FIXING problems, IMPROVING, MODERNIZING, are NOT excepted functions, and those people are furloughed. @realDonaldTrump, that is asinine."

A lot of the Alt account efforts, both in public and behind the scenes, went toward supporting civil servants and contractors. Asher said, "Are you a federal employee on furlough, or one who is excepted but not getting paid right now? Do you have questions about how the shutdown impacts you and what you can do? Ask here. If I can't answer it, I will do my absolute best to find someone who can." Ning posted an alert with two flashing red light emojis about paperwork needed to file for unemployment in DC. And in other public tweets, and in a series of Google Docs and DM rooms, followers and a few Alts were compiling offers of help. There were many. For example, when Asher was asked about whether federal employees could defer mortgage loan payments, USAA responded on Twitter, "Thanks for reaching out. We are monitoring the situation, and if the shutdown occurs, eligible members may receive a one-time offer via email with a link to offered assistance. Or, you can contact us at 210-531-8722 for options that may be available ~CH." Asher, a veteran himself, knew that USAA, which only serves veterans and their families, was a popular bank with government workers, many of whom have previous military service. Alts and followers shared events where federal employees could get charity meals, gift cards, and items both in DC and around the country. Colby tweeted about the Shoshone-Bannock tribes giving away buffalo meat and potatoes in Idaho, for example.

Alt accounts received questions both in open Twitter and in direct messages from people wanting to know how they could help federal employees. They gave some practical suggestions: Colby shared about a Facebook group where park rangers were selling personal items in order to pay bills. He was asked whether people should visit park facilities during the furlough, and he replied, "This is really a case by case basis. The simple answer is that the public should treat them as closed and not go. Knowing that won't happen, I suggest picking up garbage in open areas. After the shutdown, volunteer your time or make a small donation :)."

As a coping strategy, humor was the order of the day. Valentin wryly wrote, "FURLOUGH FURLOUGH FURLOUGH Bwah ha ha! Now AltGov is my full-time job. You'll pay me in <3, won't you, followers?" When he posted that there were 1,500 GoFundMe campaigns for federal workers living expenses, a follower chided him that it might be against ethics rules. Valentin replied, "The enforcers of those rules are also on furlough, probably making GoFundMe pages, so there's that." And when a viral Tweet asked people what action figure would represent their profession, Colby was ready. "Funny idea of a Park Ranger action figure! Comes with flat hat (Smokey Bear hat) and a government shutdown furlough notice."

The best cure for woes from a shutdown would be to end it, which was fundamentally a political problem. Alts also endorsed political solutions. Charlie encouraged followers who worked for the government by tweeting, "Go to DC and meet with a senator. Preferably Mitch McConnell. Tell him your story. He won't listen but the press might cover it." And when the AFL-CIO held a rally in favor of government workers, Alt account holders encouraged others to attend. Cameron tweeted, "You are cordially invited and encouraged to attend the #FurloughRally Thursday. America and its civil servants are being held hostage. It is time to exercise our right to assembly and say Enough!! We. The. People." Ning joined in encouraging followers to attend as well, "FURLOUGH RALLY IN DC!!!!!!!!!! At noon this Thursday, meet at AFL-CIO, 815 16th St. NW. We will rally, then march to the White House. All are welcome! Feds, non-feds, adults, kids. Please come help us—so we can get back to work helping you. #TrumpShutdown." The Alts's tweets were reshared by accounts for unions and from the science marches that had organized the fall after Trump took office. For followers who couldn't come to DC, Asher had suggestions on how to offer support. "Is your business being affected by the #TrumpShutdown? Shut your doors on Thursday and put up a sign 'closed due to the Government Shutdown.' A non-federal employee that is being affected by the #TrumpShutdown? Call in a sick hour, or a day. Join us Thursday #FurloughRally." After the fact, Valentin said, "Today, I marched on Washington. It felt FANTASTIC. I met an amazing number of passionate families from all across the US who hate the wall and want us to allow feds to work. WE WANT TO WORK."

Though parks were not essential to fund through a spat between the president and Congress, it was politically unappealing to have them closed. During the shutdown, parks provided limited services—you could enter, for example, but there was not enough staff to empty the trash cans. Asher and others in administration had to keep working to try to keep basic things running and, to the extent possible, avoid damage to protected lands. He and the few in park service administration who were trying to keep things together, had conference call after conference call at all hours. He was grateful for the well-stocked chest freezer in his home, as his spouse took to shopping for a grocery delivery service to bring in some extra money. The shutdown was hard on the nearby cities, and state governments in Arizona and Utah contributed funds to keep more services available at popular sites like the Grand Canyon and Zion. New York State helped to keep the Statue of Liberty open.

Asher's job sometimes required him to visit the National Park Service facilities. He had a particular fondness for the Statue of Liberty. "Yes, it is a symbol of immigration 'of hopes and tears,' it's also a lot more than that. It's an icon of America, of multicountry and multicultural collaboration. It's also a premiere destination for international tourists. In fact, the vast majority of international tourists visit the statue, sometimes spending a lifetime's savings to visit the Big Apple, and the statue. It's quite literally the gateway of America," he said. In a bit of irony, the statue was an icon both sides used as they bickered over immigration and the border wall. The statue remained open, not entirely because of federal funding, but because of an injection of funds from New York State. It does a booming business. At the busiest times of the year, the close to one thousand people who work there, either for the park service, for contractors, or for concession holders, help around eighteen thousand visitors per day. Park Service employees are generally known for their fierce loyalty to the land, history, and tradition that they protect, but Asher said the Statue of Liberty staff were inspirational— many of them descended from families who entered the country through Ellis Island. A retired "keeper of the torch" came voluntarily for four hours on most days, working to restore parts of the old hospital, which wasn't accessible to tourists for safety reasons. He cleaned the large auditorium, at the time a state-of-the-art facility where doctors from around the country would come to learn from autopsies performed there, by himself with a toothbrush and a cup, working gently to clean, but not damage, intact portions of the original paint.

The paid staff were still working, and there was money to pay them, but there was still a problem: the government is an integrated system. Asher said, "The money was there, but there was no way for them to access it" because making a payroll requires multiple areas to work together, and some of them were on furlough. So staff were coming to work and knowing they were not going to get paid. It was a tremendous source of stress—acting as the welcoming face of America while not knowing how they would make rent that month." Some visitors took their political views out on the staff, telling them that they didn't deserve to have a job. Asher heard reports that the staff were at their breaking point. He also knew, from previous visits for work, that some of the staff followed AltGov accounts. He had even had a worker show him one of his own posts while on a lunch break, and he had to play it cool. Asher wanted to help, and he did, in two ways.

Friday is the day when government employees can see the amount their next paycheck will hold. For employees that live paycheck-to-paycheck, as many park employees do, they will check at noon. One might then make a call home to say how much the grocery budget could be for the next week or if they can afford camp for the kids next summer. But on January 9 no one expected to find funds for that week. There was an all-hands meeting scheduled for that day where they found out that Asher and the other administrative employees who were involved had worked what seemed like a miracle involving multiple government systems and tens of thousands of data points. At that noon meeting, they learned that there would, in fact, be a paycheck coming. But there was more.

The week before, Asher began using the network of Alts and followers to plan a surprise. He asked scores of people to think what the Statue of Liberty meant to them—a story about a visit, a school lesson, a relative's journey to America—and asked them to put that in a tweet that they would share at noon, perhaps using a scheduler to make sure it posted at exactly that time. When the all-hands meeting ended and people headed to their lunch break and pulled out their phones for a quick check of Twitter, they saw thousands of posts of endearment, orchestrated by AltGov.

At the end of the shutdown, accounts shared some of the results of the government being closed for more than thirty days.

Asher encouraged others federal employees to help:

Many of us Feds who received assistance, free meals, gift cards, etc. due to the shutdown. Now the shutdown has ended, and we will soon get our pay back. However, over a million contractors won't. So, now we need to pay it forward. Let's help out our contractors.

Within ethical limits, I will be giving any gift cards I have received during the Shutdown to contractors who weren't paid. I will also donate to help them make ends meet due to the month of lost pay that they will not recover.

For the Alts going back to work, there was a lot to fix, in a real sense. Colby said coming back from a shutdown meant a lot of clean up, in different ways. "For @NatlParkService employees this means repairing buildings that were trashed, cleaning swastikas off signs, picking up garbage littered everywhere, and trying to track down people who, for example, started illegal fires in sensitive archeological areas." And on a personal level, he said, a protracted period without a paycheck was hard to come back from. He said, "Today I made my first purchase in two months. During the shutdown, I basically went into hiding. I survived on what was in the cabinets or the food bank. I spent twenty-eight dollars on groceries, and I feel wasteful. I could eat rice one more night. I should save that money for the next disaster."

I think we have collectively had more of an impact than any of us would have imagined when we started.

I have no idea if it has been enough, but I do think we have made a difference.

Just with political dialog and helping to provide counter-voices to the administration's bully pulpit.

Also with just helping to give some people hope.

That's hard to quantify but can be very important to those who needed it.

@AltScalesofJust (Morgan)

12

NATIONAL SECURITY

Though AltGov started as a reaction to the deletion of climate change and other data, it didn't take long into the presidency for some Alts to begin to fear for national security. Even prior to the election, Trump had shown disdain for the intelligence community, tweeting nine days before his inauguration, "Intelligence agencies should never have allowed this fake news to 'leak' into the public. One last shot at me. Are we living in Nazi Germany?" He was upset with reports from those agencies stating that Russia had tried to meddle in the presidential election as well as with allegations that his campaign had been in contact with the Russians. In what the White House called Trump's first official event, he visited the Central Intelligence Agency to give a speech that was, perhaps, intended to get things off on a better foot.

While the president did express "a thousand percent support" for the intelligence community, much of his speech landed badly. Trump said it seemed like he distrusted intelligence because the dishonest media was making up facts. After a series of statements in support of his CIA nominee, he spoke about crowd size at his events and his number of *Time* magazine cover appearances. He told the audience, "I'm, like, a smart person" and that "I feel like I'm 30, 25, 39," before discussing his inauguration, the size of the crowd, and how he thought the rain had let up briefly during his inauguration speech. He said he would have to get a larger room at Langley to accommodate the thousands of CIA workers who were trying to get in to see him and concluded with, "No, I just wanted to really say that I love you, I respect you. There's nobody I respect more. You're going to do a fantastic job. And we're going to start winning again, and you're going to be leading the charge."

What was intended as a nice gesture fell flat with some members of the audience. Representative Adam Schiff, the ranking Democrat on the House Intelligence Committee said, "While standing in front of the stars representing CIA personnel who lost their lives in the service of their country—hallowed ground—Trump gave little more than a perfunctory acknowledgment of their service and sacrifice." A spokesman for former CIA director John Brennan said Brennan believed "Trump should be ashamed of himself." A press pool photo showed the president pumping his fist in victory in front of the Memorial Wall in the Original Headquarters Building, which reads "IN HONOR OF THOSE MEMBERS OF THE CENTRAL INTELLIGENCE AGENCY WHO GAVE THEIR LIVES IN THE SERVICE OF THEIR COUNTRY." The CIA holds annual memorial ceremonies there "to honor, remember and celebrate the self-less and brave individuals who made the ultimate sacrifice on behalf of the nation." An article in *The Atlantic* notes that the relationship between the White House and the CIA is an important one because the agency needs the president to soberly consider his intelligence briefings and to keep quiet about clandestine operations.

Trump's speech at the CIA also fell flat with the AltGov, who had connections to the intelligence community. Sabah said he had been willing to give the new president a chance, figuring that as Paul Ryan, Speaker of the House, had said, a political newcomer would follow a learning curve. "That changed the second day of his term. You can't be a good person and stand in front of the memorial wall at [the] CIA and not be struck by their sacrifice," Sabah said. Booker agreed. He was working on government contracts at the time, he said, and the people he was with at a DC bar were gaming out different scenarios related to the new administration—some "what ifs." "When the speech at the memorial wall happened. . . . Well suddenly we were surrounded by like-minded folks, even those who wouldn't say it." According to Sabah, "I definitely wasn't the only one who decided he was an irredeemable, self-aggrandizing jackass and officially gave up hope for decency after his memorial wall speech." Sabah continued that "the memorial wall speech was a special f_ck you to the civil service. It felt like he was pissing on graves at Arlington. Hard to describe the degree of disrespect and offense."

That speech was the first of a series of national security concerns in the Trump presidency, and the AltGov reaction was to primarily help followers with understanding the issues. In 2017, the president met with Russian Foreign Minister Sergei Lavrov and Ambassador Sergey Kislyak at the White House and, according to press reports, shared classified information about intelligence the United States received from other countries. The US media was not allowed to cover the visit, but an official photographer brought by the Russians took photos, which the Russian embassy posted for all to see, a dig at US media. Observers and ethicists were beginning to questions Kislyak's role with the presidential transition and new administration. The visit took place just hours after President Trump dismissed the FBI Director, James Comey. The agency had been investigating contacts between the Trump campaign, the new administration, and Russia. Sabah had posted longform pieces on blogger.com where he expounded at length about national security issues. It was titled "Expanded insights from the Twitter handle @AngrierWHStaff. Trump WH, National Security, Foreign Policy, etc." On May 6 he wrote about reports that Michael Flynn, who had been the national security adviser for only twenty-two days, had had questionable relationships with both Turkey and Russia:

> There's been a lot of discussion whether or not the leaks that lead [*sic*] to Flynn's ouster were illegal or immoral, but this is a red-herring. Don't get distracted by the, "look over there!" rhetoric—potential treason is always worth investigating, and if the powers that be won't do it without prompting, so be it. Realistically, what is the argument? Personally, "I'm really disturbed by how you discovered my treason," doesn't hold water to me.

Other accounts have tweeted many times about national security issues as well. Some of them confrontational when correcting what they see as misinformation, even targeting small accounts. For example, an account with fewer than three hundred followers shared an old *New York Times* article about President Richard Nixon's CIA targeting dissidents, suggesting that government surveillance of Americans who might have inappropriately dealt with Russia was related. Amadi had a long, corrective response:

> Nope, because Russia had precisely nothing to do with what the @nytimes was reporting on at the time and actually, the breaking of the law was targeted at suspected foreign intelligence operatives which at the time would have included Russian operatives.
>
> Those other alleged operations, in the fifties, while also prohibited by law, were not targeted at dissident American citizens, the sources said, but were a different category of domestic activities that were secretly carried out as part of operations aimed at suspected foreign intelligence agents operating in, the United States.

What Trump is siding with Russia on is a cyber and psyops attack by
Russia on the United States, very different than your bullsh_t attempt
at whataboutism.

Amadi didn't save his inflammatory posting for small accounts. While he
continued to fight misinformation, he targeted large accounts as well, for
example telling an account with more than one million followers,

Served in the Marine Corps for 5 years where I was stationed with the
NSA as an intel analyst, never got my clearance taken like

@JackPosobiec

btw Flynn lied to the FBI and took a plea deal for it, admitting guilt.

He also supplied a link that led to Flynn's plea offer. Flynn pleaded guilty
to lying to the FBI about his conversations with Kislyak, was eventually
sentenced, and later was pardoned by the president.

As national security concerns continued to mount, some AltGov accounts continued to share context and expertise. For example, in 2018,
President Trump met with Russian President Vladimir Putin at a summit
in Helsinki, Finland, where Trump was expected to address concerns about
Russian interference in the 2016 election. According to transcripts from a
joint press conference afterward, a reporter from the Associated Press asked,

Just now, President Putin denied having anything to do with the election interference in 2016. Every U.S. intelligence agency has concluded
that Russia did. My first question for you sir is, who do you believe?
My second question is would you now, with the whole world watching, tell President Putin, would you denounce what happened in 2016
and would you warn him to never do it again?

In a lengthy answer that included discussion about computer servers and
Hillary Clinton's emails, Trump said, "My people came to me, Dan Coates,
came to me and some others they said they think it's Russia. I have President Putin. He just said it's not Russia. I will say this: I don't see any reason why it would be," adding, "President Putin was extremely powerful
in his denial today." The response was widely seen as Trump siding with
the Russian leader over his own intelligence community. It drew negative
commentary from senators and congressional representatives, including
Republicans. While the media reports focused on Trump's words and
the political reaction to them, Booker provided insight that went beyond,

tweeting, "Putin knows he overplayed his hand in Helsinki. He knows he revealed the depth of the hold he has on Trump. He won't make that mistake again." Followers seemed to appreciate the insight, with 111 other accounts retweeting it and 284 liking it. Sabah had things to say as well, but more to generate heat than light. When former CIA chief John Brennan called Trump's comments "imbecilic," Sabah tweeted, "If you're attacking John Brennan today for his (true) comments and not upset at POTUS for his abhorrent press conference, you're a cockwomble. That is all." The self-righteous anger was even more engaging, with 827 followers retweeting and close to 4,500 liking the tweet.

National security concerns came to a head in a phone call that President Trump had with Ukranian President Volodymyr Zelenskyy on July 25, 2019, which ultimately led to an impeachment and a removal trial. The Alts had been talking about impeachment since Trump's inauguration, sometimes seriously and sometimes jokingly. The day he leaves the White House they would have a big party. Jelani tried to manage expectations with tweets like, "Remember, there won't be an impeachment with a Republican majority. Especially with the perceived amount of those possibly compromised." When the news about Trump's phone call broke, for many of the Alt accounts, the move toward a formal impeachment brought out strong feelings of schadenfreude. Follower @drredeyedick had been a major AltGov fan from the beginning, chatting with accounts in public tweets and sometimes in private chats. He used a service to create what he called the AltGov Daily, a frequently published (but not always daily) online newsletter that included many AltGov tweets as well as commentary and context. He recognized the vindictive joy, tweeting, "Impeachment proceeding . . . & the Alts are gettin' all froggy," along with a GIF of a top hat clad, high kicking Michigan J. Frog cartoon.

National security-focused accounts tried to provide some context for information as it was released as a part of the ongoing investigation. Some Trump campaign officials appeared to have relationships with Ukraine that went back many years. In 2014, Ukraine ousted a Kremlin-favored president, Viktor Yanukovych, and faced government corruption complaints and investigations since. A little over a week after Yanukovych fled to Russia, Russia invaded Ukrainian territory, taking control of Crimea, a strategically important peninsula in the Black Sea that, while part of Ukraine, had a large population of ethnic Russians. Many countries had objected to the annexation of Crimea, with the United States and the European Union both enacting sanctions to encourage withdrawal, to no avail. That same year, then-Vice President Joe Biden's son Hunter joined the board of a Ukrainian energy company owned by an oligarch who was part of the corruption probe. For the United States, corruption concerns continued for several years afterward. When Trump hired Paul Manafort as his campaign chairman in March 2016, he was hiring someone who had a work history in Ukraine. In August 2016, the Ukrainians revealed a handwritten ledger showing that ousted president Yanukovych's party had given Manafort millions of dollars. It was done outside of the regular monetary system, which would have been trackable. Manafort was fired from the campaign five days later. Shortly after the 2016 election, Ukraine's anticorruption probe of that energy company came to an end. Meanwhile, Trump started suggesting that what looked like Russian interference in the election was actually Ukrainian interference. As allegations that the Trump campaign collaborated with Russia for aid in the election continued, he hired "America's Mayor" and one-time presidential candidate Rudy Guiliani to conduct investigations to defend him. On April 21, Zelenskyy was elected in a run-off.

The Alts who had knowledge in national security and foreign relations were sharing stories from the media with their followers and, in some cases, directly answering questions. For example, when a follower asked, "@RogueSNRadvisor @AngrierWHStaff @AltScalesOfJust @AltHomelandSec Can anyone tell me exactly WHERE in the US Constitution it says that POTUS cannot seek help from foreign govt (i.e. Ukraine) to investigate a political opponent??? (Having a heated debate & want to give specifics)," Morgan answered him, "For one, the Emoluments Clause in Article I, Section 9, Clause 8. Substantive help from a foreign government in getting @realDonaldTrump reelected is a service of significant value that would violate that clause."

A new leader meant new people would be negotiating between the two countries, and news reports began noting items of concern. The AP reported in early May that Ukrainian officials held a protracted meeting about how to avoid being sucked into American politics. Meanwhile, Rudy Giuliani told the *New York Times* he was going back to Kiev to encourage the Ukrainians to investigate the Bidens, because it would help Trump and possibly the country. He ended up not making the trip.

Information about the phone call first became public as a part of an August 12 whistleblower report from an anonymous CIA officer to the intelligence community inspector general. Inspector General Michael Atkinson found that report both credible and urgent, requiring him to report it to the House and Senate intelligence committees. A rough transcript of the call that the White House released suggests Trump made the point that the US government was beneficial to Ukraine and that Ukraine was not being sufficiently helpful in return. President Trump asked the Ukrainian president to speak with Giuliani. President Zelenskyy mentioned trade, sanctions against Russia, and a desire to buy Javelin missiles from the United States. Trump then said words that resonated throughout the impeachment trial: "I would like you to do us a favor though because our country has been through a lot and Ukraine knows a lot about it." He also asked for help finding information about Biden and his son. In the report, the whistleblower wrote,

> White House officials told me that they were "directed" by White House lawyers to remove the electronic transcript from the computer system in which such transcripts are typically stored for coordination, finalization, and distribution to Cabinet-level officials. Instead, the transcript was loaded into a separate electronic system that is otherwise used to store and handle classified information of an especially sensitive nature. One White House official described this act as an abuse of this electronic system because the call did not contain anything sensitive from a national security perspective.

Sabah had a new blog, AngryStaffer.com, that was connected to an account on the creator-support service Patreon. Patreon allows artists, writers, podcasters, and others to have followers who pledge monthly financial support, usually in return for some kind of premium like ad-free sites, invitations to private social media groups, exclusive "Ask Me Anything" (AMA) chats, and the like. Other resistance commentators have used similar strategies. For example, Eric Garland, whom *Business Insider* describes as, "Meet the eccentric liberal analyst whose unhinged tweetstorms have made him Twitter-famous" had about 350 subscribers to a Patreon that offered exclusive content and membership in a Discord discussion channel at more expensive levels. Tom Joseph, another Twitter user who posted about his belief that the president suffered from dementia, had close to two hundred patrons who paid for podcast episodes. Mueller She Wrote is primarily a podcast started by veteran and former Fed and comedian Allison Gill, who has cohosted with other comedians like Jordan Coburn, Jaleesa Johnson, and Dana Goldberg, and was supported by a Patreon with thousands of members, some of whom sponsor memberships for others. Gill's enterprise bloomed into a podcast network, producing shows for other resistance commentators. In Sabah's case, he did nearly weekly public AMA chats on Twitter, getting hundreds of questions and responses in the thirty minutes he was live. Sabah offered three levels of support on the Patreon, named after varieties of alcohol, with the gag being that dealing with all the bad news from the government required a stiff drink or two. He had more than 2,000 patrons across the levels. Blended Whiskey level cost three dollars per month and offered a weekly patron AMA and ad-free blog posts. For ten dollars per month, patrons also got access to a patron-only message board. If patrons paid twenty-five dollars per month, they could get a "AWHS Challenge Coin" and an opportunity to suggest blog topics. Giving challenge coins, a decades-old military tradition, is when a small medallion is given as a sign of affiliation with an organization or as an appreciation from a leader, like the Secretary of Defense. For instance, Morgan had one given to him by Robert Mueller when Mueller was FBI director.

Sabah used the blog for a regular feature called Angry's Daily News Dump, where he would summarize a few news stories and then add his commentary in a longer and more detailed format than Twitter would allow. One of the big issues of the first impeachment was the White House's hold on providing military aid that Congress had approved. Sabah summarized an article from the *Washington Post* about White House efforts to justify that hold. The summary was followed by context from the Alt.

> Angry's Thoughts: "It's the cover-up, not the crime" except this time it's both, and there's plenty of documentation. These emails show that the White House knew in real-time that they were breaking the law here, and that they were looking for retroactive justification for doing so.

> Every agency besides OMB objected to this in real-time, because they understood that the extortion was happening and to quote Bolton, they wanted no part of whatever drug deal the White House was cooking up.

> For example, everyone at State was opposed, except Pompeo, who is spectacularly dumb for someone who has been in politics for as long as he has.

> Testimony last week showed the American people that nobody in the intelligence or national security communities supported this aid being withheld.

The issue of whistleblowers resonated with the Alts, some of whom had done the same during their careers. Congress has made laws in order to protect whistleblowers in coming forward and speaking out if they see something wrong, which ultimately will help with good governance. However, the consequences can be harsh: getting fired, demoted, threatened, moved to a worse job, receiving a pay cut or fewer hours, isolation or mockery at work, or having your immigration status threatened, for example. And that's just from your government employer. Vigilante justice online is another possibility and sometimes even turns into vigilante justice in person, with a false report bringing police to your home, guns drawn. Even having protesters show up at your house can be unsettling and inconvenient.

Some of the Alts had assisted in online vigilante justice. For example, in 2018, social media users posted a video of New York attorney Aaron Schlossberg yelling at workers in a cafe for speaking Spanish. Wilder was credited in the media and on his own Twitter feed for organizing a GoFundMe that raised more than $1,000 to send a Mariachi band and taco truck to Schlossberg's office. The campaign description said, "Raising $500 to send a Mariachi band to cheer up the staff and attorneys at The Law Office of Aaron M. Schlossberg Esq. P.L.L.C. after a difficult day." It continued, "We are requesting the band to sing the famous, endearing, and warm Spanish children song, La Cucaracha, the cockroach." When he shared a news article, followers enjoyed the joke, with close to three hundred retweets. They weren't always so combative, though. Later, Wilder objected to a social media video of a Texas woman's actions, which inspired his followers to try to share the woman's identity. Although Wilder had aggressively pursued Schlossberg, he did not in this case, apparently because people were considering visiting her home during a real estate open house. When a follower suggested the doxxing was just, Wilder replied, "No. The line is drawn at people going into her home and harassing her while she is trying to sell it. That could be an unsafe thing. She is a racist f_ck yes. The inside her home crap is unnecessary."

For the whistleblower on the Ukraine call, some conservative media outlets led a campaign to reveal his or her identity and a few Republican politicians, including Kentucky Senator Rand Paul, shared links to those articles on their social media. The president himself called for the identity to be revealed, arguing that the person might have suspect motives. "Like every American, I deserve to meet my accuser, the so-called 'Whistleblower,'" he tweeted. His attorney, Andrew P. Bakaj, sent a letter to Acting Director of National Intelligence Joseph Maguire stating they had "concerns that our client's identity will be disclosed publicly and that, as a result, our client will be put in harm's way." The *Washington Examiner* reported that right-wing influencers Jack Burkman and Jacob Wohl had offered a $50,000 bounty for the identity. The pair, known for arranging stunts intended to humiliate those investigating the president, held a front-stoop press conference for which they promised they would reveal the identity, but then did not, according to the *Washington Post* article that ran in the style section.

The Alts had been through some heart-pounding moments when Twitter was ordered to unmask Wilder. The fear they felt both from their employers and from upset citizens was echoed in conversation about the whistleblower. They showed support in several ways. Hunter tweeted, "Dear Whistleblower: we don't know who you are, or if you'll ever read this. You've risked your career and more to put an end to corruption and prevent electoral interference. You are #Altgov, and we've got your back. See you at the #ImpeachmentParty." Cameron added, "Damn straight. AltGov: We Stand With You #Whistleblower." Even before the Ukraine call, AltGov was interested in whistleblower protection, believing it was essential to help prevent corruption. A poll taken during the impeachment showed that one in three federal government employees surveyed said they were less likely to report wrongdoing to the appropriate authorities due to attacks by Trump and congressional Republicans on the whistle blower. Sam, Dallas, Tate, and @BadHombreNPS's patch sales raised $11,000 for a whistleblower protection group. Sabah went the information route, saying on his blog that Rand Paul's attempts to get the whistleblower's purported name publicized in the Senate trial following impeachment were deceptive: "Paul thinks he's being cute here, but this is a felony violation of federal law. It's also a shameless attempt to discourage further whistleblowers from coming forward. Coming from someone who used to be very pro-whistle-blower, it only makes me wonder what they have on Rand Paul." If it was an attempt to silence whistleblowers, it may have worked.

As the investigation moved to formal impeachment hearings, ending with impeachment by the House and a removal trial in the Senate, Alt accounts tried to provide context for their followers. Taylor tweeted about the bind that Zelenskyy found himself in: "Ukraine, of course, is desperate for US support. The biggest risk they face is falling out of favor with the American public. And that explains any upcoming recapitulation of 'no pressure.' They can't afford to piss off the MAGAs. They are truly hostages in this."

Amadi continued his aggressive attacks on disinformation, telling an account with nine followers tweeted that Trump would go on to serve a third term because his first was nullified: "That's not how impeachment or the constitution work f_cko." But Amadi also had real expertise in national security, and other posts were more informative, including this description of his reading of the whistleblower complaint:

It shows a concerted effort by @RudyGiuliani to surreptitiously make contact with Ukraine to discuss investigating @JoeBiden long before AG Barr perjured himself in front of Congress and it also shows a premeditated and concerted effort by @realDonaldTrump staffers to conceal the true nature of the "routine" phone call to Ukraine and once word started to get out about the calls true purpose . . . a concerted effort to restrict access to the call as much as humanly possible to the point of concealing it on a separate electronic system used to store sensitive classified material despite the call not rating even close to a classification level the system is designated for.

@RealDonaldTrump and his staff knew exactly what was going to happen during that call and him and his staffs [*sic*] actions both preceding and following said call show that they know the requests made during the call are blatantly illegal and would lead to serious consequences.

He followed this up with a link to the released whistleblower document so followers could find it for themselves.

Asher and other Alt accounts that weren't as closely linked to national security also tried to offer context for their followers. Asher wrote,

Interesting how Trump, his defense, and the GOP, at every opportunity, try to make the Impeachment trial of Trump a trial of something else. This isn't a trial on the whistle blower, it isn't a trial on The house, it isn't a trial on the Bidens. It's a trial on Trump.

If there was a legitimate reason for any of those other things to be investigated, or even a legitimate concern, there would be an ongoing investigation. Giuliani pretends to be Trump's attorney and investigator while smearing political opponents' situation.

There would be an actual investigation. Meanwhile, there is an actual investigation and trial of an actual president who has ignored congressional requests for information that, if he wasn't actually doing something wrong, would prove his innocence.

And yet, the GOP for some *strange* reason doesn't think there is a need to verify if the President of the US is corrupt. Nah, they just want to keep their seats and would rather attempt to play the "well the Democrats should have made a better case."

It's all political maneuvering from them. If they actually cared, they would be asking tough and real questions.

Other Alts focused on dealing with information others were sharing. Texas representative Dan Crenshaw tweeted that the impeachment was mostly hurting Democrats by drawing attention to Hunter Biden, possibly increasing support for Elizabeth Warren or Bernie Sanders, who were also front runners in the Democratic primary. Ning replied with some AltGov sarcasm, "I love it when an entire administration agrees to push Ukraine for a tougher prosecutor, sends Biden to close the deal, because they suspect that years later, it would help Warren or Sanders inch ahead of Biden in the Democratic primaries." Taylor, in contrast, used his voice to boost others. When the president tweeted "these Media Posts will serve as notification to the United States Congress that should Iran strike any U.S. person or target, the United States will quickly & fully strike back, & perhaps in a disproportionate manner. Such legal notice is not required, but is given nevertheless!" Taylor, who had changed his username from Rogue US Mint to Impeachment Today retweeted his note that "this tweet threatens to break several laws. First, the President cannot notify Congress under the War Powers Resolution by tweet," getting the message more than eight thousand retweets and more than twenty thousand likes. He also tried to encourage his followers to see themselves as part of an impeachment process, sharing a research result saying, "If you ever thought protests don't change much, this Stanford study says you're dead wrong."

Data should be soundly sourced, attributed, vetted.

@AltGovDoc (Van)

13

PANDEMIC

At the end of 2019, the World Health Organization first learned about a cluster of unusual pneumonia cases in Wuhan, China. It was an infection that would soon become known as SARS-CoV-2, the virus that causes COVID-19. Unusual respiratory disease clusters pop up periodically and receive extra scrutiny from public health officials in the United States. In early January 2020, the CDC's National Center for Immunization and Respiratory Diseases (NCIRD) began preparing for a response in case the disease appeared in the United States. Later that month, it was confirmed that the virus was very transmissible, as cases were growing in some other Asian countries, too. The first case in the United States was reported January 20, 2020, in Washington State, which caught Mickey's attention as he lived close by. The US government took extra steps, giving Health and Human Services Secretary Alex Azar control of a White House coronavirus taskforce which, on January 31, declared a public health emergency, placing restrictions on travel that meant few people would be able to travel to the United States from China. Those who did would have to quarantine for fourteen days upon arrival.

The information environment was immediately confusing and colored by an intersection of health and political concerns. Italy, faced with an overwhelmed health-care system, put restrictions in place on February 23 that basically locked down the country. The next day, President Trump tweeted, "The Coronavirus is very much under control in the USA. We are in contact with everyone and all relevant countries. CDC & World Health have been working hard and very smart. Stock Market starting to look very good to me!"

Dr. Nancy Messonnier was director of NCIRD at the CDC and tasked with working on the emerging COVID-19 infection. On February 25, she gave a stark briefing about the country's future with the virus. At the time, cases in the United States were few—fourteen diagnosed and thirty-nine who brought the illness from abroad and had been quarantined. But Messonnier told reporters that difficult times could be on the horizon and that "we want to make sure the American public is prepared." She warned that telehealth, telecommuting, and school closures might become a reality in the near future. She described talking to her children about it, saying that while risk was low that day, "we as a family ought to be preparing for significant disruption to our lives." Messonnier's attempts to be realistic might have contrasted with the administration's desire to appear well in control of the situation, particularly as the president was navigating an election year. *Columbia Journalism Review* ran a lengthy piece in April 2020 discussing the challenges journalists face in covering a pandemic when information is restricted, noting, "Concerns that CDC officials are being muzzled seem especially notable under an administration characterized by a brazen disregard for facts, science, and truth itself. (Throughout the pandemic, variations on the phrase "the CDC did not respond to a request for comment" have abounded. The CDC did not respond to a request for comment for this story, either)." Former CDC Director Thomas Frieden took it further, telling the *New York Times*, "Nancy Messonnier told it like it is. And she was 100 percent right, and they silenced the messenger." Days after Messonnier's first briefing, Trump, at a rally, called COVID concern the new Democrat "hoax." A week later, he was telling reporters, "No, I'm not concerned at all. No, we've done a great job with it."

Five days after Messonnier spoke, the problem was too big to ignore. The WHO declared COVID-19 a pandemic on March 11. When the NBA suspended its season on March 12 after the Utah Jazz's Rudy Gobert tested positive, the reality of pandemic disruption hit Americans hard. It was going to be a while until there could be a vaccine—developing immunizations sometimes took years. The president took to leading reports from the White House task force, given at daily press conferences. The media attended, sitting on socially distanced chairs while the president gave news about federal efforts, trying to offer a bright side that would restore citizen confidence and help stabilize a wildly volatile financial market. He embraced hydroxychloroquine, an antimalarial medicine that had been evaluated in clinical trials, but it was found to be ineffective against the disease. The world of information about the disease became extremely confusing, as different parts of the government were saying different things, sometimes at the same press conference. Trump announced the drug as "a game changer" against the disease on March 19. At a press conference the next day, director of the National Institutes of Allergy and Infectious

Diseases, Dr. Anthony Fauci, "told reporters that the drug wasn't an effective treatment. Trump stepped forward to say 'But I'm a big fan, and we'll see what happens.'" Just four days later, an Arizona man died and his wife became very ill after ingesting a fish tank cleaner that listed an ingredient that sounded like the one the president was talking about.

Vetted treatment options were few as people fell sick. New York doctors described the hospital situation as apocalyptic. The government response was struggling, and the AltGov pondered what to do. Asher tweeted, "First . . . F_ck you Trump. Second, if there is anything I can do, print parts, order things, anything to help stop this crisis. I will do what I can." He found ventilator design specifications from a medical technology company called Medtronic, and said, "I could use some smart folks to help dissect this & figure out how we can help." Ultimately, one of the best ways Alts and their followers decided they could help was to provide a consistent source for known, good information. A war-room-type effort started: the COVID-19 Project.

By April 3, the CDC was recommending masks for everyone. This was a change from the early weeks of the pandemic when, concerned that there wouldn't be enough personal protective equipment (PPE) for people in health care, Dr. Fauci had said that the general population didn't need masks. But there were problems. The president downplayed it at the task force briefing where the recommendation was announced, saying, "They suggested for a period of time. But this is voluntary. I don't think I'm going to be doing it. . . . So with the masks, it's going to be, really, a voluntary thing. You can do it. You don't have to do it. I'm choosing not to do it, but some people may want to do it, and that's okay." Even for people who wanted to wear masks, or those who lived in parts of the country where mask-wearing moved from a public health suggestion to a civic mandate, they were hard to come by. Surgeon General Jerome Adams made a video, which was distributed online and to the news media, of how to construct your own mask by folding a T-shirt or towel and using rubber bands to place it around your ears, but studies emerging from university research labs reported that fabric choice and the presence of a filter mattered in making the masks effective. That didn't make them easier to find. Faced with their own crisis, China, a major supplier of PPE, was keeping masks that they made for themselves. Even medical centers in the United States weren't able to get protective gear for their staff. Multiple news stories suggested that states were left hanging. The federal government was seizing the orders that states were trying to make as health-care workers and vulnerable populations needed to be protected.

Where the federal government was having trouble, AltGov stepped in. Hunter had the idea to have AltGov followers make masks to distribute to nursing homes, Native American reservations, hospitals, and other places where there was a need. He pulled some followers into a DM room and turned the project over to them, as he became busy with law school. They organized themselves using the concept of a sewing circle, a historic group where women would support each other as they did work on needlework projects like military uniforms. These groups let women engage in one of the only outlets for organizing and activism that the society at the time felt was appropriate for women. The AltGov Sewing Circle had a home in a Twitter account, a few DM rooms, and a companion website that offered resources for people who wanted to sew masks. Some of the organizers had a science background and were thus able to evaluate emerging research on best materials and construction for mask-making. They created several Google Docs and spreadsheets with links to tutorials. Some of the sewers were already AltGov followers and had worked on earlier projects like the hurricanes and BotSpotter. Others were their friends or came from open calls on Twitter, saying things like, "We started a nationwide #SewingCircle. follow @altgov_sewppe for info on distribution, materials, patterns and best practices. DM me if you'd like to join up! Also, check your state: example: #SewingCircleNY."

For more than a year, around fifty people sewed masks for the project. Rahel was one. He said, "Making them has helped me to retain what little sanity I have left. I made hundreds and invented a hack to make ties out of fabric using a soda bottle to keep things aligned." He even posted a tutorial for how to make a multiple layer cotton mask with ties and a pocket for a filter. In total, members of the sewing circle made and donated more than twenty-five thousand masks in the United States, Canada, and Mexico, in an effort that lasted about a year. They collaborated with other citizen mask groups for ideas for sourcing materials, but most of the participants worked on their own. A few managed to figure out how to share supplies by mail, or by dropping them off personally if they lived close to each other, but most paid for their own materials and for postage. Other followers had ideas for where to donate them. For example, one follower knew about a program for the homeless in New Orleans that was having trouble getting masks for their clients, so another follower took that on, making and sending all the requested masks. The Navajo Nation took a tremendous hit from COVID, with the highest infection rate in the United States at one point, which tribal leaders blamed in part on a lack of federal support. News articles reported that there were people besides health-care workers who desperately needed PPE such as nursing home workers, morticians, and those who worked in group homes for the disabled. The articles supplied contact information for donations. Other members of the sewing circle focused on creating masks and gowns that went to supply those facilities as well. The home-sewn masks and gowns filled the gap and the collaboration made it possible to source materials and find the best ways to make safe and useful PPE. Rahel tweeted, "I have officially made and donated 1394 pleated masks for a clinic in Texas that serves the homeless and low income people. I have probably made a couple hundred more pleated masks for family/friends/friends of family." In his house is a framed thank you note signed by several homeless shelter workers from two thousand miles away, one of whom said, "No telling how many lives you've saved." Sharing the frame is a mosaic of fabrics used from making the masks and an embroidered square that reads, "I became a mask maker because your life is worth my time. 1394." But that was the extent of his pride. "I didn't do it for recognition," he said, "I did it because someone had to." When they were not sewing, followers in the sewing circle posted stories and memes on the group DM that had one strict rule: no politics.

Not everyone involved had sewing skills. So a second AltGov effort worked on providing quality information and developed a Slack group with more than fifteen channels dedicated to ventilators, finding PPE, and developing a website where followers could access facts and links so followers could find current information based on the best understanding of science. It was an uphill battle, as daily White House Task Force briefings sometimes featured what seemed like bad information. For example, at one, the president said,

> So, supposing we hit the body with a tremendous, whether it's ultraviolet or just very powerful light, and I think you said that hasn't been checked, but you're going to test it. And then I said supposing you brought the light inside the body, which you can do either through the skin or in some other way. And I think you said you're going to test that too. Sounds interesting, right? And then I see the disinfectant, where it knocks it out in a minute, one minute. And is there a way we can do something like that by injection inside or almost a cleaning, because you see it gets in the lungs and it does a tremendous number on the lungs. So it'd be interesting to check that.

Calls to Poison Control and emergency room visits increased when some tried self-medicating with disinfectants. To help discourage people from dangerous things, the twenty-five members on the Slack, a mix of Alts and followers, searched for online advice, looking for experts to verify information. They planned projects where the AltGov and its followers could carry on a now familiar mission: providing reliable information in a useful context and stepping in to fill gaps where the government was struggling.

One general project was the COVID-19 project website, which a follower who had worked on the hurricanes put together. It was mostly an aggregator, and since COVID and the related shutdowns caused a variety of problems, the website offered solutions in a variety of areas. For example, one section included mental health resources like podcast episodes, infographics, and articles. Another aggregated resources for parents who were suddenly their children's at-home teachers, with links to virtual museum tours, live webcams that showed nesting eagles, homeschooling idea sites, and more. There was practical information too, such as on testing, which was confusing at the time because COVID symptoms could be confused with those of the common cold, and it was hard to know if you maybe had symptoms. There was a page on what to do if you weren't feeling well, with information vetted by Lee, who worked at a hospital. Because federal coordination was still developing, local and state information was often the best bet. One page aggregated each state's health department website and another all the Twitter feeds from each governor. Dana worked as a professional Drupal developer and had been involved with the AltGov for quite some time. She created the site, one of several she created for AltGov efforts. "I figured I would donate my time/skills," she said. "It was the only way I knew how to fight back when Trump won." She built the site in such a way that it was relatively simple for others to add content and offered some training in how to use a content management system. She paid for hosting and domain registry herself. As the projects expanded, one discussion was if they could register the project as a nonprofit in order to help with costs. They considered other options, too, like piggybacking off existing nonprofits that some of the Alts and their followers worked with. In the meantime, Asher offered to help pay for technology costs. The site never got a nonprofit registry, but COVID surged forward.

By May of 2020, the death count in the United States was more than one hundred thousand. It was apparent that the COVID-19 response was both a public health crisis and a governance concern. As time went on, media reports began to question the way the administration was acting with regard to questionable therapies. Even as the CDC issued warnings about ingesting aquarium cleaners or other unproven therapies, the FDA authorized the release of stockpiled hydroxychloroquine for use for hospitalized COVID patients. Oddly, Dr. Stephen Hahn, the FDA director, worked directly with a single clinical trial where the investigator wanted to test the drug along with zinc and an antibiotic. While the FDA does use the results of such trials in decision making, it was most unusual for a director to be involved. Dallas, in a series of angry tweets, wondered if Hahn had some sort of conflict of interest with the drug. He thought many of the response choices were "a money/power grab by those with corrupt intentions." The federal government had a detailed pandemic plan in place when Trump took power, which took the public spotlight after Senate Majority Leader Mitch McConnell, speaking on a campaign Facebook Live event said, "Clearly, the Obama administration did not leave any kind of game plan for something like this." Former Obama staffers immediately began sharing a link to such a plan, called Playbook for Early Response to High-Consequence Emerging Infectious Disease Threats and Biological Incidents, which specifically mentioned novel coronaviruses among other threats. "If it was to save the public [Trump] could have just pulled out the SARS table top [*sic*] and ran through that on auto-pilot. That would have allowed him to blame experts and Obama for any failures we experienced along the way," Dallas said. He also took issue with Trump's first FDA commissioner, Scott Gottlieb, who moved from the government into a place on the Pfizer board of directors. "Also don't follow Scott G. He's got money in this fight and is trying to secure his legacy as the commish," he tweeted. Gottleib has been a regular commentator on COVID and vaccine-related issues on news shows, generally credited as the former commissioner.

The president's musing about whether disinfectant would offer a cure made work harder for civil servants, and the Alts let the public know. Ning tweeted, "This is why Maryland has received more than 100 calls today from people asking if drinking bleach will help their covid symptoms," and then, "I feel bad for all the state and federal staff who stopped doing covid response work today, so they could create products about drinking bleach." Statements like, "So, we have more cases because we do the greatest testing. If we didn't do testing, we'd have no cases," and, "I also urge Americans to help us stop the spread of the virus. Practice good hygiene, socially distance, avoid large crowds, and wear a mask where distancing is not possible. It's a patriotic thing to do," came from the same person on the same stage and it was confusing for the public. The confusion became a seed for disinformation, as people who wanted to avoid mask mandates or business closings, and later vaccines, would latch on to the information that supported what they wanted to hear.

It was hard to know whom to trust. Hunter asked Van, a follower he had interacted with for a while to start a different Twitter account under the handle @AltGovDoc that could share medical information. "This virus becomes more frightening with each variation and people are panicking. This is a level of global cognitive dissonance not seen in quite some time. Some react by downplaying or ignoring the threat. Some react by seeking alternative remedies like horse paste and who knows what else that's circulating social media," Hunter said. He vetted the account, run by a physician board certified in emergency medicine, by using LinkedIn and by speaking to a colleague of the @AltGovDoc account holder. That new account focused only on fighting COVID misinformation, while the person behind kept his general account as well. On AltGovDoc "they do not post anything political. That's what their other account is for," Hunter said. Between his thirteen-hour shifts in the emergency room, Van mined an assortment of accounts that tagged themselves #MedTwitter for articles, graphics, and current information to share. He had an audience of more than two thousand, and his impact was boosted as Alts and his followers shared his posts. "@AltGovDoc has been able to help clarify a lot of these misconceptions and answer COVID questions directly from our followers," Hunter said.

Van's account shared research studies and offered practical advice. He shared links to approved masks and guidance for how to wear them. "Vetted mask source. Please #WearAMask this means fitting snuggly at all points around the face #SocialDistancing key to this is understanding this virus is aerosolized and stays in the air to infect you for many hours long after the spreader is gone #ventilation = health/life." He kept his account open to messages from others and would regularly try to answer questions from AltGov followers and others who saw the reshares of his information. He also did regular Ask Me Anything sessions on Twitter where, for a period of time, he would try to answer questions people had about COVID, sessions he described as "a joy for me." For example, a post asked, "For those of us listening to scientists & are avoiding indoor places, I've been wondering, at what point would you start going to indoor public places again where people are there for a while (i.e., gyms, movie theaters)? A low community infection #? Or truly a vaccine available?" Van replied, "I am not currently going anywhere with people indoors except for work. When there's adequate testing, and the community R0 is well less than 1.0 and you have no underlying conditions, etc. Even then mask-wearing and social distancing will be important."

Dallas's account had a new voice to deal with, covering another aspect of the pandemic—handling loss. Chad, a voice on Dallas's account that said he was a funeral director with disaster experience, posted a ten-tweet thread about dying alone, a COVID reality as contagion worries caused many hospitals to keep friends and family away. He wrote:

> Our loved ones know that we love them, they know that they are traveling with our thoughts & prayers. While they may be physically alone, they are not mentally or spiritually alone. In non-conventional times this is the comfort we can offer.

> Saying goodbye as the living becomes far more difficult in these times. There is no wrong or proper way to grieve a loss. We all must process loss in our own way.

> What you must avoid is self-doubt that you could have been there if you had tried harder or worked it differently. This is not the case; your loved one would not have wanted you to risk sickness for them.

The tweet had hundreds of likes, demonstrating that it resonated with the audience. The replies were touching. Respondents shared their own stories of loved ones dying in nursing homes away from family. Others simply said, "Thank you so much, this helped me more than you'll ever know." The thread ended with hope and support. "We grieve and weep for you as we do for the loved ones we have lost. You are not alone and your loved one is not a stat. Hugs when we can once again hug—Chad."

The voice of Chad stayed around on the @Alt_FDA account, popping in to share COVID-related content. He posted a news story about a medical examiner contracting the disease from a corpse along with a refresher on the hazardous materials steps that would be needed to keep funeral directors safe. It included an equipment list and a suggestion that if someone died at home, you tell the family who are present what you are doing and why. He also hosted a few Ask Me Anything sessions, answering questions on everything from how to explain death to a toddler to what would happen if the number of COVID dead required places to start using mass graves. There were a few other check-in posts where the voice of Chad would ask followers how they are doing. Then there was a more major project.

Dallas asked followers with art skills to submit samples so he could get help with a book idea. At the end of March, Dallas and Massachusetts designer PB Manning wrote *Welp, You Found a Dead Guy*, a book for children where the main character, a young girl, has to figure out what to do if she finds someone she thinks is dead. Suggestions include keeping a distance, yelling to make sure they are dead, and identifying a smell that proves it's not safe to be around them. The last page includes the @alt_fda logo and an illustration of an adult in a hazmat suit carrying her out, following an arrow on a sign that reads "Therapy." Dallas said the book has major elements of disaster training: assess, address, and move forward, along with showing how to mark and make areas safer. One follower, an early childhood teacher, responded that the book was an example of a social story: pictures and text that let children know what to do in a situation. "God, I hope we never need this social story. But thanks to you all, we are ready. Thank you."

If you're a part of this movement because you want to be famous then you should delete your account. We're here to educate the world.

We're public servants, not celebrities. This is a mission greater than any one person or one Twitter.

@AltDIA (Tate)

14

WHO ARE WE?

The arrival of Van's account coincided with some other accounts like @AltMusician and the short-lived @AltActor, which pleased some Alts and enraged others. @AltActor was introduced with fanfare and mystery, with Cameron tweeting that it was a recommended follow that would make "the voices in your head explode with glee" if you knew who they were and Hunter saying, "@AltActor is a real television actor, has an IMDB profile. That's all we will reveal." Morgan tried to give some gravitas by saying, "Everyone, please also follow the other newest verified #AltGov member, @AltActor. (Not all in AltGov directly work for the government like some of us, but ALL verified AltGov are allies, friends, and valued parts of the #AltFam!)"

One follower said, "If the alt family knows who they are and vouches, that's good enough for me." But it was not good enough for some of the other Alt accounts like Wilder and Jelani. Wilder tweeted,

Wtf is altmusician? How do you fully vet an altmusician? Is it on a scale? No pun. Like can these folks sink our sh_t any deeper? How about altcuck? Alttw_t? Alttablecloth? This sh_t makes me regret my decision 4 years ago and all the sh_t and agony that came with it.

I am glad some found an unintentional platform just waiting for them with 2clicks to declare themselves part of something that was never meant to be some clicks and likes fraternity. Way to water down the sh_t and make us look like clowns. Thank you for finally making me hate.

It got really bad when a new AltGov podcast called *Alts After Dark* posted a link to a Patreon seeking money for production costs. The podcast was an effort from Hunter, Morgan, and Chris, along with parody account

@alt_kellyanne_. Hunter said they were looking at how the AltGov's unique perspective on information might stay relevant after an election that they expected Trump would lose. "We decided to create the podcast to provide more content to our followers, to be able to dive in deeply into relevant topics that were marred with misinformation and confusion." They used a Discord server for voice calls for months while doing the planning, Morgan said. The podcast included a sarcastic read of the news, legal interpretation of current issues from Chris, an attorney, and Hunter, then a law student. Some episodes had thoughts from Cameron as well. There were also interviews of political and resistance figures. Van appeared, his voice disguised, and described how COVID spread and caused infection and how masking and distancing could interrupt the spread. Music producer @dreamwithfaith, who had been involved with get-out-the-vote projects for AltGov, appeared and described using music to inspire underprivileged youth. Virginia lieutenant governor candidate Sean Perryman appeared as well. After the components were recorded, Morgan spent more than thirty hours each week editing, and the final podcast was distributed on Sound-Cloud and Spotify.

Holding an AltGov account was sometimes a negative, for a variety of reasons. It's hard to know if you are making any kind of real difference. "It is a daily struggle with no end in sight and my goal was only loosely defined so I don't think there is any achievement to measure," Reid said. For some, the anonymity, while necessary, also hurts because people in their lives don't know what it is that they have done through the account. Dallas enjoyed having author Katherine Eban interact with his posts and he boosted hers as well. When Scott Gottlieb was the FDA Commissioner, he followed Dallas. But when Gottlieb's successor replaced him, he did not, and it really seemed to bother Dallas. Dallas tweeted, "When will the @FDACommissioner follow us?" When Gottlieb tweeted congratulations about Hahn's Senate approval, Dallas tweeted, "But will he follow us?" Some of the stress was more existential. Alex worried about the nature of social media and of the ethics of his using it at all. "It's turned tragedy into entertainment, argument into sport, fact into conspiratorial nonsense, and created billions of useless conversations that've driven wedges between friends and families and even brothers, all because some people down in SF think that communication is a greedy algorithm and more of it is always better," he said. His presence in the innermost AltGov DMs was a quirk of being Twitter friends with some accounts at a time when there was a gap in vetting. He said he never was vetted, but people inside assumed he was and people on the outside assumed he worked for the government, even though his profile and tweets both made it clear that he didn't. Taylor just wondered about the size of his impact. "I think I may have made a couple dents, but IMO they've been small."

There were other, more banal challenges too. AltGov time was stolen time—stolen from sleep, stolen from free time, or stolen from family time. Because the Alts lived in different time zones, and some even in other countries, working together or even just chatting was a problem, and lots of conversations happened late into the night. Many Alts claimed they had trouble sleeping and some even had a diagnosis of insomnia. As Noor put it, "The Resistance never sleeps." When Alts had federal government jobs, participation was not legal during work hours under the Hatch Act. Alts were careful, but at one point, the Office of Special Counsel issued guidance that even using the words "resist" or "resistance" was a violation of the act if it was a government employee. Asher expressed his defiance like this:

Hey @RealDonaldTrump

Puts on Stetson

I'm a rogue government employee that is part of the #resistance. I'll be right here resisting until your dumb ass gets impeached for laundering Russian mob money, colluding to interfere with an election, and obstructing justice.

#AltGov

But it was a serious conundrum. Morgan, a high-ranking official in his agency, wrote a serious thread about what the practical implications were. From the name of his account, which did not include "DOJ" to the content of his tweets, he showed care to not use his account to influence elections—the focus of the Hatch Act. For example, he said he focused on actions of politicians in his comments, not their parties. He said he didn't tweet about the president while on government property or time, and that making sure he worked a full and complete eight hours (at least) was a good way to feel OK about that. He noted that "I am trying to help the government improve from the inside, and I believe I am making a difference through my official role." But making the time to do so was a continual challenge.

Most of the Alts have families. Noor laughed, remembering episodes of toilet tweeting—using a few seconds in the bathroom to check a DM or to reply to a tweet. He felt bad: Was he neglecting his spouse and kids? Was he neglecting important work? Both? For Gary, his time on the phone was a major bone of contention for his spouse. He described "stress and anxiety through the roof" when she got mad at finding him on his phone yet again while he was meeting followers and training them to pull data to detect Twitter bots. Even when spouses knew, they didn't always really understand. When Suuad was pulled into hurricane rescue, his spouse had to take over home life, including 100 percent of the parenting. The spouse "still to this day doesn't know what I did or why," Suuad said, mostly because the spouse never asked. "I'm not really one that wanted to talk about it either."

Sometimes the inability to talk led to problems. Following a chaotic news cycle closely was exhausting and demoralizing. "We're not consumed by Twitter, but that's where our energy is primarily," Suuad said. The changing problems meant constant need for new solutions, and it didn't feel right to have concerns or to feel overwhelmed. "All we hear is they had it worse," Suuad said referring to hurricane victims. Whether it was fellow employees who were being transferred across the country to live and work in states they had no connection to in Valentin's case, or other park rangers who lost their possessions in wildfires as in Colby's, or working in a court system so backed up that there was no hope for actual justice in Chris's, being an Alt meant advocating, yes, but also thinking about problems all the time. The drumbeat of news on social media was matched by a constant flow of thoughts, commentary, and requests for retweets and shares in private DM rooms. It became common for Alts to take breaks for weeks or even months when they became overwhelmed, with events in the news often being what brought them back. Taylor said, "I was taking breaks for the last year. It's been hard. Every time I've come back, it's just like I had just had 3 glasses of wine and I'd watch the news and go on Twitter and vent it out. It's not fun anymore. It's more negative than positive. I've needed to bring back some of that positivity." Some left entirely. Booker, Gary, and Taylor all left and deleted their accounts, and in some cases their usernames were picked up by others, which was confusing for followers and eroded trust in the Alts as a whole.

While being an Alt was primarily about communication, sometimes the accounts found themselves blocked. This is a feature Twitter offers where a user can set it so that another user can't see their tweets or direct message them. Some of the Alts were quite proud of who blocked them, even putting it in their account description. Taylor's read, "altGov member from the US Mint. Blocked by usmint for going rogue. Possibly a Nasty Girl. Infantry. VetsAgainstTrump RESIST." Booker's read, "Hello, I am the Alternative United States Press Secretary. All of my statements have a basis in reality. Blocked by Trump." Many of the Alts were blocked by the president's account. Holly O'Reilly, the founder of Blue Wave Crowdsource who had worked closely with the Alts during the hurricanes, was a member of a lawsuit against the president that intended to stop him from blocking Twitter accounts, including hers. The basis of the suit was that tweets are official statements, so the president couldn't legally prevent people from hearing things from the government. She told Yahoo Music, "When you have elected officials blocking you—people that are supposed to be serving you—and that is their main way of corresponding with the public and you can't see [what they're saying], that is like having a town hall meeting and somebody closes the door and you don't get to go in, just because you don't agree with the person speaking." In her mind, it was like being told that she didn't get to participate in democracy. The Knight First Amendment Institute joined O'Reilly and six other Twitter users as plaintiffs in the suit. O'Reilly told Yahoo Music that the Knight Institute had actually reached out to her. The president did quite a bit of blocking, including blocking celebrities and even journalists like Daniel Dale who, at the time, was the Washington correspondent for the *Toronto Star*. The blocking was such a phenomenon that for a time, *Wired* magazine even kept an online running list of accounts that had been blocked.

AltGov account holders had different feelings about being blocked themselves and about others being blocked. Wilder, being blocked, described it as "new achievement unlocked," which elicited a "Mazel tov and welcome to the club," from @RogueCPI. When a follower tweeted that they were blocked, Colby told them, "Congratulations are in order! Many a resister has tried to hit their MoCs w the truth so hard they get blocked, but most fail. You, my friend, must look at this as a great life accomplishment. (We've been trying to get the Donald to block us since Jan, but alas, not yet.)" Carter had a similar attitude, stating, "Not yet, though goodness knows I'm poking the bear as hard as I can." Some Alts felt differently, though, believing that blocking was a serious matter, even if they presented it in a funny way. Tanner tweeted, "The one thing I have in common with the North Korean people is that I also can't see what Trump is tweeting about Kim Jong-un #BlockedByTrump." Valentin took it even more personally. "I swear he has it out for the #AltGov," he tweeted at Carl Reiner. The lawsuit moved along and in March 2018, Judge Naomi Reice Buchwald ruled that because the Twitter account is a public forum, it is not legal for the president to block people. The government has appealed this ruling. Years later, some AltGov accounts were still blocked, to their dismay. Valentin tweeted, "Yet I only get news of this, as I am still blocked for calling him a racist, despite the courts finding it unconstitutional." He continued to be distressed by the block, even making it a part of his profile description.

There's been splitting and shrinking over time. Suuad said, "People talk a lot about the positives that have come out of this whole mess. For me, and those involved, one of the best has been the birth of the Alt Cabinet, formed one random nite [*sic*] when a bunch of us were randomly drinking and tweeting at each other." The AltGov group of ten, "The Cabinet," talks daily. Wilder said, "We are close friends . . . went to each other about significant other issues or family issues and even remind each other of doctor appointments. I got lucky in that respect: They are more than just Twitter friends. They are definitely real friends." Several of that group talk via teleconferencing and one has a dog that was bred by Suuad. Friendships within the cabinet remained strong, but the friendships with others weren't always what they seemed, Suuad said. He said some people take interaction as close friendship that he would not see that way. "She may trust me like that, but no way do I trust her. It's just like real life I guess. Sometimes a friend has a different expectation of your friendship than you did."

There were always the followers, who stayed with the Alts despite continuing disappointing news. There were impeachments, but there never was a removal party. The Alts had a strong group of faithful followers who would romanticize the idea of a big party to celebrate when the White House changed hands, and relationships like that kept the audience together during slow news periods. It wasn't just on the public side. Asher and Morgan and Rahel and Gefen and Liron were some of the accounts in a private direct DM group for some Alts and some followers that had some running jokes about retreating to an island. Among the followers, that one knows how to grow things, another has medical skills. A knitter can keep everyone clad and another has, of course, the most important skill—keeping the internet running. A movement does not have power without followers, and AltGov had a varied and engaged group along for the ride. All told, the accounts had more than a 1.5 million followers. They weren't all unique—about one-third of the followers overlapped, following more than one Alt account. Still, so many unique followers meant large potential for reaching Twitter users, who composed nearly half of American adults.

And the Alts often considered the impact of their posts. Social media algorithms picked and presented the things that the AltGov followers would see when they opened the app. Just because an Alt account shared a piece of information didn't mean that people saw it. Businesses that use social media to get you to buy things, do things, or have an opinion about something start with the basics: Did you see the post? They call this an impression. On one ordinary spring Thursday, just eleven of the Alt accounts tracked their impressions. There was no major breaking news that day for them to comment on or share context for. Even so, across those accounts, they had more than three million impressions—more than three million views of the information they shared that day. To put that in context, consider the reach of other information sources that share on social media. That subset of the AltGov had more impressions than the *New York Times* or the *Washington Post* has subscribers. The Alts had more impressions than either Sean Hannity's or Rachel Maddow's evening shows had viewers on a typical night. The Alts varied within themselves and across accounts in how much care they put in crafting messages, but no matter. Their audience was huge.

The Alts existed for their followers. The movement started as a way to preserve public access to government actions and operations, so the accounts did try to continue meeting that need. For example, Dallas said, "We are always working on educating our followers on the science side of the fda. Explains in layman's terms the decisions being made." Science-oriented Alts like Sam, Ning, and Charlie all posted clarifying information and answered questions for followers about how things work. Some faithful followers almost acted like groupies for the Alts—following closely and readily retweeting and liking every post, looking for the inside bits of information and cozy relationship conversation that makes followers feel seen, which one follower described as "AltGov pillow talk." For their part, followers also said they know that following does affect what they think and do. "Now I know there are 'actual' patriots out there . . . and I have the desire to fight. If you can risk everything, so can we," one wrote. Another wrote that he or she recognized "some things extended to tangible help, too." Another said that following the AltGov "helped me become 'woke'—first time marching, calling my reps, protesting, 'resisting,' etc." Like the Alts, the followers became close to each other too. Liron, Gefen, and Rahel lived in different parts of the country but kept in touch over DM and became invested in each other's lives, sharing about mundane things like pets and kids as well as bits of political news, sometimes from their states. Before COVID, they even talked about having one of them come to visit the others in a round-the-country road trip. Stacy and Greer realized that they lived in the same city and became good friends, meeting up for lunch or beers after work.

When accounts hit a milestone (a big round number of followers like ten thousand), they would reward the followers with an Ask Me Anything period where followers posted questions and the Alt answered them in the comments. Guest Alts would often pop into these conversations as well. Most account holders also say they want balance in their interactions with followers. Reid explained, "I see bipartisan and conservatives reach out to me because I call out unethical things on both sides when I notice." Sabah elaborated, "That's honestly my favorite part of AltGov. I've been a just-right-of-center Republican for the majority of my life. My most recent political aptitude test put me at barely left of center, but I make a conscious effort to NOT just post things that my (mostly left leaning) followers will agree with." This noble aspiration doesn't always carry through, though. Sometimes, you'll see an Alt getting pretty snippy with someone who's responding to them because they think the person is acting in bad faith. For example, when Amadi shared about an inspector general report on Hillary Clinton, an openly conservative account said he should look at transcripts from Lisa Page. Amadi tweeted back, "And of course the right is twisting words about burning sources into making Trump a victim."

It's intoxicating to have a platform. When your day job was ordering cars for a government fleet or making sure the software was doing what it was supposed to for your agency, it was one of those important, but hidden, jobs that is the civil service. You might hold the rank of Seaman and be one of more than three hundred thousand Navy service members, but an Alt account could mean your opinions were taken to have knowledge about the whole Department of Defense. And Twitter makes it easy to know what your platform thinks about what you post. A feature called analytics will tell you how many people follow you, how many saw a particular post, how many shared it, liked it, commented on it, and so on, and Alts regularly checked those. Some would delete tweets that don't get enough engagement. Others fretted when their total number of followers went down, using services like Social Blade to look at fever charts of the size of their audiences, day by day.

Was follower count what made AltGov worthwhile? Was it followers sharing or replying to posts? Was it the relationships with other Alt accounts? After some very early efforts, AltGov accounts never really acted as one. Tate is one of the only accounts who managed to stay appreciated by most of the other accounts, which he credits to just trying to stay calm. "So many of us, like, we're so close getting hysterical in these groups. People needed rationality, and that's what I tried to do. Maybe to peace-keep, but mostly to some sense to the chaos," he said. Managing the relationships was something that multiple accounts said they tried to do. For example, Gary tried to bring people in and to advise people on the side when they were rubbing others the wrong way. "I listen and work with almost everyone," he said. But still, there were different ideas about how people should work together.

Booker saw AltGov as "a cell-based network that coalesces around common goals," noting it is similar in structure to al-Qaeda, though quite different in goals. Although AltGov didn't have a central leader, there were sometimes subgroups who self-organized and worked independently of the others on projects. They had general goals in common, mostly preserving effective government, but different issues including disaster relief, cyber influence campaigns, voting rights, public health, and protecting data resonated with different Alts. A more socially pleasing comparison Booker made was the anti-Nazi resistance of World War II. This kind of structure had some pluses, he said. It can be effective without depending on a leader and is difficult to destroy because there's no central weak point that takes everyone down.

A structure with no mutual accountability didn't sit well with everyone, though. Early on, Tate proposed a code of ethics based on what Suuad called "the golden rule of AltGov: don't be a dick." Suuad, Jelani, Amadi, Tate, and others were fans of the code. Tate said, "I was very adamant about not using this platform to make money, and not using the platform to doxx yourself or try to get social clout." He offered it in a core group DM, and many of the other accounts took a pass. I think it was more of a "that's a good idea, but doesn't pertain to me," reaction to the code of ethics as opposed to a 'that's not going to work,' or some more negative association," Suuad said. There was even a suggested graphic for the code. Highlights included:

Don't be a d_ck (unless it's in self defense)

Don't be rude (ask for clarification and use "I" statements)

Fundraising should be transparent (tell people where money goes)

Facts are friends, not foes (so check for accuracy before you share)

We are accountable to ourselves

Notes on the side stated principles like, "No one account is 'better' or 'more important' though they may be more visible." Ultimately, the loose structure meant no leadership, which meant any code was impossible to enforce. After it was rejected, accounts in the AltCabinet started talking mostly to themselves, distancing from the other accounts.

Agree to disagree lasted for years, with occasional open disagreements, mostly over fundraising. But the podcast, which the creators saw as a fun way to inform their followers in a different medium that allowed for longer-form discussion, was a breaking point. Others saw it as the end. Half the people involved in creating it hadn't worked for the government: hadn't taken the professional and personal risks. When Hunter tweeted that the podcast was coming, Wilder quickly replied, "This is funny because none of the ALT OG accounts who actually had to deal with sh_t in 2017 knew about this and none are involved. I am amazed. The name should be changed to Jabronis or something else." When a follower questioned what they were seeing, asking if the verification meant nothing, Wilder replied that in his view, monetizing was "BS." He tweeted, "We'd like the original alt mission to remain the same: inform, joke and no $" and said he objected because the original Alt accounts took real risks to share information. "They took something that that for us was a lot of agony, and confusion and stress. They took the good parts out of it. And just ran away with it as if it's theirs." After the complaints, Hunter and the others took the Patreon down, but they still produced several episodes.

But Amadi had a blunter take. He wrote a Medium post where he noted that original accounts had offers to collaborate with prominent political figures, to interview with well-known journalists. As he saw it, when the attempts at structure and ethics were rebuffed, it was over. "What was supposed to be a cause to fight for has turned into some weird fraternity or social club," he wrote. He called the post "#AltGov is Dead."

I think at first I kind of served as a more comedic outlet. "If you are able to laugh about something that's really dark, it makes you feel better." The first 30,000K that followed me knew I was joking around a lot.

Then the lawsuit happened. It was this big deal. I was named in the lawsuit for some reason (one of my Tweets was quoted in the counter lawsuit).

After that, a lot of people like journalists and new personalities and more famous types of activists—they all started following me. Like I was putting out useful info, which I absolutely was not. It was a weird paradox. I got more followers, but the more I got the less I started enjoying it because I had to be more serious about it.

@Alt_Labor (Tanner)

15

ELECTION AND INSURRECTION

The lead-up to the 2020 election was busy. Just weeks after Amadi declared the death of AltGov, a pronouncement with which many disagreed, the already frenzied news cycle leading up to any election got several new twists. President Trump had already placed two justices on the Supreme Court. On September 18, 2020, the nation learned that he would have a third opportunity, as eighty-seven-year-old justice Ruth Bader Ginsburg succumbed to pancreatic cancer, which had plagued her for several years. Ginsburg, or RBG as she was sometimes known, was an outspoken champion of women's rights. Some of those behind Colby's @NastyWomenofNPS account had backgrounds as historians, and in 2017 included Ginsburg in a Women's Equality Day thread, posting, "Ruth Bader Ginsburg #NotoriousRBG "My mother told me to be a lady. And for her, that meant be your own person." Ginsburg was also quite popular with Alts, so much so that Sam even live-tweeted a CNN documentary about the justice.

According to news reports, days before her death, Ginsburg asked her granddaughter to record a last message: "My most fervent wish is that I will not be replaced until a new president is installed." There was a possible precedent for this message, as Trump's first Supreme Court appointment, Neil Gorsuch, was put in the seat once held by Antonin Scalia, who died during the Obama administration. Fairly quickly, both the president and Senate Majority Leader Mitch McConnell indicated that they wanted to move quickly to fill Ginsburg's seat, inspiring Sabah to tweet,

> It's hard to imagine being more pissed off than I already was, but I'm furious at the lack of decorum from many of the GOP here.

The ink wasn't even dry on the announcement of RGB's death when they started talking about replacing her.

She was a giant, and she deserves better.

Some of the Alt response was similar to what they had posted when Brett Kavanaugh was nominated to replace Justice Anthony Kennedy—scrutiny of the proposed replacement. Trump's nominee to replace Ginsburg, Amy Coney Barrett, was rated well-qualified by an American Bar Association committee. A law professor at Notre Dame, she described her judicial philosophy similar to that of Scalia's, who described himself as interpreting laws and the Constitution as they were understood at the time when they were written. Coney Barrett, like many members of the court, is Catholic and had been vocal about her views on abortion, which had caused concern when she was appointed as a judge on the United States Court of Appeals for the Seventh Circuit. Terry raised questions about her, tweeting, "The problem isn't that she has religious principles. The problem is that she serves principles other than justice in such a manner as to undermine justice altogether. If a judge has no integrity in the matter of their own appointment, we cannot trust them to have it in much else." Kim, who didn't work for the government and was free to be openly partisan, saw the dispatch with which Congress considered a replacement as a different opportunity—one for fundraising for Democratic causes, tweeting, "We did it!!! $100 million has been raised since SCOTUS Justice Ruth Bader Ginsburg's tragic death Friday night. She would be so proud!!" Still, ultimately, Barrett was confirmed with a highly partisan vote.

It was a busy year and there was still the matter of the 2020 election. For this, their Twitter followers took on the mantle with only occasional assists from Alt accounts. Followers formed multiple get-out-the-vote groups, working to make sure they did what they could. Rahel explained that some Alts were occasionally involved, and because of that, efforts had to be focused on voter registration and participation, which was fine. There was plenty that needed doing. Though the 2020 election had more participation than past elections, there were still real concerns about the fairness of people's chances to actually cast their ballots.

First, some states passed legislation that made it harder for nonwhites to vote, including new voter ID requirements in Iowa and Kentucky. Oklahoma made it more difficult to vote by mail, restricting mail-in voting by requiring mail-in ballots to either be notarized or have a photocopy of an ID card. Voters would have to plan in advance to get that ID in hand before election day. Some people with low incomes and with jobs that don't allow time off during the week found it difficult to even obtain IDs. It went further. A state of Florida vote determined that people with criminal convictions could get their voting rights reinstated—1.4 million of them at the time that law was passed. However, Florida's legislature made it conditional that they pay fines and fees to the criminal justice system first, which disproportionately hurt Black offenders.

Second, voter roll purges in some states, which AltGov campaigns had fought in the 2018 midterms, continued into 2020. Georgia, which had removed about 500,000 from the rolls in 2017, removed more than 300,000 more prior to the 2020 election. Ohio removed more than 150,000 in a process that the Center for Public Integrity found was mistaken on one in six voters. A later study found that this deletion particularly hurt young voters. Voters who are deleted aren't always notified. If they learn about it, they need to reregister by the election deadline. Due to COVID, fewer voter registration drives took place and sometimes government offices were closed.

Third, some states simply closed polling places, taking advantage of the first election in fifty years held without the full voting rights act. For example, Texas counties closed 403 polling locations, and more than two hundred were closed in Arizona. The consequences were debatable, but generally, fewer polling places can hurt some voters. When there are fewer places to cast ballots, voters may have to wait in longer lines. And when locations change unbeknownst to voters, it's possible that they head to the school or fire station where they had always gone, only to find that they should have gone elsewhere. They may not have the time to now do that, so they may give up and not vote.

Fourth, there were some efforts to intimidate and confuse voters. There were reports in Florida of people stationing themselves near polling locations with firearms and of voters with Black Lives Matter T-shirts being sent away when poll workers decided that they were electioneering. Conservative tricksters Jacob Wohl and Jack Burkman faced felony charges for robocalls to voters in five states stating that voting could lead to, among other things, forced vaccination. Some Detroit voters received leaflets indicating the voting period had been extended due to COVID. There were even ballot drop-off boxes that were set on fire in California and Massachusetts.

And finally, because of the pandemic, fewer voters were willing to stand in line and enter voting locations, just for fear of getting sick. The first major spike in COVID cases occurred at that time, and people were being asked to avoid crowds. Absentee and voting by mail were some solutions, but they had their own problems. Republican donor and fundraiser Louis DeJoy had been installed as the US Postmaster General in May 2020. DeJoy was selected by the postal service board of governors, all of whom had been appointed by Trump. The first postmaster in about twenty years with no experience in the postal service, DeJoy's experience was in private freight companies. He put in place a series of so-called cost-cutting measures at the postal service, including eliminating overtime, removing street mail collection boxes in some cities, and removing and destroying high-speed mail sorting machines. The main effect of these measures was substantially slowing mail delivery, which DeJoy acknowledged. In the face of congressional scrutiny, he pledged that the changes wouldn't affect the election. But with a pastiche of policies, by state, about when a vote had to be received in order to be counted, there was abundant confusion. The president's occasional statements to the press and at rallies about the questionable nature of mail-in voting did not help.

Meanwhile. for the Alts, especially those who still worked for the federal government, the run-up to the election was also an extraordinarily busy time at work. Preparing to transition between administrations was always busy, but this time it was complicated by what Cameron called "departmental arson." At both the federal and the state level, he said it was "setting proverbial fire to things by way of shady orders & attempts to shake things in their favor." Polling had been suggesting a bigger Biden win than what actually happened, and Republican politicians were trying to do what they could to keep states red, keep their congressional representation from the same party, and keep Trump in the White House. Most of the Alts were focused on "generally holding things upright until inauguration," Cameron said. But in a time of uncertainty and confusion, voters needed information and that's what the Alts' followers organized themselves to do.

Dana said there was a separate DM room for "call to action campaigns" where they uploaded things like graphics some volunteers had created and wording for particular initiatives. They worked with @resistbot, a volunteer-run service that was created to make it easy for citizens to write to their representatives. It was extended to include ways to help people vote. Users could text keywords like "check" to verify voter registration. You could reach the service from iMessage, Telegram, Twitter, Messenger, or just your phone, and the bot would walk you through the information, look up your registration for confirmation, and then set a monthly check so it could alert you if you were ever removed. Other keywords would help you register, track your mailed ballot, get vote-by-mail instructions, and more. For the AltGov followers who would see information from the get-out-the-vote campaign on Twitter, it made a complicated process seem more natural. The @resistbot creator joined in some of the DM conversations with followers and Alts and helped strategize about campaigns. They shared links to other tools as well, such as a service called Categorized Tweets that sorts a politician's Twitter timeline according to subject to make it easier to see how a politician feels about an issue.

A lot of the information was intended to cut through some of the noise around the election. "We would post information on registering in the different states with dates," Rahel said, "Just basic 'if you live in _____ here's info on how to register by this date' kinda stuff." They did weekly pushes to remind people to verify their registration too. Followers did most of the planning and creation of content and, as they were able, Alts would share the posts to get them in front of bigger audiences.

Election Day itself was anything but reassuring. As Charlie put it, "I'm anxious, guys." He and other Alt accounts shared links to voting information and sources for voters in distress because of malfunctions, closed polls, and so forth. Tate asked followers to share photos of their "I voted" stickers, while Mickey addressed the burgeoning misinformation, tweeting, "Mail in ballots are not cheating, Donald." After the polls closed, Asher had another party. Of sorts. Because of the pandemic, it was a Zoom call that went late into the night. "Everyone was anxious," he said, but "most of us were on until about 3–4 a.m." They went to bed not knowing who had won the election.

Pundits had been predicting the unpredictable for election returns, and that prediction, at least, was correct. More voters overall and many more mail-in and absentee votes meant that depending on how the states counted their votes, the apparent leader in a state could change and the winner could seem like a surprise. Red mirage. Blue mirage. Vote-counting did take a long time, and six states remained uncalled several days after Election Day. Tanner handled his uncertainty with humor, tweeting, "I honestly don't know where the country even begins to rebuild, let alone sustain, in the next four years, so thank you for paying my salary all these years. I'll be considering offers from the rest of the world. Thank you. Tag your favorite country below." As the votes were counted, the agitation around the country grew. "Stop the steal!" conservative voices yelled, agitated by false reports that poll workers were slipping in Biden votes, hiding from the watchful eyes of election observers. "Count Every Vote!" liberal ones exclaimed, livid at the idea that mailed-in votes might be discarded because of timing. Whether a huff of exasperation or a sigh of relief, the nation let out its collective breath on November 7 when the Associated Press called the election for Joe Biden.

Although it was the beginning of years of misinformation and concern about the process of the election, the election itself was over. Some of the Alts turned their attention to runoff senate races in Georgia. If both democratic candidates won, the democrats could control both the legislative and executive branches. But for Asher and other Alts, it was time for yet another administrative transition. The day after the election, he said everyone at work was exhausted. He had ten meetings the rest of that week to plan for what was coming next.

Though it seemed like it was time to get ready to move on from the Trump administration, Trump himself had other ideas. "This election is far from over," he said, the day the race was called for Biden. The national security apparatus began noticing a lot of online chatter from militia and other far right groups suggesting that the election was stolen. On November 14, disgruntled supporters rallied in downtown Washington, DC, in numbers estimated from thousands to more than a million, depending on who was asked to estimate the crowd. The estimate of more than one million came from Trump Press Secretary Kayleigh McEnany in a tweet that Reuters rated "false." Other protests featuring figures like conspiracy streamer Alex Jones were organized in Georgia, Washington State, and elsewhere. Trump had hired attorneys to file suit against election procedures in swing states he lost, but nearly all of them failed. On December 19, Trump tweeted, "Statistically impossible to have lost the 2020 Election. Big protest in D.C. On January 6th. Be there, will be wild!" Morgan recognized the danger of the rhetoric, tweeting, "More ★current★ government officials need to speak out publicly and join their voices with the former defense secretaries. The election is OVER."

January 6 was the day that, according to the Constitution, Congress was to meet to certify the results of the election. The House and the Senate met in joint session to do the certification. Some Republican members of Congress, both senators and representatives, planned to object to certification in some of the swing states. About an hour before House Speaker Nancy Pelosi gaveled in the joint session, the president held a rally near the White House saying, among other things, that "We will never give up, we will never concede. It doesn't happen. You don't concede when there's theft involved." He told the crowd, "And we fight. We fight like hell. And if you don't fight like hell, you're not going to have a country anymore." While he was speaking, a crowd was already gathering near the Capitol. When he left the stage, the crowd from the rally came and joined those at the Capitol. As Congress was beginning its session at 1:00 p.m., protesters started testing the barriers keeping them out of the building and eventually succeeded in going inside about an hour later. It took more than four hours for a combination of Capitol Police, DC Metro Police, and the National Guard from DC and multiple states to resecure the Capitol, while members of Congress cowered in safe rooms, their staff barricading themselves in locked offices.

Congress reconvened and completed the certification after three o'clock in the morning, but the damage was done. As Asher looked at pictures of the aftermath—broken furniture, shattered mirrors in the Speaker's office that had hung in the Capitol for hundreds of years—he was shocked. And saddened. Those pictures were soon accompanied by others—photos and selfies and videos that the people in the mob had taken of themselves and proudly streamed or posted on social media themselves. Assaulting a police officer is a crime, as is entering or remaining in a restricted federal building and destroying federal property. And Asher found a sense of mission.

The weeks between the certification and the inauguration were a busy time at work. Transitions always work that way. But Asher spent his non-work time helping to pull faces from the footage and looking for clues that would identify the perpetrators of violence against the nation he had sworn to protect. He used his network, built from four years of talking and working as @AltWASONPS to help, tweeting, for example:

Alts and Rogues.

Start digging.

Is this information accurate. Is this company in support or against the terrorist who broke into the Capitol with flexcuffs?

What's the companies number?

Who owns it?

Let me know.

Sam chimed in, resharing it to his larger platform with a "You know what to do, Rogues."

Asher described hours looking at videos and photos and in pulling stills. "We have ripped and flagged every single image/video that we can find, have ran the videos through facial recognition software to collate/organize." Like his other AltGov activity, it was a mix of his professional mission and a personal one as he knew people who lived and worked in the area. "To them, this really was a terrorist attack. So . . . if I can help make them feel just a little bit safer, by helping to track down people responsible, I will."

ALTS WERE INTRIGUING —

After the inauguration, I needed hope. Twitter drew me because I'd seen a writeup on some Alts. New to Twitter, I lurked for a few months. Then I made an account. I had started to really like these folks and what they stood for, and I wanted to help. Little did I know what a scintillating journey it would be, or how much my definition of Alts would expand.

ALTS WERE GENUINE —

Mostly, I saw good people making sure facts were disseminated properly. Letting us know that there were ethical Feds and Locals. Giving us hope. Yes, they were anonymous, but it was OK. The effort was real. The information they shared was important.

ALTS HAD SKILLZ —

HarveyRescue came along—the most amazing "winging it" venture I had seen in ages, anywhere. A few Alts developed an idea of how to use SocMed to assist disaster victims, built it on the fly, and asked for volunteers. Exhilarating. Unforgettable experience. Alts didn't just sit back and spill info at us. They CARED! Together we cried, and worked all hours, and laughed. My heart still overflows from the memory.

ALTS WERE MY FRIENDS —

You can't do such intense rescue stuff without becoming close. Some of us did. More projects came along—things we could do to make a difference against this horrifying administration. BotSpotters. GOTV. Calling out CongressCritters all the time. We didn't have to feel hopeless. Alts led, offered advice, did good works. They educated us when needed. We encouraged one another, defended one another against trolls. Personally, I still cannot fully express my gratitude. Without the Alts, inclusive, I may have given up hope in democracy.

I say "inclusive" because there were many varied Alts, many not in gov at all—but we shared a common purpose. A goal: to defend our democracy, protect citizens, try to make equal rights more than just a phrase.

ALTS POLICED THEMSELVES —
Grifters and chaos agents existed. They were weeded out. Often quickly, one or two took longer. The goal was "no financial gain"— AltFam knew it. We witnessed Alts culling grifter accounts.

ALTGOV EVOLVED —
Alts gained at least 1,000,000 individual followers (there was overlap since AltFam followed multiple Alts). It became a real movement. A collective of caring people, often inspired to work incredibly hard in their communities, or online, to extend the work of the Alts. AltFam became a team. We are, in my mind, the footsoldiers. We are people from all over who found hope in the Alts, and then found a way to bring our own talents and energy to the fight.

ALTS WILL STILL BE NEEDED after the upcoming election, and SO WILL ALTFAM. We will repair the damage caused by the Grifter-in-Chief. My life has been infinitely enriched, my heart filled, with the truly wonderful people I've met on this journey. I love you all.

They're not heroes. (Or they would have all come out publicly and fought the good fight.)

But they were enough.

@EmbryoResist (Liron)

16

TRANSITION, AGAIN

*T*ap. *Tap. Tap. Tap.* The hard rubber buttons on the bottom of Parker's driving moccasins kept a staccato beat on the wood floor, announcing the eight steps he paced from the dining room entrance, through the living room with the TV on, into the foyer, and eight steps back. It drove his spouse crazy. Parker made a habit of watching significant government events when they were televised, and he encouraged his spouse to watch this one. They were worried. A few weeks ago, a flag-carrying crowd had livestreamed themselves forcing their way into the Capitol. Was there going to be a repeat today?

It was a cold, clear day in Washington, DC, when Joe Biden was inaugurated on January 20, 2021, as the 46th president of the United States. Congressman Bernie Sanders made a meme-worthy appearance huddled in his chair with fluffy brown and white mittens made for him by a Vermont elementary school teacher. He was cold, but most of America was not, as the event was a made-for-TV affair because of the COVID-19 pandemic.

Morgan couldn't actually attend, but he did go into downtown DC a few days prior. He wore the same kind of outfit as he did the day after the 2016 election: somber. His black suit, grey shirt, and black and white tie matched his mood. Heartbroken. The city would usually be bustling with workers and tourists, but it was so quiet you could hear the birds tweeting. It was like the nation's capital was taking a moment of silence for the losses of the last four years. He shared photos on his Twitter account: reporters setting up their shots of the capitol, filming between a line of national guard trucks parked to form another barrier. Eleventh Street was empty of pedestrians and blocked by concrete barriers, placed end to end: a row of them twelve across and at least twenty feet deep. Civic space, yet the public was not welcome.

Like election night in 2016, he had trouble sleeping. It was the excitement tinged with uncertainty. At 12:40 a.m. he tweeted, "Today is the day many of us created these accounts to see. TODAY, DONALD TRUMP LEAVES OFFICE. We still have a long road ahead, but let's all commit ourselves to working as hard on #HealingWithBiden as we did on resisting Trump. We can't pretend that what we saw will just go away." He wanted to watch Biden's inauguration, but he had to work. Though he was working from home that day, he had a deadline to meet, so he had work data on his TV and the inauguration on his phone. He dressed for the occasion wearing an Alt Scales of Justice T-shirt with a drawing of blind justice and the words "Liberty and justice for all" in red, white, and blue script. And fitting with the theme of his Twitter account, as the ceremony ended, he tweeted, "As of today, Donald Trump is no longer shielded from indictment or prosecution."

Some of the Alts and their followers had planned to attend from out of town, but COVID changed those plans. Instead, they followed from afar, diminished by the stresses of the pandemic and the four years that had preceded it. Still, they were optimistic about the future. For Liron, the cancelled meetup plans meant he had to work that day, but he was able to catch snippets of the event streaming on his phone, a few minutes at a time between jobs. When he could, he checked just one DM room, grinning at a picture of an AltFam friend from Thunderdome who posted a smiling face and a champagne toast. Rahel caught bits and pieces as well as he worked, still sewing facemasks. "Having it on while you do something generous and useful," Liron commented. Gerry watched every minute, cozy at home with his family. As tears slid down his cheek, he watched Youth Poet Laureate Amanda Gorman on the stage at the inauguration, saying "But while democracy can be periodically delayed it can never be permanently defeated."

Dallas said he shed a few tears, too, as Joe Biden took the oath of office. "That sealed the deal and there was only going to be movement forward from that moment on." He had stayed home from work that day and watched from his couch. After work hours, he joined his friends at the bar they liked to hang out at, talking about the future. "We are, were thankful it went down peacefully . . . but all of us seemed very realistic in the amount of work ahead of this administration," he said. He had committed to keeping the account active at least until COVID was not such a massive, deadly problem.

Inauguration Day of 2021 was both an end and a beginning. Like many of the Alts, Asher posted a reflective thread around that time:

I truly believe in what I do, and I will and do fight relentlessly for what I believe is right. At the same time, some of the things that I oversee are not and were not as controversial as things that others may have been involved in. I don't say that as a "cop out" [*sic*] I say that because it's the truth and, to be blunt, there is only so much that one person can do.

But this isn't a story of a futile attempt to speak out. Throughout the last 4 years there is a lot that I have done, a lot that I have been personally responsible for, that has limited the damage that the Trump administration attempted to cause.

And I didn't do it because of my political position. I didn't do it because I wanted to see his administration fail. I did it because I have responsibilities. I did it because when everything was laid out, what they were attempting was nonsensical.

In many cases, I lucked out and was often able to clearly explain and get people to listen to why what they were proposing was a really bad idea . . . not always though.

But it's also not about me. In the grand scheme of things, I've honestly and truly only played a very small part in all of this.

There was the question of what comes next. The group of followers, together, virtually in the Thunderdome DM enjoyed the day, which was a break from strategy and worrying. A day to celebrate the posting, sewing masks, knocking on neighbor's doors and handing out voter registration forms, hunting for cries of help during disasters, and writing code to identify bots. It was a day to rest. And to believe. "Then we all agreed to reengage in maintaining everything the following day or week," Liron said. They had been a part of an unprecedented movement and were, in some ways, forever changed by it. The Alts' followers had evolved from citizens looking to the Alts for leadership to being citizen leaders themselves. The Alts, who started their accounts to work *for* the people were now working *with* them.

Most of the Alts have been much quieter since that cold January morning. Political intrigue goes on. Sabah continues to engage his followers in weekly Ask Me Anything posts and in special content for others on his Patreon. Parker occasionally comments on the news and continues to assist veterans who reach out in messages. Between misinformation and lack of vaccines overseas, new COVID variants popped up, and Dallas followed and interpreted CDC guidance. But for many of the accounts, the inauguration meant a time to step back a bit. To post less often. However, most aren't completely gone.

Wilder said if he looks back at his screen time statistics, at times he was spending eight hours a day on Twitter in the thick of things. And while he was there, he met "very authentic people who are beautiful with their perspective on the world or I found something about them that I can learn from." Keeping his account means being able to keep up with people that, though he will never meet them, have been an important part of his life for years. There's also the matter of legacy. Wilder said keeping his account open means he will have something to share with his child, whose formative years were during this time. Someday, he will show the child, who maybe "would agree with it, then or not, I don't really care. But at least I did something my way to change something." Asher pondered going public with his identity,

> One day, maybe I'll say exactly who I am . . . maybe in the near future, or a few years from now. Maybe I'll save it for one last surprise during a retirement speech. Or maybe I'll just slowly drift away out of sight and out of memory. Because, as I said. This isn't and was never about me. It was about standing up and doing the right thing. However, no matter what happens, whether I stay or go. . . . Should the time ever come where I believe I need to stand and speak out, I will. And I can guarantee I won't be alone.

#WeAreAltGov

REFERENCES

CHAPTER 1

ABCNews.com (2017). Trump Inauguration Speech (FULL) | ABC News. January 20, 2017. https://www.youtube.com/watch?v=sRBsJNdK1t0

Boghani, P. (2016). Me "Meet Myron Ebell, the Climate Contrarian Leading Trump's EPA Transition." November 16, 2016. PBS.org. https://www.pbs.org/wgbh/frontline/article/meet-myron-ebell-the-climate-contrarian-leading-trumps-epa-transition/.

Calma, J. (2021). "How Scientists Scrambled to Stop Donald Trump's EPA from Wiping Out Climate Data." March 8, 2021. TheVerge.com https://www.theverge.com/22313763/scientists-climate-change-data-rescue-donald-trump.

HHS Presidential Transition Team. (2017). "HHS Presidential Transition Agency Landing Team Book." AltGov2.org. http://altgov2.org/wp-content/uploads/2017/03/HHS_transition.pdf.

InsideEPA.com. (2017). "Trump Transition Preparing to Scrub Some Climate Data from EPA Website." January 17, 2017. https://insideepa.com/daily-news/trump-transition-preparing-scrub-some-climate-data-epa-website.

Kessler, G. (2017). "Spicer Earns Four Pinocchios for False Claims on Inauguration Crowd Size." January 20, 2017. WashingtonPost.com. https://www.washingtonpost.com/news/fact-checker/wp/2017/01/22/spicer-earns-four-pinocchios-for-a-series-of-false-claims-on-inauguration-crowd-size/.

NBC News (2017). Kellyanne Conway: Press Secretary Sean Spicer Gave 'Alternative Facts' | Meet the Press | NBC News. January 22, 2017. https://www.youtube.com/watch?v=VSrEEDQgFc8.

Nikjforuk, A. (2013). "Dismantling of Fishery Library 'Like a Book Burning,' Say Scientists." December 9, 2013. https://thetyee.ca/News/2013/12/09/Dismantling-Fishery-Library/.

Tumulty, K. and Ellperin, J. (2017). "Trump Pressured Park Service to Find Proof for His Claims About Inauguration Crowd." January 26, 2017. WashingtonPost.

com. https://www.washingtonpost.com/politics/trump-pressured-park-service
-to-back-up-his-claims-about-inauguration-crowd/2017/01/26/12a38cb8
-e3fc-11e6-ba11-63c4b4fb5a63_story.html

CHAPTER 2

Boyle, A. (2017). "Bad-ass Badlands. National Park's Climate Tweets Pop Up, then Go Poof." January 24, 2017. GeekWire.com. https://www.geekwire.com/2017/badlands-bad-ass-national-park-climate-tweets/.

Crugnale, J. (2017). "Fact Checking the Badlands National Park Climate Change Tweets." January 25, 2017. Weather.com. https://weather.com/science/news/badlands-tweets-fact-checked-climate-expert.

Davenport, C. (2017). "With Trump in Charge, Climate Change References Purged from Website. January 20, 2017. NYTimes.com. https://www.nytimes.com/2017/01/20/us/politics/trump-white-house-website.html.

Emails from DOI and NPS about the original tweets. https://www.doi.gov/sites/doi.gov/files/uploads/twitter_consolidated_redacted.pdf.

Green, M. (2017). "Trump Plans to Nominate Non-scientist to Head Science at USDA." July 21, 2017. CNN.com. https://www.cnn.com/2017/07/21/politics/clovis-nominated-to-usda/index.html.

Horowitz, J. (2016). "Trump's Labor Secretary Pick Uses Bikinis to Sell Burgers." December 9, 2016. CNN.com. https://money.cnn.com/2016/12/08/news/companies/puzder-hardees-carls-jr-ads/.

Marte, Jonnelle. (2016). "Trump Names Andrew Puzder, a Fast-Food CEO and Critic of Substantially Raising the Minimum Wage, to Head the Labor Department." December 8, 2016. WashingtonPost.com. https://www.washingtonpost.com/news/get-there/wp/2016/12/08/trump-names-andrew-puzder-a-fast-food-ceo-and-critic-of-substantially-raising-the-minimum-wage-to-head-the-labor-department/.

Perdue, S. (2014). "The Common Core Blame Game." NationalReview.com. May 8, 2014. https://www.nationalreview.com/2014/05/common-core-blame-game-sonny-perdue/.

Stein, J. (2017). "The Ex-Wife of Trump's Labor Pick Appeared on this Domestic Violence Episode of Oprah. February 15, 2017. Vox.com. https://www.vox.com/policy-and-politics/2017/2/15/14623180/anthony-puzder-oprah.

Swaine, J. (2018). "Trump Inauguration Crowd Photos Were Edited after He Intervened." September 6, 2018. TheGuardian.com. https://www.theguardian.com/world/2018/sep/06/donald-trump-inauguration-crowd-size-photos-edited.

Tiernan, K. (2021). "Final Response (signed)-safe_redacted." February 26, 2021. https://www.documentcloud.org/documents/20495125-21-018-final-response-signed-safe_redacted.

CHAPTER 3

Bogardus, K. and Yehle, E. (2017). "'I Take Responsibility'—Rogue Badlands Tweeter." April 17, 2017. EENews.net. https://www.eenews.net/articles/i-take-responsibility-rogue-badlands-tweeter/.

Brown, A. (2017). "Rogue Twitter Accounts Fight to Preserve the Voice of Government Science." March 11, 2017. TheIntercept.com. https://theintercept.com/2017/03/11/rogue-twitter-accounts-fight-to-preserve-the-voice-of-government-science/.

Capatides, C. (2017). "Badlands National Park Twitter Account Goes Rogue, Starts Tweeting Scientific Facts." January 24, 2017. CBSNews.com. https://www.cbsnews.com/news/badlands-national-park-twitter-goes-rogue-starts-tweeting-facts-about-the-environment/.

Dann, C. (2016). "Donald Trump's Administration WIll Have to Hire as Many as 4,000 People." November 20, 2016. NBCNews.com. https://www.nbcnews.com/politics/politics-news/donald-trump-s-administration-will-have-hire-many-4-000-n684251.

Davenport, C. and Lipton, E. (2017). "Scott Pruitt is Carrying Out His E. P. A. Agenda in Secret, Critics Say." August 11, 2017. NYTimes.com. https://www.nytimes.com/2017/08/11/us/politics/scott-pruitt-epa.html.

Davis, W. (2017). "Rogue National Park Accounts Emerge on Twitter Amid Social Media Gag Orders." January 25, 2017. NPR.org. https://www.npr.org/sections/alltechconsidered/2017/01/25/511664825/rogue-national-park-accounts-emerge-on-twitter-amid-social-media-gag-orders.

Hetter, K. (2017). "Unofficial National Parks Account Trolls Trump." January 26, 2017. CNN.com. https://www.cnn.com/travel/article/unofficial-national-park-service-account-trolls-trump/index.html.

Horowitz, J. (2016). "Trump's Labor Secretary Pick Uses Bikinis to Sell Burgers." December 9, 2016. CNN.com. https://money.cnn.com/2016/12/08/news/companies/puzder-hardees-carls-jr-ads/.

Marte, J. (2016). "Trump Names Andrew Puzder, a Fast Food CEO and Critic of Substantially Raising the Minimum Wage, to Head the Labor Department. November 8, 2016. WashingtonPost.com. https://www.washingtonpost.com/news/get-there/wp/2016/12/08/trump-names-andrew-puzder-a-fast-food-ceo-and-critic-of-substantially-raising-the-minimum-wage-to-head-the-labor-department/.

Nebbe, C. and Perkins, K. "Candidate Profile: Sam Clovis." May 27, 2014. IowaPublicRadio.org. https://www.iowapublicradio.org/state-government-news/2014-05-27/candidate-profile-sam-clovis.

Noble, A. (2017). Rogue Twitter Accounts Form Resistance against Trump, Fuel Rebellion against Policies." February 20, 2017. WashingtonTimes.com. https://www.washingtontimes.com/news/2017/feb/20/rogue-twitter-accounts-form-resistance-against-tru/.

O'Connor, S. (2017). "Badlands National Park Goes Rogue on Twitter." January 24, 2017. DailyNews.com. https://www.dailynews.com/2017/01/24/badlands-national-park-goes-rogue-on-twitter-and-riles-up-the-internet/.

Roston, E. (2017). "What Really Happened When a National Park's Twitter Account Went Rogue." April 15, 2017. Bloomberg.com. https://www.bloomberg.com/news/articles/2017-04-14/what-really-happened-when-a-national-park-s-twitter-account-went-rogue.

CHAPTER 4

Beavers, O. (2017). "Sally Yates: I Found Out about Travel Ban by Reading about It on the Internet." June 28, 2017. TheHill.com. https://thehill.com/homenews/administration/339988-sally-yates-justice-dept-found-out-about-travel-ban-by-reading-about.

CBS This Morning (2017). April 8, 2017. Archive.org. https://archive.org/details/KYW_20170408_110000_CBS_This_Morning.

Domonoske, C. (2017). "Twitter Sues Homeland Security to Protect Anonymity of 'Alt Immigration' Account." April 6, 2017. npr.org. https://www.npr.org/sections/thetwo-way/2017/04/06/522914335/twitter-sues-homeland-security-to-protect-anonymity-of-alt-immigration-account.

Draft has been created to track the email events regarding ALT_USCIS. (n.d.). rcfp.org. https://www.rcfp.org/wp-content/uploads/imported/2018-07-30_cbp_records_production_to_rcfp_part_12.pdf.

Frankel, A., and Volz, D. (2017). "Twitter Case Shows Breadth of U.S. Power to Probe Anti-Trump Statements." April 7, 2017. Reuters.com. https://www.reuters.com/article/us-twitter-privacy-analysis/twitter-case-shows-breadth-of-u-s-power-to-probe-anti-trump-statements-idUSKBN17A02M.

Greenblatt, M. (2017). "Travel Ban Links Higher Risk of Terrorism to Refugees, but the Facts Challenge that Connection." March 7, 2017. NewsChannel5.com. https://www.newschannel5.com/news/national/travel-ban-links-refugees-to-terrorism-but-the-facts-challenge-that-connection.

Levin, B. (2021). "Report: Trump's Justice Department Spied on at Least Five Reporters from Outlets Trump Despised." May 20, 2021. VanityFair.com. https://www.vanityfair.com/news/2021/05/trump-doj-reporter-surveillance.

MSNBC (2017). "The Rachel Maddow Show, Transcript. 4/7/17. "April 7, 2017. https://www.msnbc.com/transcripts/rachel-maddow-show/2017-04-07-msna979866.

Roberts, J. J. (2017). "Twitter Sues Trump Administration to Block Investigation into 'Rogue' Account." Yahoo.com. https://www.yahoo.com/news/twitter-sues-trump-administration-block-204223111.html.

CHAPTER 5

Adams, R. and Brown, H. (2017). "These Americans Were Tricked into Working for Russia. They Say They Had No Idea." October 17, 2017. BuzzfeedNews .com. https://www.buzzfeednews.com/article/rosalindadams/these-americans -were-tricked-into-working-for-russia-they.

Barrett, Devlin, Horwitz, S. and Helderman, R. S. (2018). "Russian Troll Farm, 13 Suspects Indicted in 2016 Election Interference." February 16, 2018. WashingtonPost.com. https://www.washingtonpost.com/world/national-security /russian-troll-farm-13-suspects-indicted-for-interference-in-us-election/2018/0 2/16/2504de5e-1342-11e8-9570-29c9830535e5_story.html.

Chuck, E., Johnson, A., and Siemaszko, C. (2018). 17 Killed in Mass Shooting at High School in Parkland, Florida. February 15, 2018. NBCNews.com. https:// www.nbcnews.com/news/us-news/police-respond-shooting-parkland-florida -high-school-n848101.

Lytvynenko, J. (2018). "Here Are Some Job Ads for the Russian Troll Factory." February 22, 2018. BuzzfeedNews.com. https://www.buzzfeednews.com/article /janelytvynenko/job-ads-for-russian-troll-factory.

Repanshek, K. (2017). "What to Make of the Alt Movement Today?" November 19, 2017. NationalParksTraveler.com. https://www.nationalparkstraveler.org /2017/11/what-make-alt-movement-today.

CHAPTER 6

Aldhous, P. and Lewis, C. (2017). "These Maps Show the Vulnerable Houston Neighborhoods That Need the Most Help Rebuilding from Harvey." September 1, 2017. BuzzfeedNews.com. https://www.buzzfeednews.com/article /peteraldhous/houston-disaster-maps.

Burris, S. K. (2017). "'Alt-gov' Twitter Accounts Pitch In to Help Coast Guard and Responders Rescue Hurricane Victims." August 29, 2017. RawStory.com. https://www.rawstory.com/2017/08/anti-trump-alt-gov-twitter-accounts -pitch-in-to-help-coast-guard-and-responders-rescue-hurricane-victims/.

CBS News. (2015) "How Citizens Turned into Saviors after Katrina Struck." August 29, 2015. https://www.cbsnews.com/news/remembering-the-cajun -navy-10-years-after- hurricane-katrina/.

Georgantopoulos, M. A. (2017). "Some Government Veterans from Katrina Are Crowdsourcing Rescue Requests from Harvey Victims." September 8, 2017. BuzzfeedNews.com. https://www.buzzfeednews.com/article/maryanngeorgan topoulos/crowdscouring-harvey-rescue-calls.

Koren, M. (2017 Aug. 28). "Using Twitter to Save a Newborn from a Flood." August 28, 2017. TheAtlantic.com. https://www.theatlantic.com/technology /archive/2017/08/harvey-rescue-twitter/538191/.

Murphy, P. O. (2017). "A Rescue That Twitter and Text Messages Made Happen." September 12, 2017. CNN.com. https://www.cnn.com/2017/09/11/us/social-media-irma-rescue-trnd/index.html.

Price, B. (2017). "IRMASOS: Emergency Response on Social Media." September 10, 2017. Breitbart.com. https://www.breitbart.com/border/2017/09/10/irmasos-emergency-response-on-social-media.

Schultz, T. (2017). "Hundreds of Europeans are Pitching in From Afar . . ." Sept. 11, 2017. Soundcloud.com. https://soundcloud.com/user-814739821/npr-crowd rescuehq-story/s-vz3Vf.

Seetharaman, D. and Wells, G. (2017). "Hurricane Harvey Victims Turn to Social Media for Assistance." August 29, 2017. WSJ.com. https://www.wsj.com/articles/hurricane-harvey-victims-turn-to-social-media-for-assistance-1503999001.

CHAPTER 7

Acevedo, N. (2019). "Mothers Separated from Their Children at the Border Sue Trump Admin Over 'Clear Abuse.'" September 24, 2019. NBCNews.com. https://www.nbcnews.com/news/latino/mothers-separated-their-children-border-sue-trump-admin-over-clear-n1058146.

American Oversight. (n.d.). "A Timeline of the Trump Administration's Family Separation Policy." AmericanOversight.org. https://www.americanoversight.org/a-timeline-of-the-trump-administrations-family-separation-policy.

Cooper, H. (2018). "'All It Takes Is One Mistake': Worries Over Plan to Send National Guard to Border." April 4, 2018. NYTimes.com https://www.nytimes.com/2018/04/04/us/politics/national-guard-immigration-border.html.

Davis, J. H. (2018). "Trump Signs Memo Ordering End to 'Catch and Release' Immigration Policy." April 6, 2018. NYTimes.com. https://www.nytimes.com/2018/04/06/us/politics/trump-immigration-policy.html.

Gallardo, A. (2018). "Do You Know a Child in a Detention Center or Shelter Facility?" June 27, 2018. ProPublica.org. https://www.propublica.org/getinvolved/do-you-know-a-child-in-a-detention-center-or-shelter-facility.

Gittleson, B. (2018). "Trump Warns of Migrant Caravan Following Fox News Report, but Organizers Say Reality Far from Their Portrayal." April 1, 2018. ABCNews.go.com. https://abcnews.go.com/International/trump-warns-migrant-caravan-fox-news-report-organizers/story?id=54162057.

Health and Human Services Data. (n.d.). Sexual Assaults FY 2015–2018. TedDeutch.House.Gov. https://teddeutch.house.gov/uploadedfiles/naduac1214_sexual_assaults_fy2015-18.pdf.

Horwitz, S. and Sacchetti, M. (2018). "Sessions Vows to Prosecute All Illegal Border Crossers and Separate Children from Their Parents." May 8, 2018. WashingtonPost.com. https://www.washingtonpost.com/world/national-security

/sessions-says-justice-dept-will-prosecute-every-person-who-crosses-border -unlawfully/2018/05/07/e1312b7e-5216-11e8-9c91-7dab596e8252_story.html.

House Committee on the Judiciary. (2020). "Judiciary Committee Releases Report on Trump Administration Family Separation Policy." October 29, 2020. Judiciary.house.gov. https://judiciary.house.gov/news/documentsingle .aspx?DocumentID=3442.

Kirby, J. and Stewart, E. (2018). "Families Belong Together Protest Underway in More Than 700 Cities." June 30, 2018. Vox.com. https://www.vox.com /2018/6/18/17477376/families-belong-together-march-june-30.

Kopan, Tal. (2017). "Kelly Says DHS Won't Separate Families at the Border." March 29, 2017. CNN.com. https://www.cnn.com/2017/03/29/politics /border-families-separation-kelly/index.html.

Levandera, E., Morris, J., and Simon, D. (2018). "She Says Federal Officials Took Her Daughter While She Breastfed the Child in a Detention Center." June 14, 2018. CNN.com. https://www.cnn.com/2018/06/12/us/immigration-separated -children-southern-border/index.html.

Levin, S. (2021). "'We Tortured Families': The Lingering Damage of Trump's Separation Policy." January 4, 2021. TheGuardian.com. https://www.theguardian .com/us-news/2021/jan/04/trump-administration-family-separation-immi grants-joe-biden.

McCausland, P., Guadalupe, P., and Rosenblatt, K. (2018). "Thousands across U.S. Join 'Keep Families Together' March to Protest Family Separation." June 30, 2018. NBCNews.com. https://www.nbcnews.com/news/us-news/thou sands-across-u-s-join-keep-families-together-march-protest-n888006.

Mindock, C. (2018). "UN Says Trump Separation of Migrant Children with Parents 'May Amount to Torture' in Damning Condemnation." June 22, 2018. Independent.co.uk. https://www.independent.co.uk/news/world/americas/us -politics/un-trump-children-family-torture-separation-border-mexico-border -ice-detention-a8411676.html.

Miranda, L. M. and McCarter, J. (2016). *Hamilton: The Revolution*. London: Hachette.

Montoya-Galvez, C. (2019). "Thousands of Migrant Children Were Sexually Abused in U.S. Custody, HHS Docs Say." February 27, 2019. CBSNews. com. https://www.cbsnews.com/news/thousands-of-migrant-children-were -sexually-abused-in-u-s-custody-hhs-docs-say/.

Phillips, A. (2017). "'They're Rapists.' President Trump's Campaign Launch Speech Two Years Later, Annotated." June 16, 2017. WashingtonPost.com. https:// www.washingtonpost.com/news/the-fix/wp/2017/06/16/theyre-rapists -presidents-trump-campaign-launch-speech-two-years-later-annotated/.

Seville, L. R. and Rappleye, H. (2018). "Trump Admin Ran 'Pilot Program' for Separating Migrant Families in 2017. June 29, 2018. NBCNews.com. https:// www.nbcnews.com/storyline/immigration-border-crisis/trump-admin-ran -pilot-program-separating-migrant-families-2017-n887616.

Shahoulian, D. e al. (2020). "The Trump Administration's Family Separation Policy: Trauma, Destruction and Chaos." Judiciary.House.Gov. https://judiciary.house .gov/uploadedfiles/the_trump_administration_family_separation_policy _trauma_destruction_and_chaos.pdf#page=370.

Shear, M. D., Goodnough, A., and Haberman, M. (2018). "Trump Retreats on Separating Families, but Thousands May Remain Apart." June 20, 2018. NYTimes .com. https://www.nytimes.com/2018/06/20/us/politics/trump-immigration -children-executive-order.html.

Southern Poverty Law Center. (2020). "Family Separation Under the Trump Administration: A Timeline." June 17, 2020. SPLCenter.org. https://www.splcenter .org/news/2020/06/17/family-separation-under-trump-administration-timeline.

Thompson, G. (2018). "Zero Tolerance: Listen to Children Who've Just Been Separated from Their Parents at the Border." June 18, 2018. Propublica.org. https://www.propublica.org/article/children-separated-from-parents-border -patrol-cbp-trump-immigration-policy.

Timm, J. C. (2018). "Trump Says 'Caravans' of Immigrants Are Headed for the U.S. What Is He Talking About?" April 1, 2018. NBCNews.com. https:// www.nbcnews.com/politics/politics-news/trump-says-caravans-immigrants -are-headed-u-s-what-s-n862136.

U.S. Government Publishing Office. (2019). The Trump Administration's Child Separation Policy: Substantiated Allegations of Mistreatment. Hearing before the Committee on Oversight and Reform, House of Representatives, 116th Congress. GovInfo.gov. https://www.govinfo.gov/content/pkg/CHRG-116hhrg 37315/html/CHRG-116hhrg37315.htm.

Ward, M. (2021). "At Least 3,900 Children Separated from Families Under Trump 'Zero Tolerance' Policy, Task Force Finds." June 8, 2021. Politico.com. https:// www.politico.com/news/2021/06/08/trump-zero-tolerance-policy-child-sep arations-492099.

Watson, K. (2020). "Trump Says Children Separated from Their Parents Were 'So Well Taken Care Of.'" October 23, 2020. CBSNews.com. https://www .cbsnews.com/news/child-separation-trump-says-taken-care-of/.

CHAPTER 8

Bee, S. (2016). "Russian Thinkfluencers." November 1, 2016. https://www.you tube.com/watch?v=OauLuWXD_RI.

Porter, T. (2020). "How Diehard Trump Fans Transformed Their Twitter Accounts into Bots Which Spread Conspiracies in a Vast Russia-Style Disinformation Network. March 9, 2020. BusinessInsider.com. https://www.businessinsider.com /power10-activists-transformed-accounts-bots-spread-conspiracies-2020-02.

Repanshek, K. (2018). "UPDATE: 'Alt' Groups Question AltYellowstoneNatPark's Fundraising Efforts." July 9, 2018. NationalParksTraveler.com. https://www

.nationalparkstraveler.org/2018/07/update-alt-groups-question-altyellowstone natparks-fundraising-efforts.

Schreiner, C. (n.d.). "Interview: Ominous Ann of AltYellowstoneNPS Twitter." ModernHiker.com. https://modernhiker.com/interview-ominous-ann-of-alt yellowstone-nps-twitter/.

Wild, J. and Godart, C. (n.d.). "Spotting Bots, Cyborgs and Inauthentic Activity." DataJournalism.com. https://datajournalism.com/read/handbook/verification-3 /investigating-actors-content/3-spotting-bots-cyborgs-and-inauthentic-activity.

CHAPTER 9

Agency for Healthcare Research and Quality. (n.d.). "Clinical Guidelines and Recommendations." Ahrq.gov. https://www.ahrq.gov/prevention/guidelines /index.html.

Frieden, J. (2015). "House Committee Votes to Defund AHRQ—Attempt to Restore Funding Fails on Voice Vote." June 24, 2015. MedPageToday.com. https://www.medpagetoday.com/publichealthpolicy/washington-watch /52294.

Hutchinson, B. (2020). "Alleged Ringleader of $400,000 GoFundMe Scam Hit with Federal Indictment." January 9, 2020. ABCNews.go.com. https:// abcnews.go.com/US/alleged-ringleader-400000-gofundme-scam-hit-federal -indictment/story?id=68169208.

Jacobo, J. (2017). "Homeless Man Who Helped Stranded Woman Buys Home after Nearly $400K Raised." December 5, 2017. ABCNews.go.com. https://abcnews.go.com/US/homeless-man-gave-20-stranded-woman-buy-gas /story?id=51593887.

Ortiz, E. (2019). "Alleged Ringleader in $400K GoFundMe Scam Pleads Guilty." December 6, 2020. NBCNews.com. https://www.nbcnews.com/news/us-news /alleged-ringleader-400k-gofundme-scam-pleads-guilty-n1097106.

Simpson, L. (2018). "AHRQ Clearinghouse Shut Down Direct Result of Previous Cuts, Sequestration and Caps." July 16, 2018. AcademyHealth.org. https:// academyhealth.org/blog/2018-07/ahrq-clearinghouse-shut-down-direct-result -previous-cuts-sequestration-and-caps.

The Mars Generation. (2018). "The Mars Generation 2018 Space Camp Scholarship Winners Announced." April 10, 2018. TheMarsGeneration.org. https:// www.themarsgeneration.org/mars-generation-2018-space-camp-scholarship -winners-announced/.

Walsh, J. (2019). "Homeless Man at Center of GoFundMe Scam Gets Probation." April 12, 2019. CourierPostOnline.com. https://www.courierpostonline.com /story/news/2019/04/12/johnny-bobbitt-jr-gofundme-scam-sentenced /3440902002/.

Wootson, C. R. and Phillips, K. (2018). "They raised $444,000 for a homeless man—who claims they spent it on vacations, casinos and a BMW." (August 25, 2018). WashingtonPost.com. https://www.washingtonpost.com/nation /2018/08/25/they-raised-homeless-man-who-said-they-spent-it-vacations -casinos-bmw/.

CHAPTER 10

Beaumond, E. (2009). "Rights of Military Personnel." MTSU.edu. https://www .mtsu.edu/first-amendment/article/1131/rights-of-military-personnel.

Gramlich, J. (2021). "How Trump Compares with Other Recent Presidents in Appointing Federal Judges." January 13, 2021. PewResearch.org. https://www .pewresearch.org/fact-tank/2021/01/13/how-trump-compares-with-other -recent-presidents-in-appointing-federal-judges/.

Guardian Staff. (2021). "FBI Failed to Fully Investigate Kavanaugh Allegations, Say Democrats." July 22, 2021. TheGuardian.com. https://www.theguardian .com/us-news/2021/jul/22/brett-kavanaugh-sexual-misconduct-allegations -fbi-senators.

Howe, A. (2019). "Decade in Review: Justice Antonin Scalia's Death and the Republican Delay in Filling the Seat." December 27, 2019. *SCOTUSblog* (blog). https:// www.scotusblog.com/2019/12/decade-in-review-justice-antonin-scalias -death-and-the-republican-delay-to-fill-the-seat/.

Office of Special Counsel. (2014). A Guide to the Hatch Act for Federal Employees. OSC.gov. https://osc.gov/Documents/Outreach%20and%20Training /Handouts/A%20Guide%20to%20the%20Hatch%20Act%20for%20Federal%20 Employees.pdf.

Thomson-DeVeaux, A. (2018). "Justice Kennedy Wasn't a Moderate." July 3, 2018. FiveThirtyEight.com. https://fivethirtyeight.com/features/justice-kennedy -wasnt-a-moderate/.

Weiss, J. (2018). "Christine Blasey Ford and the Power of Vulnerability." September 27, 2018. Politico.com. https://www.politico.com/magazine/story /2018/09/27/christine-blasey-ford-and-the-power-of-vulnerability-220737/.

CHAPTER 11

Andrews, T. (2019). "I'm a Single Mom and I Can't Get Dinner on the Table Because of the Government Shutdown." January 11, 2019. Cosmopolitan.com. https://www.cosmopolitan.com/politics/a25847792/government-shutdown -affecting-workers-single-mom-personal-story/.

Berman, M. and Rein, L. (2018). "What Happens When the Government Shuts Down? Late Paychecks, Closed Museums and More." December 22, 2018. WashingtonPost.com. https://www.washingtonpost.com/politics/what-would -happen-if-the-government-shut-down-late-paychecks-closed-museums-and -more/2018/12/21/79c982a2-053e-11e9-b6a9-0aa5c2fcc9e4_story.html.

Brandom, R. (2019). "Amid Shutdown, Agencies Scramble to Secure Federal Websites." January 23, 2019. TheVerge.com. https://www.theverge.com/2019 /1/23/18194281/government-shutdown-us-federal-websites-homeland-secu rity-hackers.

Ebbs, S. (2019). "Unpaid Federal Workers Get Help from Food Banks during Government Shutdown." January 15, 2019. ABCNEws.go.com. https://abc news.go.com/Politics/unpaid-federal-workers-food-banks-government-shut down/story?id=60374327.

Fears, D. and Eilperin, J. (2019). "Three Dead in National Park System Accidents as Shutdown Wears On." January 5, 2019. WashingtonPost.com. https://www .washingtonpost.com/energy-environment/2019/01/04/three-dead-national -parks-shutdown-wears/.

Joyce, K. (2019). "Overflowing Garbage, Feces on Roads Prompt Yosemite National Park Officials to Close Some Campgrounds." January 1, 2019. FoxNews.com. https://www.foxnews.com/us/overflowing-garbage-feces-on-roads-prompt -yosemite-national-park-officials-to-close-some-campgrounds.

McCombs, B. and Fonseca, F. (2019). "National Parks Rush to Repair Damage after Shutdown." February 1, 2019. ABCNews.go.com. https://abcnews.go .com/US/wireStory/national-parks-rush-repair-damage-shutdown-60781429.

Pitt, A. (2018). "Statue of Liberty Will Remain Open during Government Shutdown." January 22, 2018. NY.curbed.com. https://ny.curbed.com/2018 /1/22/16917980/government-shutdown-2018-statue-of-liberty-open.

Southall, A. (2018). "Statue of Liberty Will Reopen Despite Government Shutdown." January 21, 2018. NYTimes.com. https://www.nytimes.com /2018/01/21/nyregion/statue-of-liberty-government-shutdown.html.

CHAPTER 12

Ackerman, S. and Siddiqui, S. (2017). "Donald Trump Speech at CIA Memorial Risks Fueling Intelligence Feud." January 21, 2017. TheGuardian.com. https:// www.theguardian.com/us-news/2017/jan/21/cia-donald-trump-first-meeting.

Al-Heeti, A. (2018). "GoFundMe Campaign Raises Money to Send Mariachi Band, Taco Truck to Racist NYC Lawyer." May 18, 2018. CNet.com. https:// www.cnet.com/news/gofundme-campaign-raises-money-to-send-mariachi -band-taco-truck-to-racist-nyc-lawyer/.

Bedard, Paul. (2019). "$50K Reward Offered to Out Trump Whistleblower." September 26, 2019. WashingtonExaminer.com. https://www.washingtonexaminer

.com/tag/donald-trump?source=%2Fwashington-secrets%2F50-000-reward
-offered-to-out-trump-whistleblower.

Blake, Aaron. (2019). "The Full, Rough Transcript of Trump's Call with Ukraine's President, Annotated." September 25, 2019. WashingtonPost.com. https://www.washingtonpost.com/politics/2019/09/25/rough-transcript-trumps-call-with-ukraines-president-annotated/.

Butler, D. and Biesecker, M. (2019). "Ukrainian Leader Felt Trump Pressure before Taking Office." October 24, 2019. APNews.com. https://apnews.com/article/donald-trump-ap-top-news-elections-joe-biden-politics-b048901b635f423db49a10046daaf8a8.

CBS News. (2017). Trump CIA Speech Transcript. January 23, 2017. CBSNews.com. https://www.cbsnews.com/news/trump-cia-speech-transcript/.

Davis, J. H. (2017). "Trump Bars U.S. Press, but Not Russia's, at Meeting with Russian Officials." May 10, 2017. NYTimes.com. https://www.nytimes.com/2017/05/10/us/politics/trump-russia-meeting-american-reporters-blocked.html.

Dawsey, J., Leonnig, C. D., and Hamburger, T. (2019). "White House Review Turns Up Emails Showing Extensive Effort to Justify Trump's Decision to Block Ukraine Military Aid." November 24, 2019. WashingtonPost.com. https://www.washingtonpost.com/politics/white-house-review-turns-up-emails-showing-extensive-effort-to-justify-trumps-decision-to-block-ukraine-military-aid/2019/11/24/2121cf98-0d57-11ea-bd9d-c628fd48b3a0_story.html.

Elving, R. (2018). "Trump's Helsinki Bow to Putin Leaves World Wondering: Why?" July 17, 2018. NPR.org. https://www.npr.org/2018/07/17/629601233/trumps-helsinki-bow-to-putin-leaves-world-wondering-whats-up.

Exum, A. (2017). "Cheapening a Sacred Space." January 23, 2017. TheAtlantic.com. https://www.theatlantic.com/politics/archive/2017/01/no-way-to-honor-sacrifice/514097/.

Hawkins, D. (2017). "Trump Called It a 'Very Special' Wall. For the CIA, It Is Sacrosanct." January 23, 2017. WashingtonPost.com https://www.washingtonpost.com/news/morning-mix/wp/2017/01/23/trump-called-it-a-very-special-wall-for-the-cia-its-sacrosanct/.

Hersh, S. M. (1974). "Huge C.I.A. Operation Reported in U.S. against Antiwar Forces, Other Dissidents in Nixon Years." December 22, 1974. NYTimes.com. https://www.nytimes.com/1974/12/22/archives/huge-cia-operation-reported-in-u-s-against-antiwar-forces-other.html.

Johnson, A. (2019). "Whistleblower's Lawyer Says Trump Is Endangering His Client." September 30, 2019. NBCNews.com. https://www.nbcnews.com/politics/trump-impeachment-inquiry/whistleblower-s-lawyer-says-trump-endangering-his-client-n1060151.

Lange, K. (2017). "The Challenge Coin Tradition: Do You Know How It Started?" October 8, 2017. Defense.gov. https://www.defense.gov/News/Inside

-DOD/Blog/Article/2567302/the-challenge-coin-tradition-do-you-know-how-it-started/.

Levin, B. (2019). "Trump: Of Course I'm Trying to Unmask the Whistleblower!" September 30, 2019. VanityFair.com. https://www.vanityfair.com/news/2019/09/donald-trump-whistleblower-identity.

Mason, J. and Pinchuk, D. (2018). "Trump Backs Putin on Election Meddling at Summit, Stirs Fierce Criticism." July 15, 2018. Reuters.com. https://www.reuters.com/article/us-usa-russia-summit/trump-backs-putin-on-election-meddling-at-summit-stirs-fierce-criticism-idUSKBN1K601D.

Miller, G. and Jaffe, G. (2017). "Trump Revealed Highly Classified Information to Russian Foreign Minister and Ambassador." May 15, 2017. Washington Post.com. https://www.washingtonpost.com/world/national-security/trump-revealed-highly-classified-information-to-russian-foreign-minister-and-ambassador/2017/05/15/530c172a-3960-11e7-9e48-c4f199710b69_story.html.

Mitchell, A. and Dilanian, K. (2017). "Ex-CIA Boss Brennan, Others Rip Trump Speech in Front of Memorial." January 22, 2017. NBCNews.com. https://www.nbcnews.com/news/us-news/ex-cia-boss-brennan-others-rip-trump-speech-front-memorial-n710366.

Sabah. (2017). "Trump's Russia Problem (Part 2)." *AngryStaffer* (blog). May 6, 2017. http://angrystaffer.blogspot.com/2017/05/trumps-russia-problem-part-2.html.

Sanger, D. E. and MacFarquhar, N. (2017). "With Awkward Timing, Trump Meets Top Russian Official." May 10, 2017. NYTimes.com. https://www.nytimes.com/2017/05/10/world/europe/trump-russia-foreign-minister-sergey-lavrov-meeting.html.

Selk, Avi. (2019). "A Trump Booster Promised to Reveal the Whistleblower's Name from His Front Yard. The Neighbors Just Laughed." October 2, 2019. WashingtonPost.com. https://www.washingtonpost.com/lifestyle/style/the-decline-of-the-jack-burkman-jacob-wohl-news-conference/2019/10/02/57f6539a-e52a-11e9-a6e8-8759c5c7f608_story.html.

Shear, M. D. and Goldman, A. (2017). "Michael Flynn Pleads Guilty to Lying to the F.B.I. and Will Cooperate with Russia Inquiry." December 1, 2017. NY Times.com. https://www.nytimes.com/2017/12/01/us/politics/michael-flynn-guilty-russia-investigation.html.

Staff. (2017). "John Brennan: Trump's 'Nazi Germany' Tweet to US Agencies Was Outrageous." January 15, 2017. TheGuardian.com. https://www.theguardian.com/us-news/2017/jan/15/john-brennan-trump-nazi-germany-russia.

———. (2018). "Transcript: Trump and Putin's Joint Press Conference." July 16, 2018. NPR.org. https://www.npr.org/2018/07/16/629462401/transcript-president-trump-and-russian-president-putins-joint-press-conference.

———. (2018). "Trump Sides with Russia against FBI at Helsinki Summit." July 16, 2018. BBC.com. https://www.bbc.com/news/world-europe-44852812.

Tani, M. (2017). "Time for Some Fame Theory: Meet the Eccentric Liberal Analyst Whose Unhinged Tweetstorms Have Made Him Twitter-Famous." March 30, 2017. BusinessInsider.com. https://www.businessinsider.com/eric-garland -twitter-game-theory-russia-trump-2017-3.

Vogel, K. P. (2019). "Rudy Giuliani Plans Ukraine Trip to Push for Inquiries That Could Help Trump." May 9, 2019. NYTimes.com. https://www.nytimes .com/2019/05/09/us/politics/giuliani-ukraine-trump.html.

Volz, D. (2019). "Trump Allies Ramp Up Efforts to Unmask Whistleblower." November 3, 2019. WSJ.com. https://www.wsj.com/articles/trump-allies-ramp-up -efforts-to-unmask-whistleblower-11572724750.

Washington Post. (2019). "Read the Whistleblower Complaint regarding President Trump's Communicatioms with Ukrainian President Volodymyr Zelensky." October 16, 2019. WashingtonPost.com. https://www.washingtonpost.com /context/read-the-whistleblower-complaint-regarding-president-trump -s-communications-with-ukrainian-president-volodymyr-zelensky /4b9e0ca5-3824-467f-b1a3-77f2d4ee16aa/?itid=lk_inline_manual_2.

CHAPTER 13

Bland, B. (2020). "I Sent Masks to Health Workers but the Trump Administration Seized Them Instead of Helping." May 16, 2020. USAToday.com https:// www.usatoday.com/story/opinion/voices/2020/05/16/trump-team-seized -my-masks-for-coronavirus-health-workers-column/5191035002/.

Botkin, B. and Kaskey-Blomain, M. (2020). "NBA Suspends Season Due to Coronavirus Outbreak; Owners Preparing for No Games until June, Per Report." March 11, 2020. CBSSports.com. https://www.cbssports.com/nba/news/nba-suspends -season-due-to-coronavirus-outbreak-owners-preparing-for-no-games-until -june-per-report/.

Bradsher, K. and Alderman, L. (2020). "The World Needs Masks. China Makes Them, but Has Been Hoarding Them." April 2, 2020. NYTimes.com https:// www.nytimes.com/2020/03/13/business/masks-china-coronavirus.html.

Bruggeman, L. (2020). "Hydroxychloroquine Returns as Wedge between President Trump, Health Advisers." July 8, 2020. ABCNews.com. https://abcnews.go .com/Politics/hydroxychloroquine-returns-wedge-president-trump-health -advisers/story?id=72036996.

Cathey, L. (2020). "9 Controversial Moments that Led Trump to Stop his White House Coronavirus Briefings." July 21, 2020. https://abcnews.go.com /Politics/controversial-moments-led-trump-stop-white-house-coronavirus /story?id=71899110.

———. (2020). "Timeline: Tracking Trump alongside Scientific Developments on Hydroxychloroquine." August 8, 2020. ABCNews.com. https://abcnews

.go.com/Health/timeline-tracking-trump-alongside-scientific-developments
-hydroxychloroquine/story?id=72170553.

Diamond, D. (2020). "Inside America's 2-Decade Failure to Prepare for Coronavirus." April 11, 2020. Politico.com. https://www.politico.com/news/magazine
/2020/04/11/america-two-decade-failure-prepare-coronavirus-179574.

Dooley, S. (2020). "Coronavirus Is Attacking the Navajo 'because We Have Built
the Perfect Human for It to Invade.'" July 8, 2020. ScientificAmerican.com.
https://www.scientificamerican.com/article/coronavirus-is-attacking-the
-navajo-because-we-have-built-the-perfect-human-for-it-to-invade/.

Eban, Katherine. (2020). "'I'll Send You the Contact': Documents Expose FDA
Commissioner's Personal Interventions on Behalf of Trump's Favorite Chloroquine Doctor." May 27, 2020. VanityFair.com. https://www.vanityfair.com
/news/2020/05/documents-expose-fda-commissioners-interventions-on-behalf
-of-trump.

Flaherty, A. and Tatum, S. (2020). "Man Dies after Ingesting Aquarium Product
Containing Chloroquine: Hospital Network." March 23, 2020. ABCNews
.com. https://abcnews.go.com/Politics/man-dies-ingesting-chloroquine-pre
vent-coronavirus-banner-health/story?id=69759570.

Grady, D. (2020). "Not His First Epidemic: Dr. Anthony Fauci Sticks to the Facts."
March 8, 2020. NewYorkTimes.com. https://www.nytimes.com/2020/03/08
/health/fauci-coronavirus.html.

Jankowicz, M. (2020). "Officials in at Least 6 States Are Accusing the Federal
Government of Quietly Diverting Their Orders for Coronavirus Medical
Equipment." April 8, 2020. BusinessInsider.com. https://www.businessinsider
.com/coronavirus-federal-govt-fema-accused-taking-states-masks-ventilator
-orders-2020-4.

Janzer, C. (2020). "When Science Loses its Voice." April 23, 2020. CJR.org.
https://www.cjr.org/analysis/cdc-pandemic-transparency-comment-access.php.

Kieley, E., Robertson, L., Rieder, R., and D'Angelo, G. (2020). "Timeline of
Trump's COVID-19 Comments." October 2, 2020. FactCheck.org. https://
www.factcheck.org/2020/10/timeline-of-trumps-covid-19-comments/.

Knight, V. (2020). "Obama Team Left Pandemic Playbook for Trump Administration, Officials Confirm." May 15, 2020. PBS.org. https://www.pbs.org/news
hour/nation/obama-team-left-pandemic-playbook-for-trump-administration
-officials-confirm.

Konda, A., Prakash, A., Moss, G. A., Schmoldt, M., Grant, G. D., and Guha, S.
(2020). "Aerosol Filtration Efficiency of Common Fabrics Used in Respiratory
Cloth Masks." *ACS nano* 14(5), 6339–47.

Lawes, C. J. (2021). *Women and Reform in a New England Community, 1815–1860.*
Lexington: University Press of Kentucky.

Levey, N. (2020). "Hospitals Say Feds Are Seizing Masks and Other Coronavirus
Supplies without a Word." April 2, 2020. LATimes.com. https://www.latimes
.com/politics/story/2020-04-07/hospitals-washington-seize-coronavirus-supplies.

Marples, M. (2020). "Navajo Nation Faces Devastating Loss from Covid-18 Pandemic." November 24, 2020. CNN.com. https://www.cnn.com/2020/11/24/health/navajo-nation-coronavirus-losses-wellness/index.html.

Quintero, D. (2020). "List of Infected Grows; PPE Supply Dwindles." March 14, 2020. NavajoTimes.com. https://navajotimes.com/coronavirus-updates/list-of-infected-grows-ppe-supply-dwindles/.

Rucker, H. (2020). "Austin Emergency Room Doctors Urge People Not to Ingest Disinfectants." April 25, 2020. KVUE.com. https://www.kvue.com/article/news/health/austin-emergency-room-doctors-urge-people-not-to-ingest-disinfectants/269-69824c2f-57e2-4d61-862e-c959907ae3a3.

Thielking, M. and Branswell, H. (2020). "CDC Expects 'Community Spread' of Coronavirus, as Top Official Warns Disruptions Could Be 'Severe.'" February 25, 2020. StatNews.com. https://www.statnews.com/2020/02/25/cdc-expects-community-spread-of-coronavirus-as-top-official-warns-disruptions-could-be-severe/.

YouTube. Surgeon General Shows How to Make Face Masks. https://www.youtube.com/watch?v=9YLXEhSjVsw.

CHAPTER 14

American Oversight. (2019). "AFGE Union Sues to Protect the Speech Rights of Federal Employees." August 13, 2019. AmericanOversight.org. https://www.americanoversight.org/afge-union-sues-to-protect-the-speech-rights-of-federal-employees.

Gartenstein-Ross, D. and Barr, N. (2018). "How Al-Qaeda Works: The Jihadist Group's Evolving Organizational Design." *Current Trends in Islamist Ideology* 23, 66–122.

Helfstein, S. and Wright, D. (2011). Success, Lethality, and Cell Structure across the Dimensions of Al Queda. Combating Terrorism Center at West Point Occasional Paper Series. https://www.hsdl.org/?view&did=5832.

Tsvetovat, M. and Carley, K. (2005). "Structural Knowledge and Success of Antiterrorist Activity: The Downside of Structural Equivalence."

CHAPTER 15

ABC News. (2020). "US Election Sees Protesters Confront Vote-Counting Centres in Phoenix and Detroit, 50 Arrested in New York." November 5, 2020. ABC.net.au. https://www.abc.net.au/news/2020-11-05/us-election-results-protesters-take-to-the-streets/12851968.

BBC News. (2020). "US Election: Why Are Trump Protesters Saying 'Stop the Count' and 'Count the Votes'"? November 6, 2020. BBC.com. https://www.bbc.com/news/av/election-us-2020-54835270.

Clinton, J. et al. (n.d.). "Task Force on Pre-Election Polling: An Evaluation of the 2020 General Election Polls." AAPOR.org. https://www.aapor.org/AAPOR_Main/media/MainSiteFiles/AAPOR-Task-Force-on-2020-Pre-Election-Polling_Report-FNL.pdf.

DeRienzo, M. (2020). "Analysis: New and Age-Old Voter Suppression Tactics at the Heart of the 2020 Power Struggle." October 28, 2020. PublicIntegrity.org. https://publicintegrity.org/politics/elections/ballotboxbarriers/analysis-voter-suppression-never-went-away-tactics-changed/.

Ellis, N. T. (2020). "Guns, Lies and Ballots Set on Fire: This Is Voter Suppression in 2020." October 29, 2020. USAToday.com. https://www.usatoday.com/story/news/nation/2020/10/29/2020-election-voter-suppression-looks-like-guns-lies-and-fires/6044702002/.

Gardner, A., Dawsey, J., and Kane, P. (2020). "Trump Opposes Election Aid for States and Postal Service Bailout, Threatening Nov. 3 Vote." August 13, 2020. WashingtonPost.com. https://www.washingtonpost.com/politics/trump-mail-voting/2020/08/13/3eb9ac62-dd70-11ea-809e-b8be57ba616e_story.html?.

Gresko, J. (2020). "Five Things to Know about Court Nominee Amy Coney Barrett." October 10, 2020. APNews.com. https://apnews.com/article/donald-trump-religion-ruth-bader-ginsburg-confirmation-hearings-amy-coney-barrett-5bfc898d36072c4b9bf63646e1c91fa6.

Kahn, C. and Lange, J. (2020). "Explainer: Red Mirage, Blue Mirage—Beware of Early U.S. Election Wins." October 22, 2020. Reuters.com. https://www.reuters.com/article/us-usa-election-mirage-explainer/explainer-red-mirage-blue-mirage-beware-of-early-u-s-election-wins-idUSKBN2771CL.

Kroll, A. (2020). "Trump's Postmaster General Faces Accusations of His Very Own Form of Voter Suppression." August 21, 2020. Rollingstone.com. https://www.rollingstone.com/politics/politics-news/trumps-postmaster-louis-dejoy-voter-suppression-1048031/.

Lonsdord, K., Dorning, C., Isackson, A., Kelly, M. L., and Chang, A. (2022). "A Timeline of How the Jan. 6 Attack Unfolded—Including Who Said What and When." January 5, 2022. NPR.org. https://www.npr.org/2022/01/05/1069977469/a-timeline-of-how-the-jan-6-attack-unfolded-including-who-said-what-and-when.

Lozano, A. V. (2020). "Ruth Bader Ginsburg's Dying Wish: Not to Have Donald Trump Choose Replacement." September 18, 2020. NBCNews.com https://www.nbcnews.com/politics/supreme-court/ruth-bader-ginsburg-s-dying-wish-not-have-donald-trump-n1240507.

Lutz, E. M. (2016). "Report: Texas Has Closed Most Polling Places Since Court Ruling." November 4, 2016. TexasTribune.org. https://www.texastribune.org/2016/11/04/report-texas-holds-highest-number-polling-place-cl/.

Miller Center. (n.d.). "Donald Trump—Key Events." MillerCenter.org. https://
millercenter.org/president/trump/key-events.

NAACP. (2021). "LDF Releases Report Detailing Voter Suppression in 2020
Election Season." September 15, 2021. NAACPLDF.org. https://www.naacpldf
.org/press-release/ldf-releases-report-detailing-voter-suppression-in-2020-elec
tion-season/.

Naylor, B. (2021). "Read Trump's Jan. 6 Speech, a Key Part of Impeachment Trial."
February 10, 2021. NPR.org. https://www.npr.org/2021/02/10/966396848
/read-trumps-jan-6-speech-a-key-part-of-impeachment-trial.

Reuters Staff. (2020). "Fact Check: How Many People Attended the Nov. 14 'Million MAGA March' in Washington, D.C.?" November 19, 2020. Reuters.com.
https://www.reuters.com/article/uk-factcheck-million-maga-march-estimate
/fact-check-how-many-people-attended-the-nov-14-million-maga-march-in
-washington-d-c-idUSKBN27Z2KI.

Romero, S., Dewan, S., and Nieto del Rio, G. M. (2020). "In a Year of Protest
Cries, Now It's 'Count Every Vote!' and 'Stop the Steal!'" November 5, 2020.
NYTimes.com. https://www.nytimes.com/2020/11/05/us/election-protests
-vote-count.html.

Singh, M. (2020). "'Count Every Vote': Protesters Take to the Streets across US as
Ballots Tallied." November 5, 2020. TheGuardian.com. https://www.theguard
ian.com/us-news/2020/nov/04/protests-votes-ballot-counting-us-election.

Slodysko, B. (2020). "Why AP Called the 2020 Election for Joe Biden." November 7, 2020. ChicagoTribune.com. https://www.chicagotribune.com/election
-2020/ct-why-ap-called-election-joe-biden-president-20201107-6couahzuzfao
7jnbd6hq3mmk5m-story.html.

Tan, S., Shin, Y., and Rindler, D. (2021). "How One of America's Ugliest Days
Unraveled Inside and Outside the Capitol." January 9, 2021. WashingtonPost
.com. https://www.washingtonpost.com/nation/interactive/2021/capitol
-insurrection-visual-timeline/.

Totenburg, N. (2020). "Justice Ruth Bader Ginsburg, Champion of Gender
Equality, Dies at 87." September 18, 2020. NPR.org. https://www.npr.org
/2020/09/18/100306972/justice-ruth-bader-ginsburg-champion-of-gender
-equality-dies-at-87.

U.S. Attorney's Office, District of Columbia. (2021). "One Year Since the Jan. 6 Attack on the Capitol." December 30, 2021. Justice.gov. https://www.justice.gov
/usao-dc/one-year-jan-6-attack-capitol.

Vanderbilt University. (2021). "Pre-Election Polls in 2020 Had the Largest
Errors in 40 Years." July 19, 2021. News.Vanderbilt.Edu. https://news.vanderbilt
.edu/2021/07/19/pre-election-polls-in-2020-had-the-largest-errors-in
-40-years/.

Wasserman, D. (2020). "Beware the 'Blue Mirage' and the 'Red Mirage' on
Election Night." November 3, 2020. NBCNews.com. https://www.nbcnews

.com/politics/2020-election/beware-blue-mirage-red-mirage-election-night
-n1245925.

Webster, E. S. (2017). "Resistbot Turns Your Texts into Faxes to Elected Officials." March 10, 2017. TeenVogue.com. https://www.teenvogue.com/story
/resistbot-faxes-texts-to-senators.

Weiss, D. C. (2020). "Judge Amy Coney Barrett Rated 'Well Qualified' for Supreme Court by ABA Standing Committee." October 12, 2020. ABAJournal.
com. https://www.abajournal.com/news/article/amy-coney-barrett-is-rated
-well-qualified-for-supreme-court-by-aba-standing-committee.

Wilder, W. (2021). "Voter Suppression in 2020." August 20, 2021. Brennan
Center.org. https://www.brennancenter.org/our-work/research-reports/voter
-suppression-2020.

Yourish, K., Buchanan, L., and Lu, D. (2021). "The 147 Republicans Who Voted
to Overturn Election Results." January 7, 2021. NYTimes.com. https://www
nytimes.com/interactive/2021/01/07/us/elections/electoral-college-biden
-objectors.html.

CHAPTER 16

Amara, K. (2021). "'War zone': Inauguration Security Reaches Levels Unseen
in DC." January 20, 2021. WBALTV.com. https://www.wbaltv.com/article
/presidential-inauguration-security-washington-dc/35254690#.

Feuer, A. and Benner, K. (2021). "Inaugural Security Is Fortified in D.C. as
Military and Police Links Are Eyed in Riot." January 14, 2021. NYTimes.com.
https://www.nytimes.com/2021/01/14/us/politics/inauguration-security-capi
tol-riot-investigation.html.

Gorman, A. (2021). "Read: Amanda Gorman's Inaugural Poem." January 20,
2021. https://www.cnn.com/2021/01/20/politics/amanda-gorman-inaugural
-poem-transcript/index.html.

Ngo, M. (2021). "Fact Check: Attendance at Biden's Inauguration Was Restricted
by COVID-19 Pandemic." January 20, 2021. USAToday.com. https://www
.usatoday.com/story/news/factcheck/2021/01/20/biden-inauguration-crowd
-size-trump/4239439001/.

Poniewozik, J. (2021). "The Inauguration Kept Crowds Out and Tried to Bring
America In." January 20, 2021. NYTimes.com. https://www.nytimes.com
/2021/01/20/arts/television/inauguration-crowd.html.

Wallace, D. and Schultz, M. (2021). "DC Inauguration Security at Capitol Includes
National Guard Medics Trained in 'Battlefield Trauma,' Explosives." January 20,
2021. FoxNews.com. https://www.foxnews.com/us/dc-security-biden-inau
guration-national-guard-medics-battlefield-trauma-explosives-protests-canceled.

INDEX

ABOUT THE AUTHOR

Amanda Sturgill teaches journalism at Elon University and is the author of *Detecting Deception: Tools to Fight Fake News*. She's an award-winning teacher and researcher who has built a twenty-plus year career studying how people communicate online. She enjoys finding inspiring stories of how people have used online tools to make positive change in their world. She lives in Chapel Hill, North Carolina, with her husband and two fabulous daughters.